D1380526

SECOND FRONT NOW!

THE ROAD TO D-DAY

George Bruce

GEORGE BRUCE

19 November 1979

MACDONALD & JANE'S LONDON

Books by George Bruce include:

Retreat From Kabul
The Stranglers
Eva Peron
Six Battles For India
Dictionary of Battles
The Warsaw Uprising
The Burma Wars
The Nazis
Sea Battles of the 20th Century
Anthology of Short Stories of the 1st World War

Copyright © 1979 George Bruce

First published in 1979 by
Macdonald and Jane's Publishers Limited
Paulton House, 8 Shepherdess Walk
London N1 7LW

ISBN 0 354 01217 7

Design: Judy Tuke
Maps: Alec Spark

Printed in Great Britain by
Billing and Sons Limited
Guildford, London and Worcester

CONTENTS

The prospect of launching an invasion out of England was little short of appalling. There was no precedent in all history for any such thing on the scale that must of necessity be achieved here.

Overture to Overlord by Lieut-General Sir Frederick Morgan, KCB, Chief of Staff to the Supreme Allied Commander

INTRODUCTION

This book is a history of the military and political background of the major strategic issue of the Second World War. Namely, whether, where and when a second front should be launched in north-west Europe, and the conflicts between the three super powers, Great Britain, the United States and the U.S.S.R. that it involved. It is based mainly on the official papers that report verbatim the discussions and arguments between Winston Churchill and his War Cabinet, the Chiefs of Staff and their American counterparts together with Stalin's letters on the subject. So that the comment is given as it was spoken at the time I have occasionally restored the first person into these records.

These sources include the files of the War Cabinet, the Prime Minister's Office, the Chiefs of Staff, the British-American Combined Chiefs of Staff in Washington, COSSAC (Chief of Staff to the Supreme Allied Commander) and SHAEF (Supreme Headquarters Allied Expeditionary Force). Use has also been made of Crown Copyright papers dealing with the issue already published in Churchill's *Second World War* and in the British and American official histories. Where a personal comment appears significant I have culled it, with the publishers' kind permission, from the diaries or memoirs of the participants in the long debate over this issue. My choice of all the available documents was inevitably limited to those that provided the most revealing material for a history in one volume of this endless subject.

Usually, the War Cabinet and Combined Chiefs of Staff papers are prefixed with the letters CAB, the military planning papers WO or SHAEF and the Prime Minister's office PRM.

1 STALIN, IMPORTUNATE ALLY

The news flashed round the world. Hitler had broken the Nazi-Soviet Non-aggression Pact, and the *Wehrmacht* had invaded Soviet Russia at 3 am on 22 June 1941, winning complete tactical surprise along a front of 2,000 miles. In April Winston Churchill had warned Stalin of an impending Nazi attack, but Stalin had shown contempt. Even now as reports flooded into the Kremlin of German armour crossing the frontier in force, of tanks blasting their way through towns and villages, of bombs setting industrial centres aflame, Stalin clung to his conviction that Hitler was loyal. The Soviet Government on its part had faithfully delivered the trainloads of rubber, oil and other strategic materials to help Hitler crush Great Britain, fighting on alone since the fall of France. He ordered Red Army commanders along the frontiers not to be provoked into hostilities, declaring that a few mutinous German generals alone were to blame.

Soon with three German Army Groups advancing spectacularly the truth could no longer be suppressed. Stalin, according to Russian historians, suffered a 'psychic collapse'. He stayed incommunicado until mid-July, taking no part in the conduct of the war and disregarding affairs of state — except to order the shooting of a scapegoat, General Dimitri Pavlov, Commander of the Western Army Group, for 'treason'. According to his surviving associates, Pavlov had too faithfully carried out Stalin's order that army commanders were not to fall victim to German 'provocation'.

For the people of Great Britain Hitler's about-turn was the most dramatic event of the war. Since the German armies had over-run France and Belgium in the spring of 1940, and the remnants of the BEF had escaped at Dunkirk, Britain had stood alone, recreating her armies, fighting the *Luftwaffe* for the mastery of her air-space, standing on guard to repel invasion, bombing Germany. These had been months of tension, determination and vigilance. All the time the blunt truth of the overwhelming numerical superiority of the German and Italian forces, soon to be joined by those of Japan, reminded Britain that, except for a miracle and unless the United States joined her, there was little hope.

The miracle had happened. Overnight, Hitler's ally, with her tremendous reserves of manpower, had become Britain's ally, if against her will; and an ally that already was bearing the brunt of the *Wehrmacht*'s onslaught, its invasion of Britain now postponed indefinitely. The relief, the wonder, at this incredible event cannot be forgotten nearly 40 years later. Everywhere — in the armed forces, factories, offices, the streets — it was seen in a visible relaxation of tension, a renewal of hope. Providence had given the nation a fighting ally, and the most unlikely one of all. A bond of sympathy grew for the unfortunate Russian people, feeling the blows of the German sword that their leaders had helped to forge.

To the strategic implications Winston Churchill, Prime Minister and Minister of Defence, was at once alert. He had declared in his famous broadcast that same night of 22 June that although the worst features of Nazism and Communism were indistinguishable, Russia's danger was now our danger. Therefore Great Britain would help Russia in every way. And a few days later Anthony Eden, Foreign Secretary, calmed the fears of the small, bearded Soviet Ambassador, Ivan Maisky, who believed that Britain might pull out of the war for the time being and leave it to Russia, while rebuilding her strength. Eden declared that Britain would fight on, and in addition send whatever weapons and supplies she could spare to Russia.

In disregarding, though not forgetting, Soviet Russia's hostile acts, and rising above the notion that she could well be left to bear alone the whole weight of Nazi military power, Churchill displayed his characteristic realism. It must have appeared in the Kremlin hardly believable that Britain would now extend a friendly hand.

But since Stalin was temporarily out of action no direct reply to Churchill's initiative came out of Russia, except a request to receive a military mission. He therefore decided to establish contact. In his note[1] to Stalin on 7 July he said that the British Government would do everything that time, geography and growing resources allowed. Referring to the Royal Air Force's heavy raids on Germany, he added: 'Last night nearly 250 heavy bombers were operating. This will go on. Thus we hope to force Hitler to bring back some of his air power to the West and gradually take some of the strain off you.'

And moved by the stand the Russian soldiers were trying to make against the *Wehrmacht*, he told Admiral Sir Dudley Pound, First Sea Lord, in a typically impetuous proposal, that it seemed 'absolutely necessary to send a small mixed squadron of British ships to the Arctic to form contact and operate with Russian naval forces'. Guided, as often, by a mixture of emotion and realism, he continued in this note of 10 July 1941:

> The advantage we should reap if the Russians could keep the field and go on with the war at any rate until the winter closes in, is measureless . . . As long as they go on it does not matter so much where the front lies. These people have shown themselves worth backing, and we must make sacrifices and

take risks even at inconvenience, which I realise, to maintain
their morale . . .[2]

That same day he gave the prim and austere Sir Stafford Cripps,
returning as British Ambassador to Moscow, a message for Stalin
setting out the terms of an Anglo-Russian agreement. These were
mainly a pledge that neither country would make a separate peace, and
a promise of mutual aid.

Churchill and the War Cabinet feared that Stalin might be driven
to make another deal with Hitler. It haunted them like rumours of an
approaching hurricane. Cripps and Vyacheslav Molotov, Russian
Foreign Minister and one of Stalin's henchmen, drafted the agreement and signed it in Moscow a few days later.

Not until 18 July 1941 did Stalin, recovered from his breakdown,
at last reply to Churchill's offer of assistance. Expressing gratitude for
the two messages, he remarked pointedly that the Soviet Union and
Great Britain had become fighting allies in the struggle against
Hitlerite Germany, and openly admitted that 'the consequences of the
unexpected breach of the Non-Aggression Pact by Hitler as well as the
sudden attack against the Soviet Union . . . still remain to be felt by the
Soviet armies'. After this bland disregard of his aid for Britain's enemy
he went on to make his first overbearing demand that she should reopen another fighting front, in a message worth printing in full:

> It seems to me therefore that the military situation of the Soviet
> Union, as well as of Great Britain, would be considerably
> improved if there could be established a front against Hitler in
> the West — Northern France, and in the North — the Arctic.
>
> A front in Northern France could not only divert Hitler's
> forces from the East, but at the same time would make it
> impossible for Hitler to invade Great Britain. The establish-
> ment of the front just mentioned would be popular with the
> British Army, as well as with the whole population of Southern
> England.
>
> I fully realise the difficulties involved in the establishment
> of such a front. I believe however that in spite of the difficulties
> it should be formed, not only in the interest of our common
> cause, but also in the interests of Great Britain herself. This is
> the most propitious moment for the establishment of such a
> front, because now Hitler's forces are diverted to the East and
> he has not yet had the chance to consolidate the position
> occupied by him in the East.
>
> It is still easier to establish a front in the North. Here, on the
> part of Great Britain, would be necessary only naval and air
> operations, without the landing of troops or artillery. The

Soviet military, naval and air forces would take part in such an operation. We would welcome it if Great Britain could transfer to this theatre of war something like one light division or more of the Norwegian volunteers, who could be used in Northern Norway to organise rebellion against the Germans.[3]

Thus began the clamorous and unrealistic Russian demand for a second front. It was hardly likely to promote goodwill for the Soviets in the light of the war supplies Stalin had earlier sent to Hitler. Especially provocative was his assumption that now as a 'fighting ally' he could demand a British military operation as risky as a cross-Channel assault on the well-fortified shores of northern France. Possibly Stalin may have realised its implications — for example, that in Britain's state of unpreparedness it would be sure to fail disastrously and cause a German withdrawal from the East to launch instead a mainly airborne invasion of southern England. Russia would then be able to regroup, re-equip and save herself. For Britain, it was an uninviting prospect, but Stalin's demand could not be dismissed out of hand owing to the over-riding fear that he might still make terms with Hitler.

General Golikov, head of the Russian Military Mission in London, followed up Stalin's letter with a list of requirements that he gave to Anthony Eden for fighter aircraft, bombers, tanks and raw materials worth millions of dollars. An even bigger list, worth nearly two billion dollars, was placed before the State Department in Washington in response to President Roosevelt's offer to assist.

To Stalin's demand for a second front Churchill replied at once. He said firmly that 'anything sensible' Britain could do would be done, but that at the present time the Chiefs of Staff did not see any chance of action in Europe on a scale likely to be of the slightest use. Referring to Stalin's proposal for an invasion of northern France he said that the sole area where Britain had air superiority was the Dunkirk-Boulogne coast, but that its mass of fortifications made it virtually impregnable. All of it was commanded by searchlights and heavy guns dominated the sea.

'To attempt a landing in force would be to encounter a bloody repulse, and petty raids would lead to fiascos doing more harm than good to both of us. It would all be over without their having to move or before they could move a single unit from your front.'

Churchill reminded him that Britain had been fighting alone for more than a year, and that her resources were strained to the utmost by air raids at home, Middle East battles against Italian and German forces, and the need to protect the vital Atlantic convoys from U-boat and Focke-Wulf bomber attacks. He added that British naval and air forces, including submarines, were soon to go north to attack enemy shipping in the north of Norway and Finland and he pointed out that troops, whether British or Russian, could not be landed in the Arctic during its perpetual daylight without air superiority. There was, he ended, no Norwegian division in Britain.[4]

Later, Churchill informed Stalin that to help Soviet resistance the British Government would send as soon as possible 140 American Tomahawk fighter aircraft (Curtiss P 40) from Britain and another 60 from British supplies in the United States, though this would seriously deplete her resources. They would ship up to two million pairs of boots, as well as tin, wool, woollen cloth and 20,000 tons of rubber. He thanked Stalin for his understanding that more could not then be done but promised, 'We will do our utmost'.

Stalin's first message and Churchill's reply had planted the seed that would grow into the most contentious political and military issue of the Second World War: the demand for the launching at once of a 'second front' in Northern France. Stalin would demand it with the same ruthless obstinacy in disregard of expert opinion with which he had imposed blind loyalty to the Nazi-Soviet Pact. Soon President Roosevelt, Generals Marshall and Eisenhower, Admiral King and other American war leaders, impatient for large-scale military action, would make a similar demand. We shall see how Winston Churchill and the British Chiefs of Staff were to demonstrate the dangers of such a course and refuse to give way until the time was ripe.

That summer, around Smolensk, on the approaches to Leningrad and to Kiev, German forces were victorious in great battles. Smolensk fell on 9 August. About 100,000 Russian soldiers were killed or wounded there and another 150,000 taken prisoner with the loss of thousands of tanks and guns. Fighting east of the town went on for another 14 days. Serious as this loss was for the Soviets, the Smolensk battles had at least held up Hitler's *Blitzkrieg* and forced him to change his plan to attack Moscow. He advanced southward instead through the Ukraine, and towards the Crimea, a cardinal error. But by 9 September 1941, Kiev and the Russian armies defending it were threatened with encirclement, while Leningrad, in the north, was cut off from almost all supplies and under artillery bombardment.

On 4 August 1941 Churchill had journeyed to Placentia Bay, Newfoundland, in the new battleship *Prince of Wales* for a secret rendezvous with Britain's unofficial ally, President Roosevelt, for, of course, the United States was still not in the war. Here, together with Lord Beaverbrook, then Minister of Supply, they conferred about the problem of sharing with Soviet Russia war weapons destined for

Britain. An arrangement to share was made, though one not much to Churchill's liking in view of Britain's great need. From this meeting was also born, of course, the nebulous Atlantic Charter, that short-lived joint declaration of principles about the future of the world.

Meantime, Stalin sent his ambassador, Ivan Maisky, to see the always smiling Anthony Eden to protest about what he regarded as the inadequacy of the war weapons sent from Great Britain. Britain had refused to launch a second front, Maisky argued, but she should give Soviet Russia more weapons of war, aircraft especially. He added that the Soviet Government were grateful for the promise of 200 fighters, but this was a small contribution in the scale of Russia's enormous losses. Seven hundred thousand men had been killed and wounded, between four thousand and five thousand aircraft and about five thousand tanks had been lost. Clearly suspicious of Britain, Maisky then bluntly demanded that the Soviets should be informed of her strategic plans. Eden made it clear that this was impossible.

Seven weeks after the birth of the treaty between the two countries tension was rising between them. It was inevitable, since neither government trusted the other and it would later worsen to the point of a break over the second front issue, but on 29 August 1941 Churchill, back in London, sent Stalin an assurance of more help. Delivery of 200 Tomahawk fighters already promised was being hurried on, he said, while two squadrons of Hurricanes, with pilots, spares and maintenance crews were due to reach Murmansk on 6 September 1941. 'You will, I am sure,' he wrote, 'realise that fighter aircraft are the foundations of our home defence, besides which we are trying to obtain air superiority in Libya, and also to provide for Turkey so as to bring her on our side. Nevertheless, I could send 200 more Hurricanes, making 440 in all, if your pilots could use them effectively. These would be eight- and twelve-gun Hurricanes, which we have found very deadly in action . . .'

On 4 September 1941 came Stalin's reply, read out to Churchill by the persistent Maisky in the presence also of Eden, whom the Prime Minister had recalled from a few days' well-earned leave in the country. It began with curt thanks for promising 'to sell' the further 200 fighters to the Soviet Union, but, Stalin said unceremoniously, these would not make any serious changes on the Eastern Front because of the large scale on which the war there was being fought. The relative stabilisation of the front which the Red Army had achieved three weeks ago had broken down, he admitted. Thirty to 34 fresh German infantry divisions and an enormous quantity of tanks and aircraft had been transferred to the Eastern Front, and there had also been a large increase with the *Wehrmacht* in activities of the 20 Finnish and 25 Rumanian divisions. He continued, accusingly:

Germans consider danger in the West a bluff, and are transferring all their forces to the East with impunity, being convinced that no second front exists in the West, and that none will exist. Germans consider it quite possible to smash their enemies singly: first Russia, then the English. As a result we have lost more than one half of the Ukraine, and in addition the enemy is at the gates of Leningrad.

He also revealed that the Germans had seized a valuable iron ore region as well as several metallurgical works, but the Soviets had removed two aluminium works, three aircraft and three motor factories from threatened areas. These however could not be operative in their new localities for seven or eight months. 'This has weakened our power of defence and faced the Soviet Union with a mortal menace,' he declared, and continued:

I think there is only one means of egress from this situation — to establish in the present year a second front somewhere in the Balkans or France, capable of drawing away from the Eastern Front 30 to 40 divisions, and at the same time of ensuring to the Soviet Union 30,000 tons of aluminium by the beginning of October next and a *monthly* minimum of aid amounting to 400 aircraft and 500 tanks (of small or of medium size). Without these two forms of help the Soviet Union will either suffer defeat or be weakened to such an extent that it will lose for a long period any capacity to render assistance to its Allies by its actual operations on the fronts of the struggle against Hitlerism. I realise that this message will cause dismay to Your Excellency. But it cannot be helped.[5]

The implied threat to make terms with Germany in Stalin's note was echoed by Ambassador Maisky. After reading it aloud he had wrangled with Churchill for ninety minutes, complaining that for the past eleven weeks Soviet Russia had borne the brunt of the German onslaught virtually alone. 'The Russian armies are now enduring a weight of attack unequalled before. I do not wish to use dramatic language, but this might be a turning point in history. If Soviet Russia is defeated, how can Great Britain win the war?'

Disregarding this barbed question at the time, Churchill said later that he felt sympathy for Maisky's appeal and the poignant terms in which he stressed the 'extreme gravity of the crisis on the Russian front', but when he sensed 'an underlying air of menace' in the Ambassador's remarks he had retorted angrily and to the point:

'Remember that only four months ago we in this Island did not know whether you were not coming in against us on the German side.

Indeed, we thought it quite likely that you would. Even then we felt sure we should win in the end. We never thought our survival was dependent on your action either way. Whatever happens, and whatever you do, you of all people have no right to make reproaches to us.'[6]

The sharp tone of Churchill's voice underlined the blunt words. Maisky was disconcerted. 'More calm, please, my dear Mr Churchill,' he pleaded, and in a more restrained way begged once more for an immediate landing in France or the Netherlands. Again Churchill explained how for military reasons this could not be done.

'We would not hesitate to sacrifice 50,000 men if we thought that by doing so we would relieve the pressure on the Russians,' he declared, in what seems to have been a somewhat showy gesture to persuade Maisky of Britain's good faith in the issue, but, he added: 'All the military advisers to the Government are agreed that there is nothing effective which can be done this year.'[7] It was 'physically impossible', he added, for a second front to be launched in the Balkans unless Turkey came into the war.

'From the start of the invasion of Russia,' he ended, 'I have continually pressed the Chiefs of Staff to examine every possible measure which might be taken to assist the Russians. They have done their best but the results have all been negative.'

Eden invited Maisky to hear the views of the Chiefs of Staff, and the next day, 5 September, in Eden's words, 'a dogged and worried Maisky' met General Sir John Dill, Chief of the Imperial General Staff, Sir Dudley Pound, Admiral of the Fleet and First Sea Lord, and Sir Charles Portal, Air Chief Marshal, in Eden's private room at the Foreign Office, where Churchill joined them later. Maisky emphasised the critical position of the Soviet forces and stressed that the time had come for Britain 'to take risks to help the Soviet Union continue the struggle'.[8]

He asked for the opinion of the Chiefs of Staff, who he was meeting for the first time, on the launching of a new front by a British force of 15 to 20 divisions in France or the Balkans, pointing out that Britain controlled the sea and could land anywhere she liked. 'The Russian Admiral thought that this would be a possible operation if diversions were simultaneously made in other directions to confuse the enemy,' he declared.[9]

Admiral Sir Dudley Pound, his muscular hands resting as usual on the green baize table, explained to him that 'in narrow waters sea power and air power must be considered together. Even if we managed to land fairly considerable forces, the Germans could concentrate their Divisions, of which they still had 20 or 30 in France, much quicker by rail than we could by sea.

'The Germans have quite a powerful air force in France, including between 200 and 300 bombers and 500 fighters. They would be able to act from a secure position against our landings.' The Chiefs of Staff, he said, realised that considerable sacrifices would be justified if any good object could be achieved, but he argued that we could do nothing to bring about withdrawal this autumn of appreciable enemy forces from the Eastern Front.[10]

Maisky was not convinced. He retorted that the best way that Great Britain could ensure against invasion would be to engage the Germans in France and, superficially, this seemed a sound argument. But apart from the shortage of the needful landing craft it ran counter to the pessimistic view about unlimited operations in France then held by Britain's Chiefs of Staff. Advancing this argument, Pound explained that the last chance the Germans had of successfully invading this country was in 1940, when Britain had established a feeble front on the Somme. If the Germans had allowed that front to remain our strength would have been drawn away into France and we would have fallen an easy prey. The Germans, he said, could easily recreate that situation if we placed considerable forces in France in the near future.

It also echoed Churchill's belief that our biggest danger lay in 'having our last reserves drawn away from us into a wasting, futile French resistance in France . . .' The core of this belief was the British conviction that indiscipline and low morale rendered the French army incapable of opposing the *Wehrmacht* effectively.

But desperate as he was, with Stalin harassing him almost hourly, Maisky could not accept so recondite a plea. Perhaps Pound could have explained it more convincingly, but he was not at his best. Neither he nor his colleagues knew that he had begun to suffer the first effects of the brain tumour that would kill him two years later.

Churchill now closed the argument. There was no escape, he declared, from the conclusion reached by the Chiefs of Staff as to the impossibility of any action in Northern France or in the Balkans of a nature to draw enemy forces away from the Russian front.

This Soviet attempt to influence Great Britain's policy came under more heavy fire that same day at a War Cabinet meeting when Churchill read out the draft of his answer to Stalin, remarking before he did so that he felt the Russian leader was worthy of being told the truth, and capable of facing the facts of a situation. 'I do not think', he said, 'that we should make promises which we cannot possibly fulfill.'

Beaverbrook agreed with the burden of the message, but argued in his rasping voice that its terms were 'too harsh and depressing'. He favoured including an immediate promise to supply half of Stalin's massive request for 500 tanks and 400 aircraft monthly from our own resources. 'We should then press the Americans to supply the other half without lessening our own appropriations. To keep the Russian army in the field is worthy of every ounce of our energy.'

Sir Archibald Sinclair, Secretary of State for Air, who stammered from time to time, shared the newspaper millionaire Beaverbrook's desire to aid the Russians if it was possible, but considered that any such promise should be subject to the development of the war. 'We could hardly spare that number of aircraft if the whole weight of the German attack was shifted back to the west,' he said.

Eden recalled in his fair-minded way that the Russians had promised that they would do what they could to assist us if the German weight was transferred to the West. Ernest Bevin, 18-stone, rough-speaking Minister of Labour and National Service, gave loud voice to the Government's resentment about the British Communists' agitation for 'A Second Front Now'. If a promise were to be made, Maisky should be firmly told that he must stop his propaganda campaign against the Government about aid for Russia, and if this did not produce the desired result, it might be worth while warning Stalin.[10] Churchill agreed that M. Maisky should be warned and an uncompromising reply from the Prime Minister to Stalin was finally drafted. 'I reply at once in the spirit of your message,' Churchill said in the note:[11]

> Although we should shrink from no exertion, there is in fact no possibility of any British action in the West, except air action, which would draw the German forces from the East before the winter sets in. There is no chance whatever of a second front being formed in the Balkans without the help of Turkey. I will, if your Excellency desires, give all the reasons which have led our Chiefs of Staff to these conclusions ... Action, however well-meant, leading only to costly fiascos would be no help to anyone but Hitler ...

He promised to try to speed a decision on the number of aircraft and tanks the Americans and British could jointly send each month and offered forthwith from British production half of the monthly total Stalin had asked for. He continued:

> We are ready to make joint plans with you now. Whether British armies will be strong enough to invade the mainland of Europe during 1942 must depend on unforeseeable events. It may be possible however to assist you in the extreme North when there is more darkness. We are hoping to raise our armies in the Middle East to a strength of three-quarters of a million before the end of the present year, and thereafter to a

million by the summer of 1942 ... Meanwhile, we shall
continue to batter Germany from the air with increasing
severity and to keep the seas open and ourselves alive. In your
first paragraph you use the word 'sell'. We had not viewed the
matter in such terms and have never thought of payment. Any
assistance we can give you would better be upon the same
basis of comradeship as the American Lend-Lease Bill, of
which no formal account is kept in money.

To President Roosevelt, best described then as an unofficial, non-
belligerent ally, Churchill then sent a copy of Stalin's letter and his
own friendly reply, with the warning: 'Although nothing in his
language warranted the assumption, we could not exclude the
impression that they might be thinking of separate terms ...'
That same evening Maisky was summoned to Downing Street to
receive the message and while it was being typed Eden noted how
Churchill handled him. 'Winston spoke to him roundly but kindly, as
only he can combine, about Soviet propaganda here in favour of "a
second front", and said the only result would be rough reaction and
recrimination all would wish to avoid.' But Maisky pleaded that he
could not say he was satisfied with British help when in fact he was
not.[12]
It had been a long and demanding day. Churchill characteristically felt the need to relax with good talk, food and wine in a pleasant
environment. To the white and gold of the Ritz, not yet too much
subdued by wartime austerity, he therefore invited Beaverbrook and
Eden for a dinner of oysters, partridge and champagne, when the talk
dwelt on the political events of the First World War.
These three most powerful men in Britain's war direction made a
study in contrasts. The egocentric Churchill, rotund, pink-faced like
a pugnacious cherub, was imperious, self-assured, interfering,
romantic about Great Britain, intensely subjective and loyal in his
friendships, behaving always with aristocratic disregard, yet
paradoxically never losing either the common touch or faith in his
destiny.
Anthony Eden, ambitious, vain, dapper, was clearer-sighted, more
analytical and perceptive in the field of international relations than the
impetuous Churchill. Part of his flair for human relationships was a
smile of rare appeal and he was well endowed with the mental
aptitudes needful for Prime Minister, for which reward he waited, in
Churchill's shadow.
Beaverbrook, the Canadian-born millionaire owner of Express
Newspapers, accentuated with his brash manner the Englishness of
his two companions, beside whom he was a diminutive five feet seven

inches. Yet his powerful head bordered by wispy grey hair, his broad brow with penetrating grey eyes, his emphatic speech and formidable personality made him look anything but small. He was a deep admirer of his old friend Churchill, who in turn prized Beaverbrook's exceptional drive and organising power.

One of Churchill's faculties was the ability to show his colleagues after a long and exhausting day the way to complete detachment, exemplified by this dinner at the Ritz. It goes far to explain how he was able to keep going in face of the burdens involving life and death everywhere that he assumed.

The likelihood that Stalin would renew his demand for a second front increased as the *Wehrmacht* advanced and Stalin worsened the situation with unrealistic orders to his generals. By 9 September 1941 General Guderian's tank units from the north-east and Field Marshal von Kleist's from the south-east had driven back the defenders of the Ukrainian city of Kiev, and almost completed its encirclement. Hurriedly, Marshal Budienny gave the order to the four Soviet armies under his command to withdraw to avoid a disastrous defeat, but Stalin countermanded the order and sent Marshal Timoshenko to take over from Budienny.

The critical day was 13 September, when Timoshenko arrived, for a gap 20 miles wide still separated Guderian's and von Kleist's advancing Panzers, and the Soviets could have fought rearguard actions to north and south while the bulk of their forces extricated themselves eastwards.

But on 16 September Stalin still refused to allow a fighting withdrawal. The Russian soldiers fought and died where they stood. Next day the German forces met from opposite directions and closed the gap. Too late, Stalin then authorised the abandonment of Kiev, but bungled the order, so that while some units tried to fight their way out others stayed on, suffered heavy losses, or surrendered and were captured. Some 600,000, including army generals, were taken prisoner or killed. At the same time German pressure increased on Leningrad too, which was already under heavy bombardment from the air and land. By 15 September 1941 the city was completely cut off from communication by land with the rest of Soviet Russia.

Enormous losses, coupled with the threat of a fresh drive on Moscow, faced Stalin. Doubts about the Red Army's power to survive loomed large, and he looked desperately about for trained reserves. Whether or not the report is true that it was Marshal Timoshenko who urged him to demand the immediate commitment of British troops is impossible to say, but on 13 September Stalin made another proposal to Churchill, this time unrealistic rather than vehement. 'In my last message I stated the viewpoint of the Soviet Government that the establishment of a second front is the most fundamental remedy for the improvement of the situation with regard to our common cause,' he declared.

> I can only reiterate that the absence of a second front simply favours the designs of our common enemy. I have no doubt that the British Government desires to see the Soviet Union victorious and is looking for ways and means to attain this end. If, as they think, the establishment of a second front in the West is at present impossible, perhaps another method could be found to render to the Soviet Government an active military help?
>
> It seems to me that Great Britain could without risk land in Archangel 25 to 30 divisions, or transport them across Iran to the southern regions of the USSR. In this way there could be established military collaboration between the Soviet and British troops on the territory of the USSR . . .[13]

One can imagine the feelings with which the War Cabinet listened to Churchill reading at five o'clock on 15 September 1941 this letter from the Soviet war leader. Stalin was asking for as many troops as were then stationed for home defence in the United Kingdom and twice as many as had been with much difficulty transported to the Middle East. 'It seemed hopeless to argue with a man thinking in terms of such unreality,' Churchill commented later.

In a message to him two days afterwards on 17 September, dealing with convoys and supply, he merely remarked that the Staffs had examined all theatres of possible military co-operation; that the two flanks, north and south, were most favourable for it, but in the north lack of shipping was the obstacle, while in the south the attitude of Turkey, which wished to stay neutral, was decisive.

And to Ambassador Cripps in Moscow he telegraphed: 'To put two fully armed British divisions from here into the Caucasus or north of the Caspian would take at least three months. They would then be only a drop in the bucket.'

On 22 September 1941 Beaverbrook and Averell Harriman, Roosevelt's special representative in London, sailed from Scapa Flow in the cruiser HMS *London* on their dangerous voyage around North Cape, to the Barents Sea, the White Sea and Archangel, thence on the 600-mile overland journey to Moscow to discuss military aid to Russia. The meeting was to influence Beaverbrook strongly in favour of more help for the Russians. General Ismay, Churchill's military secretary, accompanied them, so that if necessary he could explain personally the obstacles to launching a second front to Stalin or his military chiefs and advisers.

On this sore issue, Churchill had forewarned Beaverbrook in a directive which emphasised: 'All ideas of 20 or 30 divisions being launched by Great Britain against the Western shores of the continent or sent round by sea for service in Russia have no foundation of reality on which to rest. This should be made clear. We have every intention of intervening on land next spring, if it can be done.'

But this last statement was little more than a cautious expression of good intentions, for none of the cogent reasons that Churchill and the Chiefs of Staff agreed prevented such an operation had changed. At worst Churchill was feeding Stalin pie-in-the-sky, at best stating his hopes.

Both Stalin and Beaverbrook kept to the question of the supply of war weapons during the talks. With Harriman they worked out an agreement embodying what Great Britain and the United States would supply from October 1941 to June 1942 based on British production and that which the British Government would otherwise have obtained from America. These two Governments guaranteed only that the weapons would be made available at the production centres, but they agreed 'to help with the delivery' of them to the Soviet Union.

A considerable sacrifice, it meant, Churchill noted, 'much derangement of our military plans, already hampered by the tormenting shortage of munitions' — especially from the standpoint of a second front, for the supplies — enough to equip a substantial force — would be delivered in perilous convoy to Archangel every 10 days.

As well as the hundreds of aircraft and tanks already sent, 20 heavy tanks and 193 fighters were then on their way. The convoy of 12 October included 140 heavy tanks, 100 Hurricane fighter aircraft, 200 Bren carriers, 200 anti-tank rifles and ammunition, 50 two-pounder guns and ammunition; then, on 22 October, 200 fighter aircraft and 120 heavy tanks were to follow in another convoy. Twenty tanks had already been shipped via Persia and another 15 were about to be shipped from Canada via Vladivostock.

Despite their eagerness to fight the Nazis, Churchill and the War Cabinet were united, except for one member, in their resolve not to commit British troops to an immediate major cross-Channel assault without any likelihood of success, simply to satisfy the unrelenting Soviet demand for it. But Lord Beaverbrook, already an advocate of an immediate second front, returned to London from his talks with Stalin brimming with enthusiasm for the Soviet cause, compassion for the hard-pressed Russian people and determination to force a change of policy in this field through the Cabinet if he possibly could.

2 CHURCHILL: 'NO SECOND FRONT IN 1941'

When the War Cabinet assembled in dark wet London at 10 pm on 15 October 1941, Beaverbrook, fresh from his talks with Stalin, at once attacked what he called Great Britain's inaction with regard to Russia. 'A serious crisis is developing in Russia,' he declared.

> It is essential that we should take some action to encourage Russian resistance, and to take advantage of the favourable situation elsewhere. Yet there has been nothing but procrastination and idleness on our part throughout the time that the Russians have been engaged in a desperate struggle. Not a single blow has been struck by our Army, although it is clear that the Germans cannot possibly be strong on the enormous front they are holding from Norway to Libya while their armies are fully engaged in Russia.[1]

Urging that immediate action should be taken either in Norway, or, at any rate in Cyrenaica, Libya, he went on: 'Every proposition which has been put forward has been negatived by the Chiefs of Staff, and there does not seem to be among the Services any sense of the urgency of the situation.'

To this harsh judgement by his old friend Churchill answered that he himself had been equally anxious to take advantage of the Russian situation to get a footing in Norway, and he had given instructions to General Brooke and to General Paget to make a plan for the capture of Trondheim, if necessary using poison gas as a terror weapon, but they had turned down the proposal. Churchill had accepted their rejection, but now he chided that 'instead of a plan a paper has been produced showing all the insuperable objections to any action'. However, he added, a project which offered good chances of success, the invasion of Sicily, had been found. To this Beaverbrook growled that the new project did not engage the Germans, whereas the Norwegian project did. Churchill explained that the Norwegian Plan could not take effect until December, by which time the crisis in Russia would be past one way or the other. Anthony Eden intervened to say that he could not see any useful development from the Norway operation. The new project, the invasion of Sicily, opened great possibilities in the Mediterranean and could be launched just as soon as any attack in Norway.

Churchill tried to end the controversy with an olive branch in the form of an offer to put the Chiefs of Staff at Beaverbrook's disposal to go fully with him into the details of any project for action which he would like to put forward. It was important to pacify him both in the interest of Cabinet unity and because of the sway over public opinion that his great newspapers gave him.

Clement Attlee, Lord Privy Seal, whose objectivity formed a useful counterweight in the War Cabinet to the more emotional Churchill and Beaverbrook, intervened to say that there seemed to be three arguments in favour of operations of our forces at the present time. 'The first is to divert German forces from the Russian Front, but this is an object which we cannot achieve; the second is to sustain Russian morale. This we might achieve if our operations are successful. The third is to take advantage of the opportunity presented by the German preoccupation with Soviet Russia. This we can achieve only if we can find an operation which would be effective.'

In his sharp, staccato voice Attlee, the veteran socialist with the bald and bony head, added that time was short and we clearly could not stage anything in Norway or elsewhere which would take place before the forthcoming operations in Cyrenaica. The right policy would be to exploit a success in that theatre, and for this reason he supported the proposal for an operation against Sicily.

The Chiefs of Staff were accordingly invited to report by 17 October, two days later, on the possibility of an attack on Sicily with forces from the United Kingdom, timed to take advantage of a possible collapse of Axis forces after a victory in Cyrenaica; but later, this plan, Operation WHIPCORD, was to be dropped when the Chiefs of Staff reported that a force could not sail from Britain before 23 November, which was too long after the planned date of the Cyrenaica offensive.

Beaverbrook's protesting voice was stifled at this meeting, but he would soon attack again more forcefully.

Meanwhile, General von Bock's Central Army Group was fighting furiously in an effort to reach Moscow before the onset of the Russian winter. Orel, 200 miles south, fell on 8 October and Kalinen, 100 miles north-west, a week later. Marshal Timoshenko retreated to a line about 40 miles west of Moscow. On 15 October, in a message to Churchill, Ambassador Cripps reported from Moscow that the Soviet Government, the Diplomatic Corps and as much industry as possible were being evacuated to Kuibyshev, about 500 miles east of the capital.

On 19 October, Stalin declared a state of siege in the Soviet capital and, in an Order of the Day, proclaimed, 'Moscow will be defended to

the last!' So ruthlessly did the Soviet commissars enforce the order
that the front stiffened, a slight return of Russian military confidence
followed and the German advance was slowed. Nevertheless, unless
the winter snows brought von Bock's Panzers to a halt, a sudden
German breakthrough might soon lead to fighting in Moscow itself,
for by 20 October it was surrounded on three sides. And if the capital
fell Russia might be forced to capitulate.

The danger spurred the angry Beaverbrook to fresh efforts. That
same day, 19 October, he attacked the British military chiefs' perfor-
mance in a sharp and censorious memorandum for the Prime Minister
which he read out in his harsh voice to the assembled War Cabinet.
Because it reflected the beliefs, however erroneous, of a number of
people at the time it is worth reading in full. 'Since the start of the
German campaign against Russia our military leaders have shown
themselves consistently averse to taking military action,' he declared,
his formidable brow deeply furrowed, his look baleful.

> Our advance into Persia was a purely minor and preventive
> operation in which we employed less than a quarter of the
> troops used by the Russians. And the only other operations we
> have undertaken have been the bombing of Western Germany
> and Fighter sweeps over France which have done nothing to
> help Russia or hinder Germany in the present crisis, and in
> which we have lost many of our finest airmen.

> Our strategy is still based on a long term view of the war
> which is blind to the urgencies and opportunities of the
> moment. There has been no attempt to take into account the
> new factor introduced by the Russian resistance.

> There is today only one military problem — how to help
> Russia. Yet on that issue the Chiefs of Staff content themselves
> with saying that nothing can be done. They point out the
> difficulties, but make no suggestions for overcoming them.

> It is nonsense to say that we can do nothing for the
> Russians. We can, as soon as we decide to sacrifice long-term
> projects and a general view of the war which, though still
> cherished, became completely obsolete on the day when Russia
> was attacked.

> Russian resistance has given us new opportunities. It has
> probably denuded Western Europe of German troops and
> prevented for the time being offensive action by the Axis in
> other theatres of possible operations. It has created a quasi-
> revolutionary situation in every occupied country and opened
> 2,000 miles of coastline to a descent by British forces.

> But the Germans can move their Divisions with impunity
> to the East. For the Continent is still considered by our

Generals to be out of bounds to British troops. And rebellion is regarded as premature and even deplored when it occurs, because we are not ready for it. The Chiefs of Staff would have us wait until the last button has been sewn on the last gaiter before we launch an attack. They ignore the present opportunity.

But they forget that the attack on Russia has brought us a new peril as well as a new opportunity. If we do not help them now the Russians may collapse. And, freed at last from anxiety about the East, Hitler will concentrate all his forces against us in the West. The Germans will not wait then till we are ready. And it is folly for us to wait now. We must strike before it is too late.[2]

But Beaverbrook's attack on our war strategy was more eloquent than accurate and did not stand up to analysis. The long term view of the war was the only possible one in the circumstances. Britain's military problem was to help Russia stay in it while engaging the Germans and Italians herself, where she could do so without great risk, and while rebuilding her strength for a major operation at some future date.

To suggest that the time was ripe for cross-Channel assaults anywhere along the European coastline was nonsense, for Germany had not denuded Western Europe of troops; 25 German divisions held vital coastal areas and there were not enough landing craft for such operations, both of which facts Beaverbrook must have known. In addition, air cover for cross-Channel operations was limited to the very well defended Pas-de-Calais region, where the War Cabinet were rightly determined not to risk lives in a futile effort.

Finally, Beaverbrook ignored the very real help to Russia in the achievements of the British convoys carrying huge quantities of tanks, aircraft, vehicles and raw materials through Arctic waters to Archangel at great cost in ships and sailors' lives. Why then did he make this attack, and support the campaign for an immediate second front in Europe in his newspapers? The answer can only be that he was blind to the facts of the situation, having allowed his emotions — his compassion for the Russian people — to master his reason, as we shall see.

Next day the War Cabinet Defence Committee met to discuss the issue that Beaverbrook had raised so challengingly.

Churchill said that the memorandum expressed the impulse which the whole Committee felt, but that he had not taken it as meant to be an attack requiring a reply in detail. Beaverbrook responded sharply that it was intended to be an attack.[3] He found himself in disagreement with his colleagues on the Russian issue.

'I wish to take advantage of the rising temper in the country for helping Russia,' he contended. 'Others don't. I want to make a supreme effort to raise production so as to help Russia. Others don't. I want to fulfil in every particular the agreement made in Moscow. Others don't. I wish the Army to act in support of Russia. Others don't. The Chiefs of Staff don't. The line of cleavage between me and my colleagues and the Chiefs of Staff is complete.'

The Prime Minister said that he was sorry to hear this statement, which he must regard as an attack on himself. He asked what plan Beaverbrook would wish the Chiefs of Staff to adopt. Beaverbrook said he would like the Norwegian plan to be carried out.

'I would too,' Churchill said, 'but it has been found impossible to make a plan. . . . Even if Germany were still conducting full scale operations in Russia, they would certainly not be in any way deterred by an attack on Norway . . . They would certainly not interrupt their operations on the Eastern Front.' Beaverbrook retorted that the arguments in favour of Norway were convincing to him.

The Prime Minister declared that nothing we could do now could influence the battle in Russia, which might not turn out badly. Even if we had started to act on the first day that Germany had attacked Russia, we still could not appreciably have affected the issue.

A minority of one in the War Cabinet, Beaverbrook's zeal for a 'second front' was frustrated there. So instead, he whipped up the campaign for it in his newspapers, *The Daily Express*, *Sunday Express* and *Evening Standard*. Popular feeling grew and more and more people marched with banners calling for 'A Second Front Now!'

With the German threat to Russia now so grave, Molotov again asked Stafford Cripps, in Moscow, about Stalin's request for a British army to be sent to Archangel, or the southern regions of Soviet Russia. Cripps reminded him that Churchill had refused this request in his letter to Stalin of 17 September, but reported the request to Churchill, who answered on 25 October that the idea of sending 25 to 30 divisions to fight on the Russian Front was 'a physical absurdity'. He continued:

> It is with the greatest difficulty that we have managed to send the 50th Division to the Middle East in the last six months. We are now sending the 18th Division by extraordinary measures. All our shipping is fully engaged, and any saving can only be made at the expense of our vital upkeep convoys to the Middle East, or of ships engaged in carrying Russian war supplies. The margin by which we live and make munitions of war has only narrowly been maintained.[4]

To the War Cabinet Defence Committee two days later at a meeting on

27 October, he questioned the possibility that the 50th Division might be moved to the Caucasus front in a month, and might be joined in three months by the 18th Division. 'These formations', he contended, 'would form a small body on a large front; they would be armed with different arms to the Russians and would be certain in the end to be overwhelmed. Great labour would be involved in getting them to the front in the course of which the supply route to Russia would be choked.'[5] He said it might be better to send some air squadrons, a proposal that Air Marshal Portal at once frowned on, owing to the maintenance problems involved.

Portal was thinking of the almost unlimited quantities of spares that would need to be shipped to Russia, as well as the skilled officers and men to maintain and keep the aircraft flying with them. Churchill's objections to sending troops applied equally to aircraft.

In another despairing plea to Churchill on 27 October, Cripps, still in the big British Embassy in beleaguered Moscow, with the sound of enemy guns in his ears day and night, reported that relations between Great Britain and Russia as reflected at his post were getting worse, and that if we could not open a second front the only way in which we could improve matters was to send troops to Russia. He urged the despatch of a force not less than a corps, with an adequate proportion of the Royal Air Force, 'either to the northern or the southern extremities of the Russian battlefront'.

This plea from an ambassador whose sympathies seemed at times to lie more on the side of Soviet Russia than of embattled Britain, drew an angry protest from Churchill on 28 October. The memory of Russia's late enmity still rankled and he reacted strongly. 'They certainly have no right to reproach us,' he protested, in a denunciation of Soviet policy.

> They brought their own fate upon themselves when, by their pact with Ribbentrop, they let Hitler loose on Poland and so started the war. They cut themselves off from an effective Second Front when they let the French Army be destroyed. If prior to June 22 they had consulted with us beforehand, many arrangements could have been made to bring earlier the great help we are now sending them in munitions. We did not however know till Hitler attacked them, whether they would fight, or what side they would be on. We were left alone for a whole year while every Communist in England, under orders from Moscow, did his best to hamper our war effort. If we had been invaded and destroyed in July or August 1941 or starved out this year in the Battle of the Atlantic, they would have remained utterly indifferent. . . . If they harbour suspicions of

us it is only because of the guilt and reproach in their own hearts.[6]

It was a wounding riposte and for some time Cripps was silenced. Churchill took great care to defend his attitude to Roosevelt, whom the Soviets were now wooing. In a long letter of 20 October telling him of the impending British offensive in Libya, of his long-term strategy for the war and the disposition of available British troops, he repeated that it was not possible to make any serious contribution to the Russian defence of the Caucasus and Caspian basin. He also referred to his Government's long-term plans for the invasion of Europe in 1943 and to far-reaching plans for special ships designed to land large numbers of tanks on enemy-occupied coastlines.

He included drawings for these, prepared by the Admiralty, and plans for merchant ships specially modified for use as tank landing ships. 'It seems to me', he wrote, 'that no less than 200 ships should be thus fitted. There is sufficient time, as we cannot think of such a plan before 1943. But the essential counterpart of the tank programme you have now embarked upon is the power to transport them across the oceans and land them upon unfortified beaches around the immense coastline Hitler is committed to defend.'[7]

Design and construction of landing craft had been of special concern to Churchill ever since Dunkirk. The idea for them was based upon a visionary paper on the subject he had prepared as long ago as July 1917, during the First World War. He referred then to tank-landing lighters carrying tanks, which by means of a drawbridge or shelving bow would be enabled to land under their own power on the beaches. This paper had become the genesis in 1940 of a plan for the design and manufacture of a fleet of landing craft and landing ships.

As early as October 1940 trials of the first landing craft had begun and by the summer of 1941 an improved design was ready. Larger, more seaworthy vessels, however, were found necessary and these, called the LST or landing ship tank, were designed and built in Britain. A final design for a landing ship tank was eventually completed and delivered to the United States, where refinements were added and production in 1942 was begun. Thus long before the advent of the United States into the war, Churchill was creating the means for landing a British armoured force in Europe.

On 18 November 1941, in heavy rain, General Auchinleck launched the 118,000-strong Eighth Army against General Rommel's forces in the area east of besieged Tobruk in the Western Desert. The advanced British armoured units reached Sidi Rezegh on 19 November, but having first stopped them linking up with the Tobruk garrison,

Rommel counter-attacked strongly. Between 22 and 27 November a destructive tank battle was fought around Sidi Rezegh, which the British eventually seized, but Rommel attacked the British rear next day with his two Panzer divisions. The British held on and linked with Tobruk on 29 November. Rommel was then fought to a standstill, he withdrew his forces to the west on 2 December and the battle petered out. But the Axis forces had lost some 13,000 Germans and 20,000 Italians, as well as about 300 mainly German tanks, compared with British losses of 17,000. And Tobruk was relieved.

Apart from its military implications the battle was important because Churchill could now claim in his exchanges with Stalin that Britain was fighting, had defeated the Germans, had destroyed tanks and had caused large numbers of German fighter aircraft to be withdrawn from the Russian front.

In the light of this struggle in the Western Desert, the War Cabinet Defence Committee met on 3 December 1941 to consider once again the persistent issue of aid to Russia. Churchill announced that Anthony Eden was going to Moscow soon to see Stalin. He would explain to the Soviet leader personally why it was quite impossible for a huge army to be sent either to the north or to the south of the Russian front. Churchill then raised the question of whether Britain should make a pledge to send a small token force of two divisions and ten Royal Air Force squadrons to co-operate with the Russians on the Don, but the Chiefs of Staff argued strongly that all available forces should be kept for the next battle against Rommel in Libya.

Admiral Sir Dudley Pound, First Sea Lord, argued that the Russians had constantly pressed us to open a second front. This we had now done in Libya, and already very considerable air forces were being drawn away from the Russian front. We were now doing what the Russians had always wanted us to do, and we would continue to press the battle in Libya. The Chiefs of Staff, he said, felt we could do far more to help Russia by fighting on in Libya than in any other way, and it would be wrong to make any move which would detract from the strength available for the battle.

General Sir Alan Brooke, the recently appointed Chief of the Imperial General Staff, in place of General Sir John Dill, contended at this 3 December 1941 meeting that in Libya we had the only offensive front from which we could engage the Germans. It was essential to keep it going, and we should cut down the defensive troops we had to maintain elsewhere to the minimum. Even if the situation on the Russian front deteriorated, he felt it would be most unwise to divert two divisions northward to the Caucasus on such a doubtful mission.

Even Beaverbrook declared that it seemed most unlikely that we could send any troops to the Russians, and he had always thought that we had made a reckless promise to do so. He also did not think that the Russians really wanted our troops. They would much more rather have more tanks and aircraft, particularly as they were getting practically nothing from the United States. Characteristically, Beaverbrook remarked that the right course would be for the Foreign Secretary to arrive for his talks with Stalin in Moscow with the offer of a force in one hand, and an offer of a further supply of tanks and aircraft in the other, and try to trade the latter for the former. The only way of getting out of sending divisions to the Russian Front was to make an offer to send equipment in lieu.

Those present agreed that in view of the advantages to be gained by pressing on with the offensive in North Africa, and in view of the change in the Russian situation caused by the successful battle at Rostov, it would be unwise to send British forces to the Don. Anthony Eden thought that the right thing to do was to tell Stalin our situation with complete frankness, including the importance of not diverting troops from the Libyan offensive, and to explain to him that in consequence we should not be in a position to send the troops which we had previously hoped would be available.[8]

Whichever way Britain turned at this time she was hampered by shortages of shipping and of aircraft. In October a plan for an attack on Trondheim on the Norwegian coast, including, if necessary, the use of mustard gas as a terror weapon for the first time in the war, had been turned down by the Chiefs of Staff, mainly owing to lack of available air support. And a proposal for an attack on Sicily, Operation WHIPCORD, was rejected because it could not be launched to coincide with the Eighth Army's offensive in Cyrenaica, as well as owing to lack of shipping.

In late 1941, the war turned against Great Britain in the Far East, but temporarily in Russia's favour on her Western front. German forces had penetrated to within sight of the Moscow suburbs before freezing temperatures of 40 degrees below zero, shortage of petrol and Soviet tenacity stopped them on 5 December. Next day the Red Army counter-attacked, by 15 December had driven the Nazis back more than 100 miles and in bitter fighting had re-taken Kalinin and other towns.

But Great Britain suffered heavily in the Far East. Japan had destroyed about half of the RAF's 110 aircraft in Malaya, was driving British forces back in relentless jungle warfare and was threatening Burma. Then on 10 December Japanese torpedo-bombers sank the battleships *Prince of Wales* and *Repulse* off the Malayan coast, a blow softened only by the victories of Auchinleck's forces over the Germans in Cyrenaica.

Then, with her destructive attack, 7 December 1941, on the American fleet at Pearl Harbour, Japan brought the United States into the war overnight, and changed its whole balance dramatically. Another ally now stood by Britain's side, for the US was now committed fully both in Europe and the Far East. But it would bring problems as well as blessings for Britain, for the American Chiefs of Staff would seek to impose upon her their own war strategy, including an immediate second front.

It was against this turbulent background that Churchill set sail on 12 December 1941 in the battleship *Duke of York* for Washington for the next of his wartime conferences with Roosevelt. His party included Beaverbrook, Minister of Supply, and the Chiefs of Staff — Admiral Sir Dudley Pound, Air Chief Marshal Sir Charles Portal and Field-Marshal Sir John Dill, who had just relinquished his post as C.I.G.S. to General Brooke, and was to be head of the British Military Mission to Washington.

During the 8-day voyage the indefatigable Churchill wrote three papers on war strategy. Their main theme was that 'the defeat of Japan would not spell the defeat of Hitler, but that the defeat of Hitler made the finishing-off of Japan merely a matter of time and trouble'. The first paper envisaged the occupation and control of French West and North Africa in 1942 by American/British forces, and the total destruction of Axis forces from Tunis to Egypt, so as to allow free passage through the Mediterranean to the Suez Canal.

The second covered the Pacific campaign, while the third, dealing with what would become the even more contentious issue of a second front, called for 'the liberation of the captive countries of Western and Southern Europe by the landing at suitable points, successively or simultaneously, of British and American armies strong enough to enable the conquered populations to revolt.' The paper, remarkable for its foresight, continued:

> By themselves they will never be able to revolt, owing to the ruthless counter-measures that will be employed, but if adequate and suitably equipped forces were landed in . . . Norway, Denmark, Holland, Belgium, the French channel coasts, as well as Italy and possibly the Balkans, the German garrisons would prove insufficient to cope both with the strength of the liberating forces and the fury of the revolting peoples. . . .
>
> In principle, the landings should be made by armoured and mechanised forces capable of disembarking not at ports but on beaches, either by landing craft or from ocean-going ships specially adapted. The potential front of attack is thus made so wide that the German forces holding down these different

countries cannot be strong enough at all points. An amphibious outfit must be prepared to enable these large-scaled disembarkations to be made swiftly and surely.[9]

The occupation of North Africa and of Tunis was seen in this far-reaching paper as the vital first step towards an eventual large-scale cross-Channel attack in 1943. Italy could be knocked out of the war, garrisons be left in North Africa, fighting units be returned to Great Britain and a strong enough force could be established for a cross-Channel landing and a 'second front'. Without victory in North Africa, British Home and Middle East forces, dangerously split by the long Cape route, would be forced to continue as independent armies, practically speaking, and thus the build-up of strong invasion forces in Great Britain would be impossible.

Secondly, Germany would be forced to withdraw additional valuable fighting units from the Russian front to defend both North Africa and Italy — and this is, in fact, what was to take place. The 10 German divisions in the Mediterranean would be increased to 40 by 1943, and enormous losses would be sustained there.

So while the battleship *Duke of York* steamed across the dangerous Atlantic on this historic mission, Churchill worked out his view of the war strategy for presentation to Roosevelt. At the same time, the Chiefs of Staff produced a paper covering Home Defence, the Middle East, India, the Far East, and the European theatre. The Chiefs of Staff also looked to the occupation of North Africa and the defeat of Italy as a first step towards a second front in Northern France, but they had reservations about the size of the cross-Channel assault force. They believed that this would be limited to about 17 divisions, largely owing to the difficulties of providing enough special landing-craft for the Channel crossing.

In a discussion of these papers on 19 December between Churchill, Beaverbrook and the Chiefs of Staff — Pound, Portal and Dill (deputising for Brooke) — it was agreed that they should propose that the United States would take the lead in occupying North Africa 'by preparing an expeditionary force of say, 25,000 men, to be augmented by a force totalling up to 150,000 men during the next six months.'

Churchill had also stated that he 'thought it important to put before the people of both the British Empire and the United States the mass invasion of the Continent of Europe as the goal for 1943.' It was a matter he had kept in the forefront of his mind ever since Dunkirk. 'I always considered', he wrote later, 'that a decisive assault upon the German occupied countries on the largest possible scale, was the only way in which the war could be won, and that the summer of 1943 should be chosen as the target date.'[10]

After a final discussion on 19 December 1941 on board the battleship, the Chiefs of Staff produced a survey of strategy in all theatres of war for which they hoped to get the backing of the American Chiefs of Staff for common action. Starting with the agreement reached in the Anglo-American Staff talks in February 1941, that 'Germany was the predominant member of the Axis Powers and consequently the Atlantic and European area was considered to be the decisive theatre,' they reaffirmed that Germany's defeat remained the key to victory despite the entry of Japan into the war.

Regarding a second European fighting front they contended: 'It does not seem likely that in 1942 any large-scale land offensive against Germany, except on the Russian front will be possible. We must, however, be ready to take advantage of any opening... to conduct limited offensives in North-western Europe or across the Mediterranean.' They continued:

> In 1943 the way may be clear for a return to the Continent, either across the Mediterranean, or from Turkey into the Balkans, or by simultaneous landings in several of the occupied countries of North-western Europe. Such operations will be the prelude to the final assault on Germany itself, and the scope of the victory programme should be such as to provide means by which they can be carried out.[11]

While the *Duke of York* safely crossed the Atlantic the Navy in the Mediterranean suffered losses which would seriously affect Britain's power to launch a second fighting front for some time. On 19 December, in Alexandria harbour, Italian frogmen fixed time-bombs to the battleships *Queen Elizabeth* and *Valiant* which blasted them out of action for months. That same day the cruiser *Neptune* was sunk, and the *Aurora* and *Penelope* badly damaged by mines when trying to intercept an Italian convoy en route to Tripoli with reinforcements for Rommel. The convoy escaped. Rommel would soon be able to turn the tables on Auchinleck as a result, and drive the 8th Army back into Egypt. Added to the earlier naval loss in November of the aircraft-carrier *Ark Royal*, and the disabling of the battleship *Barham*, these new losses meant the virtual destruction of the Royal Navy's power in the Mediterranean. Crucial too, were the losses of the *Prince of Wales* and the *Repulse* in the Far East in December.

With these severe losses in mind, Churchill and his naval, military and air advisers, with Beaverbrook, landed at Washington Airport after a short flight from Hampton Roads on 22 December 1941. The occasion was a turning point for Great Britain, for they were to convince the President and his war leaders that Hitler and the Nazis must still be defeated before Japan, despite the treacherous blow she had dealt America.

But it was a tense situation for, already, powerful voices in the United States Navy were demanding a reversal of the flow of war weapons from Great Britain and Soviet Russia to American forces in the Far East. 'We are all in the same boat now,' Roosevelt had said, but some of his team had begun to pull in the opposite direction. Could the conflicting interests of the two great allies be reconciled and British leadership maintained, at least for the time being?

The discussions themselves, the ARCADIA Conference, were long and complex, covering the whole field of war strategy. Churchill and his staff lived and worked from a number of rooms off the upstairs hall of the White House, with an operations room where the up-to-date movements of the armies and fleets in the various theatres of war were indicated. The quiet calm of the White House was shaken by the constant flow of staff officers and officials bearing red despatch cases with messages from Whitehall, or from the Commanders-in-Chief where British troops were fighting in the Middle and the Far East.

The Chiefs of Staff, British and American, met and worked in the Federal Reserve Building, first thing in the morning as two separate teams, then as one. Altogether they met twelve times, hammering out solutions to military problems for the President and the Prime Minister. The cool and intellectual Field-Marshal Sir John Dill headed the British team and soon became close friends with his American counterpart, General George Marshall, later described by General Brooke as a man 'of charm and dignity', and 'a great man, a great gentleman, and a great organiser'; yet Brooke was as critical of Marshall's strategic thinking as Marshall was of his — a fact which would lead to near-deadlock in strategic planning in the future.

Between these two a clash was hard to avoid, for both found it hard to give way. Marshall, well over six feet, with craggy features and a curiously long upper lip, inspired trust and liking, but lacked Brooke's logical approach. An outstanding military organiser, he was devoted probably as much to the achievement of world supremacy for the United States as to the defeat of Germany and Japan. Brooke, a highly experienced fighting soldier who had commanded the triumphant escape to Dunkirk of the remnants of the B.E.F., hid a brilliantly analytical mind behind a façade of bushy eyebrows, acquiline features, short black military moustache and brusque, often intolerant manner. Churchill's personal physician, Lord Moran, said he wore an iron mask to hide a sensitive, highly-strung person whom no one knew existed. Better than anyone he stood up to Churchill's dictatorial manner. 'The P.M. got his way with every one else; only Brooke refused to budge,' Moran noted.

The Chiefs of Staff, British and American, studied the entire course of the war and put forward their own proposals to the President and Churchill, who meantime continued their own discussions together. Out of the staff meetings of the best naval and military brains on both sides, was created the permanent Combined Chiefs of Staff Committee in Washington. It became an indispensable Anglo-American weapon for the conduct of the war and in a practical sense the most useful result of the ARCADIA Conference, for it took most of the vital wartime strategic decisions.

From the outset of the talks the fears of the British that the Americans might now turn aside from Europe and defeat Japan first were calmed despite Japan's rapid moves in South-East Asia. The foundation of Anglo-American strategy was still to be the defeat of Germany first, despite the loud cries of America's isolationist press. Although later Churchill was accused of having coaxed Roosevelt into this decision, it was in fact as much the work of General Marshall, American Chief of Staff, Admiral Stark, then Navy Commander-in-Chief, General Leonard Gerow, Senior Army Planner and his deputy, Brigadier General Dwight D. Eisenhower, of whom so much was to be heard later.

Churchill put the implications of this decision in a few well-chosen words in a letter to the War Cabinet in London during the talks: 'While therefore it is right to assign primacy to the war against Germany, it would be wrong to speak of our "standing on the defensive" against Japan; on the contrary, the only way in which we can live through the intervening period in the Far East, before Germany is defeated, is by regaining the initiative, albeit on a minor scale.'

Roosevelt accepted Churchill's plan for an Anglo-American landing in North Africa as soon as possible, with or without the Vichy Government's agreement, so as to forestall the Germans there. Roosevelt, according to Churchill, said that he was 'anxious that American land forces should give their support as quickly as possible wherever they could be most helpful, and favoured the idea of a plan to move into North Africa being prepared for either event, i.e. with or without invitation.'

The Combined Chiefs of Staff, to whom the North African project was submitted for study, held very different views about the size of the force needed for it. The Americans called for 300,000 men, compared with the 100,000 the British wanted,[12] but later both sides accepted a compromise force of 3 British and 3 American divisions and 348 aircraft, chiefly from America.

To Churchill's regret, the plan — called SUPER-GYMNAST — at once came up against the obstacles of shortage of ships on both sides.

Marshall pointed out that 20,000 American troops — 14,000 for Northern Ireland to relieve a Marines division there, and 6,000 for Iceland — were due to sail on 15 January 1942, but, he said, they could be re-allocated to SUPER-GYMNAST with a delay of six days if this was agreed upon before 13 January. The British planners said that the diversion of their shipping needed for this would mean 25,000 men less for the Middle East and the cancellation of two other minor, but significant operations.

By 12 January the failure of Auchinleck's offensive in North Africa, and Japan's rapid conquests, including the seizure of Hongkong, Wake Island, Loosong and the threat to Singapore, all combined to create caution about immediate landings in French North Africa. And in the light of the shipping requirements for the Far East and the Middle East it could not in any case be launched until 25 May 1942. So Marshall's proposal to cut the transport of troops to Northern Ireland and to Iceland from 20,000 to 6,600, and to use the ships made available for an urgent convoy of 21,800 troops and 393 aircraft to the South Pacific was agreed.[13]

The hope of Churchill and Roosevelt for an immediate invasion of North Africa was therefore ruled out, but the reasoning upon which it was based held good. 'It was recognised', noted a Chiefs of Staff Memorandum for the War Cabinet on GYMNAST, dated 20 January 1942, 'that if events took a sudden favourable turn in North Africa, we should have to exploit the situation with such British and American forces as could be made available at short notice, one British Armoured and two Infantry Divisions with some fighter aircraft and anti-aircraft guns and the one American Division (Combat Loaded).' It was agreed that plans should go ahead on this assumption while for the time being preparations should also be made as far as possible for a full strength invasion of French North Africa when it was possible.

General Marshall's point of view emerged in an important agreement following ARCADIA which stated that it should be a 'cardinal principle of American-British strategy that only the minimum force necessary for the safeguarding of vital interests in other theatres should be diverted from operations against Germany.' It was also agreed that the essential features of grand strategy should be: 'the realisation of the victory programme of armaments: the maintenance of essential communications: the closing and tightening of the ring round Germany: the wearing down and undermining of German resistance by air bombardment, blockade, subversive activities and propaganda: the continuous development of offensive action against Germany: maintaining only such positions in the Eastern theatre as will safeguard vital interests and to deny to Japan access to raw materials vital to her continuous war effort while Britain and the United States are concentrating on Germany.'[14]

Churchill said farewell to Roosevelt on 14 January 1942, travelled by train to Norfolk, Virginia, then by air in a Boeing flying-boat to Bermuda. The spacious and comfortable aircraft fascinated him and on the spur of the moment he asked Captain Kelly Rogers, chief pilot, if they could fly home to England from Bermuda, where the *Duke of York* was standing by for the ocean journey.

Kelly at once said yes; there was, he said, a 40 mph tail-wind and it would take about 20 hours. There were risks, Churchill realised, but so there were from U-boats at sea even in the *Duke of York*. After discussion at Bermuda with Admiral Pound and Air Marshall Portal it was agreed that they should fly. 'I thought perhaps I had done a rash thing,' Churchill noted. 'I had always regarded an Atlantic flight with awe.'[15]

Regular trans-Atlantic flights were at this time a future event, navigational aids were primitive compared with today, and radio silence was imposed for fear of alerting the enemy. Nevertheless the flight went well, but a minor navigational error took them towards the end of it on a course within five minutes' flying time of German anti-aircraft guns at Brest. They turned north just in time and approached England from the south instead of the south west. The aircraft was detected on radar and six Hurricanes were sent up to intercept them. Fortunately they failed to do so.

Churchill returned to a tale of disasters. Singapore could not be defended and was certain to fall any day to the Japanese forces. Rangoon was threatened, then, on 21 January 1942, Rommel launched a counter-offensive and sent Auchinleck's Eighth Army staggering back over the ground he had recently gained. All hopes of an immediate GYMNAST came to an end.

Meanwhile, Beaverbrook's newspapers were raising a popular clamour for A Second Front Now! Banner headlines in the *Daily Express* supported articles which painted a picture of easy victories once the British armies had been launched across the Channel against German fortifications in Europe. Enthusiastic meetings continued to be held in Trafalgar Square and Hyde Park, in London, as well as in the major cities throughout the country.

To this popular clamour Sir Stafford Cripps, until lately Ambassador in Russia, added his own authoritative voice. But Churchill remodelled his Cabinet on 19 February 1942, accepting Beaverbrook's resignation as Minister of Production, which he had only held since 4 February, putting Oliver Lyttelton in his place and making Cripps Leader of the House of Commons and Lord Privy Seal instead of Clement Attlee, who became Churchill's Deputy, and Dominions Secretary. Cripps was thus forced into silence on Cabinet issues.

Despite his problems, Churchill could look back on the AR-

CADIA conference as one of the turning points in the war, for he and Roosevelt had agreed on a historic British-American programme of war strategy, including the defeat of Germany first. But the growing American impatience for a single fighting front in Europe without delay, would still be opposed by a cautious British will to proceed step by step at different points in accord with a carefully planned strategy. A wrangle was to begin that brought threats by the Americans to turn their backs on Europe and defeat Japan first. Churchill, Eden, Brooke and Mountbatten contended in this war of words with Roosevelt, Cordell-Hull, Stimson, Marshall, King and Eisenhower, while Stalin and Molotov strove to guide their decisions in Russia's favour.

3 EISENHOWER'S IMPATIENCE

Blizzards, ice, freezing gales, these fatal obstacles in Russia had slowed the advance of the lightly-clad German armies to a painful standstill in the winter of 1941–42 and enabled the Soviet forces to stage a limited counter-offensive on the central and northern fronts. But this welcome success — this relief from the German onslaught — that the frozen wastes afforded did little to calm the anxiety of American and British military leaders about Soviet Russia's capacity to resist a massive new German armoured assault in the spring. If the Germans over-ran the Soviet forces and Russia was forced to surrender, Hitler would dominate Europe, occupy the Middle East, cut off Great Britain's oil supplies and force her to come to terms as well, with consequent peril for the United States. Therefore by every means — a second front if possible; massive deliveries of tanks and aircraft by sea certainly — Soviet Russia had to be helped to go on fighting.

Roosevelt and Churchill, with their military staffs and planners, had this imperative in mind night and day. From Dunkirk onwards the dogged Churchill had pressed the British Joint Planning Staff to prepare plans for an eventual return to the continent and the project had gained in urgency after the forced entry of Soviet Russia into the war against Nazi Germany. The British staffs had worked out by December 1941 plans named ROUNDUP for an invasion of Europe to exploit a German collapse in Russia. The plan, reflecting British military shortages then, provided for an assault along the 70-mile French coastline from Deauville to Dieppe, by an alarmingly small force of six infantry and six armoured divisions with six tank brigades, support troops and aircraft, reinforced by naval bombardment from three cruisers and a battleship. In many ways theoretical and impractical, this early ROUNDUP plan carried very little weight among General Brooke and his fellow Chiefs of Staff, though it grew in time into the nucleus of the mighty OVERLORD. But in 1941 another plan for a second front named SLEDGEHAMMER overtook it, drawn up by the American and British command and planning organisations.

To know how the second front was planned eventually it is necessary to understand something of this complex military planning system. At the apex of the British set-up stood Churchill, Minister of Defence, responsible to the War Cabinet and its Defence Committee, by whom he could be over-ruled. Unlike Roosevelt, the American Commander-in-Chief, who usually, but not always, accepted the verdicts of his subordinates in this field, the egocentric Churchill brought to bear a strong though not decisive influence on planning.

Directly responsible to Churchill was the British Chiefs of Staff Committee, which included the Commander-in-Chief of the Imperial General Staff, General Sir Alan Brooke, Admiral Sir Dudley Pound and Air Chief Marshal Sir Charles Portal. Together with their immediate subordinates, the Joint Planning Staff, they were responsible for planning British strategy, as well as reporting on the practicability of Churchill's numerous strategic ideas.

In January 1942, the command structure was enlarged when General Sir Bernard Paget, the very soldierly Commander-in-Chief of British Home Forces and therefore in charge of defence against invasion, was instructed by the Chiefs of Staff to study the cross-Channel attack plan SLEDGEHAMMER, drawn up by the Joint Planning Staff. He was to be aided by the Navy and Air Force Commanders-in-Chief. From this informal association the nucleus of a planning group, the Combined Commanders, grew in 1942. Commodore (later Admiral) Lord Louis Mountbatten, Chief of Combined Operations — the brilliant and daring officer who began his career in the Royal Navy in the First World War as a teenage midshipman — joined the Combined Commanders early in 1942, while the commanding general of the United States forces in Europe was also invited informally to work with them. Until the appointment of General Morgan as COSSAC (Chief of Staff to the Supreme Allied Commander) responsible for OVERLORD planning, the Combined Commanders were responsible for planning a second European fighting front.

In marked contrast to the British, the Americans entered the war entirely lacking any supreme military planning body comparable to the Chiefs of Staffs Committee. The President, as Commander-in-Chief, even lacked the support of an independent military secretariat free of any ties with the fighting services, so that the army and navy often acted independently of each other.

It was a confused situation, but to cope with planning demands in association with the British staffs, the Americans hurriedly set up the United States Joint Chiefs of Staff on the lines of the British body. Even then, at their first meeting no military secretariat was present to record proceedings on their side. 'There are no regular meetings of their chiefs of staff,' Field-Marshal Sir John Dill, chairman of the British side in the Combined Chiefs of Staff, told Brooke in a letter.

They have no joint planners and executive planning staff . . . .Then there is the great difficulty of getting the stuff over to the President. There is no such thing as a cabinet meeting, and yet the Secretaries for War, Navy, etc are supposed to function . . . .Eventually they will do great things, but the difficulty is going to be to hold cards of re-entry to enable them to play their strong suits when they have collected them . . . . The whole organisation belongs to the days of George Washington, who was made Commander-in-Chief of all the Forces, and just did it. Today the President is Commander-in-Chief of all the Forces, but it is not so easy to just do it.[1]

It was with this far-sighted observation that the very perceptive Dill, former Chief of the Imperial General Staff, began his role as head of the British Joint Staff Mission and senior British member of the Combined Chiefs of Staff set up at the ARCADIA Conference. The Americans were quick to remedy their deficiencies in the command and planning organisation for European operations.

The first members of their joint Chiefs of Staff were General George C. Marshall, Chief of Staff of the Army; Lt-General H. Arnold, Commanding General of the Army Air forces, and Deputy Chief of Staff for Air; Admiral Harold R. Stark, Chief of Naval Operations and Admiral Ernest J. King, Commander-in-Chief of the United States Fleet. The posts held by Stark and by King were combined in March 1942 under King, while Stark went to London as commander of United States naval forces in Europe.

By early 1942 the British and American Joint Planning Staffs made up the Combined Staff Planners, a body which was responsible to the Combined Chiefs of Staff. On each side plans and studies of policy and strategy were agreed by the joint planning staffs and submitted to the Joint Chiefs of Staff for approval by the Combined Chiefs of Staff. Responsible mainly for plans for cross-Channel operations in 1942 were the British Combined Commanders and the Operations Division of the War Department in Washington.

One of the chief concerns of the British and American military leaders in 1942 was, as we have seen, helping Soviet Russia to stay in the war, and the military planners on both sides were instructed to find a way of attracting German forces from the Eastern Front. In London, at a meeting on 17 March 1942, the British Chiefs of Staff were pessimistic about the prospects of a cross-Channel operation in the Pas-de-Calais area where the full weight of the RAF could be brought to bear and a permanent bridgehead made.

Brooke argued at this meeting that it seemed most unlikely that we should be able to hold a bridgehead indefinitely against the forces that the Germans could concentrate. 'We could not afford to lose a force consisting of our best trained units armed with special types of equipment, including the latest Cruiser tanks,' he said. But despite Brooke's caution, the Chiefs of Staff, in curiously indefinite terms, instructed the Joint Planning Staff to prepare a study of the possibility of causing the maximum destruction to Germany in the period May to July 1942, with the object of relieving German pressure on the Russian front.[2]

After another debate on this perplexing issue four days later on 21 March, the Chiefs of Staff agreed that the planning of cross-Channel operations should be undertaken by the C-in-C Home Forces, the Cs-in-C Fighter Command and Bomber Command, and the Chief of Combined Operations. In an important directive to them, which did not however commit Britain to any operations in 1942, they said:[3]

> You have been appointed to plan operations with the following object: to make Germany continuously employ her air forces in active operations and to cause protracted air fighting in the West in an area advantageous to ourselves, in order to reduce German air support available for the Eastern front as early as possible.
>
> It is intended that these operations should include a major deception plan designed to threaten the Germans with a permanent return to the continent.
>
> Planning should commence forthwith and a report to the Chiefs of Staff should be made at the earliest date about the forces which it would be practicable and desirable to employ, and your views on the probability of success.

The planners were authorised to undertake 'immediate preparations', if need be in advance of final approval.

Great caution thus remained the keynote of the British military chiefs' discussions on the feasibility of a cross-Channel invasion. And at a meeting of the War Cabinet Defence Committee as well on 28 March, Lord Louis Mountbatten, now Chief of Combined Operations, strongly opposed the project of an attack in the Pas-de-Calais area. 'Re-embarkation', he argued, 'would be an extremely difficult task. We should certainly have to leave behind most of the equipment and probably many of the personnel.'[4] He suggested that an operation in the Cherbourg Peninsula should be examined in further detail.

Brooke retorted that the only area in which the object could be achieved was the Pas-de-Calais, where the air battles could best be fought and where the army could operate under proper fighter cover. Operations in the more distant Cherbourg Peninsula did not fulfil these conditions.

General Paget said bluntly that he did not consider that under present conditions the occupation of a bridgehead anywhere in France was a feasible proposition.

The shadow of Dunkirk still hung over the thinking of British military planners at this time.

The Americans, 3,000 miles distant from the heavy guns and mined beaches of northern France, urged on by a restless public and an enormous army they needed to use, were burning for action, eager to test their military prowess, to overwhelm the Nazis and bring the war to a quick, victorious end.

Brigadier-General Dwight D. Eisenhower, then Deputy Chief of the US War Plans Division, was foremost among those American planners eager to strike a counter-blow in Europe without delay. 'We've got to go to Europe and fight,' he wrote impatiently in his personal notes on 22 January 1942, 'and we've got to quit wasting resources all over the world — and still worse — wasting time. If we're to keep Russia in, save the Middle East, India and Burma; we've got to begin slugging with air [sic] at West Europe; to be followed by a land attack as soon as possible.'[5]

In February, promotion to chief of Army Operations Division (OPD) came Eisenhower's way, and he gave further voice on 22 February 1942 to his impetuous wish for action in the personal notes which reflected his thoughts and feelings about the war. 'We've got to keep Russia in the war and hold India!' he wrote. 'Then we can get ready to crack Germany through England.'[6]

Eisenhower, this unassuming, but very earnest and friendly man with the candid blue eyes and slightly jaunty appearance, whose destiny in world history was starting to blossom, now prepared a formal strategic study which emphasised once again for 'logistic reasons as well as strategic axiom' the decision to concentrate first against the enemy in Europe. In it, he urged as a way of keeping Russia in the war, that:

> We should at once develop, in conjunction with the British, a definite plan for operations against north-west Europe. It should be drawn up at once in detail, and it should be sufficiently extensive in scale as to engage from the middle of May onward, an increasing portion of the German air force, and by later summer an increasing amount of ground forces.[7]

Political considerations played no part at all, it should be noted, in

Eisenhower's naming of north-west Europe for the invasion that summer. His decision was based entirely on the strategic and logistical military objectives of defending Great Britain and the Atlantic sea lanes, while at the same time creating forces for the cross-Channel jump-off.

Anthony Eden, on the contrary, perhaps alone at this time, was gravely troubled about Europe's post-war future in the light of Soviet Russia's declared wish to extend her western frontiers. On 28 January 1942 he expressed his anxiety in a remarkably perceptive note to Churchill. To read it today brings a profound sense of regret and dismay that it was ignored:

> On the assumption that Germany is defeated and German military strength is destroyed and that France remains, for some time at least, a weak power, there will be no counterweight to Russia in Europe . . . Russia's position on the European continent will be unassailable. Russian prestige will be so great that the establishment of Communist governments in the majority of European countries will be greatly facilitated and the Soviet Government will naturally be tempted to work for this.[8]

Eden's prophetic vision was a lonely one and his warning went unheeded, or, at least, ran counter to American pro-Russian leanings and therefore was necessarily disregarded. Roosevelt and the American war leaders were already deeply suspicious of Great Britain's 'political' as opposed to 'sound strategic' objectives in the war against Nazi Germany. So the chance of planning the time and place of a second front with the double objective of striking down Hitlerite Germany and achieving a military presence in eastern Europe to discourage Soviet Russia's ambitions there was lost.

Eisenhower's impatience for speedy action was now beginning to bear fruit in the War Department in Washington. On 6 March 1942 the United States Joint Strategic Committee, studying Eisenhower's memorandum for operations in north-west Europe, concluded that the British Isles should be 'a base area for an offensive to defeat the German armed forces', and recommended, after minimum forces had been sent to the Pacific, 'a maximum effor⁺ in cooperation with the British in offensive action operations against Germany' — a British-American landing in September 1942, preceded by an air assault starting in the last two weeks of July in the general area Calais to Deauville and inland to St. Quentin–Soissons–Paris.[9]

Destruction of enemy air and ground forces and their diversion from the Russian front, the planners saw as their main purpose, for which D-Day was to be between 15 July and 1 August 1942. Shortage of shipping however would limit American troops to about 40,000 by July 1942 and therefore limit their part in the proposed operation. Thus it was a British force, substantially, that the US planners proposed should storm Hitler's 'Fortress Europe'.

General Marshall now had before him two plans: this American one, and the British 1941 ROUNDUP plan for an invasion in 1943. He therefore directed the Combined Chiefs of Staff to decide whether it was possible to land and maintain a force in northern France in 1942, or in 1943.[10]

The 'hawks' in Washington now faced a setback, for the Combined Planners found that the shortage of both cargo vessels and landing craft would prevent an invasion in 1942, and that it would only be possible in 1943 if Soviet Russia was still locked in battle with the *Wehrmacht*.

During these Combined Chiefs of Staff studies Eisenhower chafed at the delay in deciding where and when the first major offensive should take place. Training, production schedules and deployment of forces were all affected by this delay, he told Marshall in a note of 25 March, in which he argued forcibly for a concentration of American forces in England as the main task leading on to cross-Channel attack — 'the direct approach . . . to the centre of German might.' Bluntly, Eisenhower argued that 'unless this plan is adopted as the eventual aim of all our efforts, we must turn our backs upon the Eastern Atlantic and go, full out, as quickly as possible against Japan!'[11]

Was this a proposal that Churchill and his Government should be persuaded into agreeing to an early second front in Europe by the threat of being left alone to face Germany? Or was Eisenhower trying to bring his ardent desire for action to bear on the Combined Chiefs of Staff to get their agreement to his plan?

Whichever it was, Marshall, chief among the 'hawks', by-passed the cautious Combined Chiefs of Staff and at lunch in the White House on 25 March gave an eloquent presentation of Eisenhower's plan to President Roosevelt, who, as Commander-in-Chief, had approved what was going on. Indeed, on 9 March he had confided in a message to Churchill that he was 'becoming more and more interested in the establishment of a new front this summer on the European continent, certainly for air and raids . . . And even though losses will doubtless be great, such losses will be compensated by at least equal German losses and by compelling Germans to divert large forces of all kinds from Russian fronts.'[12]

Marshall left his White House luncheon bearing the President's assent to the plan and his instructions to put it 'in shape if possible over this weekend'. Harry Hopkins, the President's special adviser, who was also present, had urged Roosevelt that nothing was as important as 'getting some sort of a front this summer against Germany', and he proposed as part of what would seem to have been a prepared plan, that instead of referring it to the Combined Chiefs of Staff it should be taken directly over to the highest British authorities.[13]

Hopkins was devoted to the President, with whom, as a semi-invalid himself, he doubtless felt much in common apart from political aims. Roosevelt, crippled by polio, carried out his duties from his wheelchair. Hopkins, called by Churchill 'an indomitable spirit' — frail, with wispy greying hair and sallow skin, though only middle-aged — drove himself without mercy and often had to take to his bed, whence, in his soft nasal voice, he transmitted Roosevelt's wishes by telephone.

So the United States War Department planners set to work and in due course Eisenhower gave the final plan to Marshall, who together with Henry Stimson, Secretary for War, presented it to the President on 2 April 1942. Roosevelt approved it and in tune with his war chiefs' sense of urgency instructed General Marshall and Harry Hopkins to fly to London at once to win over Churchill and the British Chiefs of Staff.

'We'll be seeing you soon so please start the fire,' Hopkins cabled Churchill, with friendly banter about Chequers' chilly rooms. And Roosevelt in a cable told Churchill that Hopkins and Marshall would soon be arriving with 'a plan which I hope Russia will greet with enthusiasm'. Next day, in an enthusiastic personal letter to Churchill, he emphasised that the plan had his 'heart and mind in it', and he went on somewhat naively: 'Your people and mine demand the establishment of a front to draw off pressure on the Russians, and these peoples are wise enough to see that the Russians are today killing more Germans and destroying more equipment than you and I put together. Even if full success is not attained, the *big* objective will be. Go to it!'[14]

Ruthless, behind his mask of cordiality, where United States' interests were concerned, Roosevelt was leaning hard on Churchill to win his acceptance of this plan, and he had need to. For Churchill knew that it disregarded the views opposing an early second front of both the British Chiefs of Staff and the Combined Chiefs of Staff in Washington. The latter had shown in detail how lack of landing craft would prevent a large scale assault in 1942 and probably 1943 as well. Now Roosevelt had by-passed the Combined Chiefs and supported his own War Department planners, who disregarded British opposition to an early cross-Channel assault. Roosevelt hoped Marshall would persuade the British to agree to this wholly American plan, for he genuinely believed it would accomplish Germany's defeat soon,

and free United States forces for the Far East; and indeed, on this basis
he had quietened the growls of that tough old American sea-dog
Admiral King, who was angrily gnashing his teeth about the 'Germany first' policy. King, like Marshall and Eisenhower, expressed the
ardent American desire for action and revenge for their military
humiliation by Japan.

General Brooke met Marshall and Hopkins at Hendon Airport on
Wednesday 8 April 1942 and accompanied them at once to Downing
Street. Here, according to Hopkins, from 4 to 6 pm before his dinner
engagement with Churchill later that night, Marshall fulfilled
Roosevelt's wish that this American plan for a 1942 second front
should be presented to the highest British authority.

4 ROOSEVELT:
'A SECOND FRONT IN 1942'

In his meeting with Winston Churchill that afternoon of 18 April 1942, Marshall outlined his plan. 'Western Europe is favoured as the theatre in which to stage the first major offensive by the United States and Great Britain,' he declared. 'Through France passes our shortest route to the heart of Germany.' Referring next to the air superiority that could be built up in England, he went on: 'Another, and most significant consideration is the unique opportunity to establish an active sector on this front this summer, through steadily increasing air operations and by raids or forays all along the coasts.'

Here he was calling for a commitment for an invasion of northern France in the summer of 1942, to which Churchill and his military advisers were strongly opposed.

Pointing out that this initial phase would be of some help to Russia, and that the successful attack through western Europe would afford Russia the maximum possible support, Marshall added: 'Decision as to the main effort must be made now. This is true even if the invasion [for ROUNDUP] cannot be launched during this year. A major attack must be preceded by a long period of intensive preparation.... Decision now will stop continued dispersion of means.' He continued, according to the details of the plan:

> Our proposal provides for an attack by combined forces of approximately 5,800 combat airplanes and 48 divisions against Western Europe as soon as the necessary means can be accumulated in England — estimated at 1 April 1943, provided decision is made *now* and men, material and shipping are conserved for this purpose.
>
> Nine divisions of this assault force are to be armoured, 6 American and 3 British, while 15 of the 39 infantry divisions are to be British as well as 2,550 of the 5,800 fighter, bomber and transport aircraft.
>
> During the preparatory period, the plan provides means to act promptly if: a) the imminence of Russian collapse requires desperate action when a sacrifice attack could be made immediately. b) if German forces are almost completely absorbed

on the Russian front, or a deterioration of the German military power is evident, a prompt movement to the continent could be undertaken.

The plan provides for the movement to the British Isles of the United States air and ground forces comprising about one million men to participate with the British in an invasion of France between Le Havre and Boulogne . . . at about 1 April 1943. Bottlenecks will be shipping and landing craft. American shipping can transport about 400,000 men, leaving the remaining 600,000 to be transported by British or other vessels. If US shipping only were used the date of invasion must be postponed until the late summer of 1943 . . . About 7,000 landing craft are needed to land in the first wave the major combat elements of an infantry and armoured force of at least 6 divisions. The initial landing would need to be reinforced by at least 100,000 troops a week.

Parachute and airborne troops will be employed to assist the ground forces to establish beachheads and to prevent rapid movement of German reinforcements towards the coast. As soon as a beachhead is established strong armoured forces are to be rushed in to break the German resistance along the coast and seize the line Oise-St. Quentin. A movement towards Antwerp will then follow to widen the salient and permit the movement of additional forces across the Channel between Boulogne and Antwerp. Short range aircraft will be based on airfields as quickly as they are captured.   A limited operation (SLEDGEHAMMER) would be justified only in case: 1) The situation on the Russian front becomes desperate, i.e. the success of German arms becomes so complete as to threaten the imminent collaise of Russian resistance unless the pessure is relieved by an attack from the West by British and American troops. In this case the attack should be considered as a sacrifice in the common good. 2) The German situation in Western Europe becomes critically weakened.[1]

But in the autumn of 1942, owing to shortage of landing craft, not more than about 5 divisions, half British and half United States, could be landed and maintained; and only 900 American aircraft could be made available, so that Great Britain would have to provide nearly 5,000. Thus, the plan was glaringly unrealistic on these counts alone.

In his notes for Roosevelt of the meeting, Harry Hopkins said that Churchill had made it 'perfectly clear to me that he did not treat the proposals as seriously as either the facts warranted or as did the United

States. . . . Marshall was more optimistic than I was. He thought that Churchill went a long way and (he, Marshall) expected far more resistance than he got.'[2]

Next day, 9 April at 10 am, Marshall unveiled his plan also to the British Chiefs of Staff at a meeting in the Cabinet War Room, saying that he had come to decide what the main British-American effort was to be and when and where it should be made. He continued: 'The greatest importance should be attached to continuation of Russian resistance; secondly, it is essential that the large American army now being built up and trained should become engaged on active operations and gain war experience.'

He thought that Western Europe was most favourable for the combined effort, but they must decide how they should go about the combined planning. 'If the Russian situation develops unfavourably, we might have to stage an emergency operation on the Continent to help them,' he said. 'We should also be ready to exploit a break in German morale.' By mid-September, two and a half infantry divisions and one armoured division from America as well as 400 fighter aircraft, 300 bombers and 200 transport aircraft should be available. But until September lack of shipping would make it impossible to transport troops across the Atlantic to Britain and therefore he could not press for an emergency operation before then.[3]

After Marshall had outlined the plan, Brooke said with unusual tact that the British Chiefs of Staff had been thinking along the same lines. He went on to propose a course of action which was the reverse of Marshall's plan to help the Russians if they faced collapse. Brooke said that if the Germans failed to bring off their offensive this summer and suffered heavy reverses, plans were being made in this event to land on the Continent to exploit the situation. He added that he was doubtful if we could do anything to help the Russians by land operations if things went badly for them, but 'we might be able to use land forces as a bait to bring on air battles and inflict a serious drain on the Luftwaffe'.

In his stern and pedantic manner, Brooke argued that 'if we are forced to land on the Continent this year to help the Russians, we might be able to put ashore a force of some 7 divisions and 2 armoured divisions, but this force would not be able to hold a bridgehead against available German forces and it is unlikely that we would be able to extricate these forces if the Germans make a determined effort to drive us out.'

The loss of this force, he said gravely, would dangerously weaken the defence of Great Britain.

He was also concerned about India and the Middle East, where the Japanese and Germans might join forces and capture the oilfields in Iran and Iraq on which, he said 'the whole of our effort in both theatres depends'. Marshall admitted that he could not press for an 'emergency operation' before September 1942, as American help could not be given before that date on any scale.[4]

Churchill, his Cabinet colleagues and the Chiefs of Staff quietly congratulated themselves over America's determination to seek action in Europe in 1943, but they had serious reservations about the idea for an emergency, or sacrifice landing, in 1942. With this, and the need not to deflect the American effort towards the Far East, in mind, Churchill responded in a very guarded letter to Roosevelt on 12 April, that he had read 'with earnest attention your masterly document about the future of the war and the great operations proposed. I am in entire agreement in principle with all you propose, and so are the Chiefs of Staff,' he continued.

> We must of course meet day to day emergencies in the East and Far East while preparing for the main stroke. All the details are being rapidly examined, and preparations where action is clear have already begun. The whole matter will be discussed on the evening of Tuesday, the 14th, by the Defence Committee, to which Harry and Marshall are coming, and I have no doubt that I shall be able to send you our complete agreement.
>
> I may say that I thought the proposals made for an interim operation in certain contingencies this year met the difficulties and uncertainties in an absolutely sound manner. If, as our experts believe, we can carry this whole plan through successfully it will be one of the grand events in all the history of war.[5]

With diplomatic flattery, Churchill had called Marshall's plan a 'masterly document', which, with its vagueness and its repetition, it most certainly was not, while his own letter did merit this description. In it first he gave his agreement to the plan, but only 'in principle', then a few lines later left the matter up in the air by saying he had 'no doubt' that 'complete agreement would follow'. In the second paragraph he at once praised the plan's soundness and skilfully undermined it. Perhaps he felt that he could not completely make up his mind until the Chiefs of Staff had finished studying the document. And he had plenty of other things to worry about, for at this time Japan had bombed Colombo, had sunk the aircraft carrier *Hermes* and two cruisers in the Indian Ocean, which her naval forces now dominated.

Marshall began to understand that the British were approaching his plan with little real enthusiasm. 'Everyone', he reported to Washington on 13 April, agreed 'in principle', but 'many if not most' of those taking part held 'reservations regarding this or that'. It would need 'great firmness' to stop 'further dispersions'.[6]

Marshall's second meeting with the British Chiefs of Staff next morning did little to reassure him. He said then that he believed that 'within the next three or four months we are likely to be forced to take action on the Continent. I am anxious that dispersion of forces should be reduced to a minimum. . . . I think it essential that our main project, operations on the Continent, should not be reduced to the status of a residuary legatee, for whom nothing is left.' There was no doubt, he said, that once we had our view firmly centred on a project problems became greatly eased.[7]

After Mountbatten had again emphasised the shortage of landing craft for a 1942 operation, Brooke said that they were all completely in agreement as regards 1943. But if they were forced this year to undertake an operation on the Continent it could only be on a small scale and not later than August if a port was to be captured by the third week in September, when bad weather would add greatly to the problems. Brooke then suggested, and Marshall agreed, that American planning officers should come over to work with British staffs in London on the plan.

The Chiefs of Staff went to their meeting with Churchill, the Defence Committee and Marshall that same evening holding certain reservations about operation ROUNDUP which was the 1943 operation as well. These were, that if the plan were accepted wholeheartedly, the Americans would put one hundred per cent of their effort into it and would afford us practically no assistance in other theatres. The effect of such a policy in the Middle East and Indian Ocean theatres would be grave. Without American assistance there it might be very difficult to prevent Germany and Japan joining hands. It was agreed that this fear should be made clear to Marshall as a proviso in accepting his proposals.[8]

Churchill accordingly opened the meeting at 10 Downing Street by saying he had no hesitation in cordially accepting the momentous proposal which Mr. Hopkins and General Marshall had presented, which had been fully examined by the Staff. One broad reservation must however be made. It was essential to carry on the defence of India and the Middle East. We could not possibly face the loss of an army of 600,000 men and the whole manpower of India. Furthermore, Australia and the island bases connecting that country with the United States must not be allowed to fall. This meant that we could not entirely lay aside everything in furtherance of the main object proposed by General Marshall.[9]

Marshall admitted that two points of doubt had arisen in his talks with the British Chiefs of Staff: whether enough United States material would be available for the support of the Middle East and India; and on the practicability of making a landing on the Continent, other than a large scale raid in 1942. 'We might be compelled to do this, and we must in any case prepare for it,' he declared. The difficulties should not be insoluble, as we should have a great measure of air control. He confessed that there had not been much time before he left the United States to study the problems of operations in 1942, and, on the data available, he had concluded that they could not be undertaken before September. If they had to be done by then, the United States' contribution would be modest . . .

Warily, Brooke then said that they were 'in entire agreement with Marshall on the project for 1943, but operations on the Continent in 1942 were governed by the measure of success achieved by Germany in the campaign against Russia. If they were successful we could clearly act less boldly. If however, the Russians held the Germans, or had an even greater measure of success, our object should be to force the Germans to detach air forces from the Russian front, or else help by the landing of troops. We had felt that matters would come to a head before September and that we might have to act before then.'

Finally, he warned about the dangers of a possible junction between the Germans and the Japanese. The British Chiefs of Staff, he said, welcomed the idea of an offensive in Europe, but it was absolutely necessary to take measures to prevent a collapse in the Indian Ocean. For this purpose United States' assistance would be required.

Harry Hopkins retorted that if public opinion in America had its way the weight of American effort would be directed against Japan. Nevertheless, after anxious discussion the President and the American military leaders had decided that it would be right to direct the force of American arms against Germany . . .

'The American decision has been governed by two main considerations,' he said. 'First, the United States wishes to fight not only on the sea, but on land and in the air. Secondly, they wish to fight in the most useful place and in the place where they can attain superiority, and they are desirous above all of joining in an enterprise with the British. If such an enterprise is to be launched this year the United States wishes to make the greatest contribution that is possible, where ever it may take place. . . . The American nation is eager to join in the fight alongside the British. But the decision once taken can not be reversed, for the United States will consider this its major war effort.'

Realistically, he added that both the United States and the British were fighting in their own interests, but the interests of the two nations now coincided and they must fight together.

Air-Marshal Sir Charles Portal, who usually held his fellow Chiefs of Staff on the rails when they were inclined to wander off, reminded the meeting adroitly that it was necessary to bear in mind the difference between air operations across the Channel and the landing of an expeditionary force. The former could be continued or stopped at will. In the latter case however we could not take as much or as little as we liked. Turning his small head with its beak of a nose towards General Marshall, he said that we should have to maintain the air effort for as long as the troops remained on the Continent. If therefore we launched an expeditionary force we must be sure that the air resources were sufficient to enable operations to be carried through to the end.

Finally, at about 3 am Churchill observed that although it remained to work out the details of the plan for ROUNDUP in 1943 there was complete unanimity on the framework, and the great project on the Continent could go forward without interference. The two nations would march ahead together in the noble brotherhood of arms. It would gradually become known that the English-speaking peoples were resolved on a great campaign for the liberation of Europe.[10]

A façade of agreement was thus created, but behind it on both sides there were grave misgivings. General Ismay, Churchill's personal representative on the Chiefs of Staff Committee, who was present, felt regrets that the British did not express their views 'more frankly'. And Brooke, who had given careful, qualified approval of the 1942 operation, SLEDGEHAMMER, wrote that day in his diary: 'A momentous meeting at which we accepted their proposals for offensive action in Europe in 1942 perhaps, and in 1943 for certain. They have not begun to realise all the implications of this plan and all the difficulties that lie ahead of us.'[11]

Brooke, in fact, believed that Marshall was pushing this plan for an offensive in Europe to counter demands by Admiral King, US Navy Chief of Staff, for troops to seize bases in the Pacific, and by General MacArthur for forces to develop an offensive from Australia. Both of them were causing a big drain on his military resources.

For King nothing counted but the speedy defeat of Japan and the eradication of the 'insult' of Pearl Harbour. General Sir Ian Jacob, Churchill's Assistant Military Secretary, noted that King seemed to wear a protective covering of horn, which was hard to penetrate. Over 60 and slightly grizzled, he was nevertheless tall, lean and active, with an alert but threatening personality and a narrow mind highly sensitive to imagined slights. Roosevelt used to joke that he was so 'tough' that he shaved his barnacled features with a blow lamp.

Churchill still had in mind alternatives like GYMNAST, in French North Africa, or the invasion of northern Norway, called JUPITER, yet his letter of 17 April to Roosevelt spoke of 'joint plans and preparations at once' for 1943, and as regards 1942: 'We may however feel compelled to act this year. Your plan visualised this, but put mid-September as the earliest date. Things may easily come to a head before then. . . . Broadly speaking, our agreed programme is a crescendo of activity on the Continent, starting with an ever-increasing air offensive both by night and day and more frequent and large-scale raids in which United States troops will take part.'[12]

Churchill was willing to give the 1942 cross-Channel operation, SLEDGEHAMMER, 'a fair run', but he had no doubt that problems like the shortage of landing craft and shipping would rule it out and therefore he preferred his two alternatives. But, he explained years later, 'I had to work by influence and diplomacy in order to secure agreed and harmonious action with our cherished Ally, without whose aid nothing but ruin faced the world. I did not therefore open any of these alternatives at our meeting on the 14th.'[13]

Despite Churchill's misgivings, plans for British-American operations in Western Europe in 1942 and '43 went forward and the British Chiefs of Staff approved a paper on the subject in which it was explained that preparations in hand should lay the foundations for operations on a large scale on the Continent in 1943. 'We should have to start at once to bring back the south coast ports into use. This would no doubt create a sense of nervousness in the enemy and, taken with our active raiding policy, would probably result in holding enemy troops in the west.'

The paper[14] proposed 'the conversion of the United Kingdom into an advanced base for operations in Western Europe; development of preparations on a front stretching from the Shetlands to the British Channel; a series of raiding operations to be carried out during the summer of 1942 linked with an active air offensive over north-west Europe; the capture of a bridgehead on the Continent within the area in which adequate naval and air cover can be given during the summer of 1942 if opportunity occurs, and finally, a large scale descent on Western Europe in the spring of 1943.'

The paper said that the 'situation may arise in which we shall have the opportunity to capture a bridgehead and possibly to extend this so as to include a port, enabling us to establish our forces on the Continent before the weather deteriorates at the end of September. We must clearly be prepared for such a situation.'

Churchill, however, told the War Cabinet emphatically that while preparations 'should proceed on the basis that we should make a resolute effort to capture a bridgehead on the Continent in the late summer, we are not committed to carry out such an operation this year.'[15]

The War Cabinet solemnly endorsed this significant conclusion following the talks held with Marshall and Hopkins. The Prime Minister then said that we should 'go ahead full speed with the plans for operations on the Continent and that we should continue without relaxation pressure on the enemy's air force.' At least on the British side there was now no misunderstanding. Plans and preparations were to be pressed ahead quickly, but whether they should be put into effect was another matter.

There was no such doubt on the American side. 'I am delighted with the agreement which was reached between you and your military advisers and Marshall and Hopkins,' Roosevelt cabled to Churchill on 22 April. 'They have reported to me on the unanimity of opinion relative to the proposal which they carried with them. . . . I am very heartened at the prospect, and you can be sure that our Army will approach the matter with both enthusiasm and vigour.' A wide gulf separated the British and American viewpoints.

When Eisenhower read Marshall's report in Washington he wrote in his official file: '. . . At long last, and after months of struggle . . . we are all definitely committed to one concept of fighting! If we can agree on major purposes and objectives our efforts will begin to fall in line and we won't just be thrashing around in the dark.'[16]

But Eisenhower was mistaken; and the agreement was shortlived.

Yet evidence of preparations along England's south coast, like assembly of landing craft and opening up ports had already increased the anxiety Hitler felt about invasion in turbulent occupied Europe from northern Norway to Finisterre. It had culminated in his Directive Number 40 of 23 March 1942. (See Appendix 1.) 'In the days to come the coasts of Europe will be seriously exposed to the danger of enemy landings,' he declared in the preamble to this very illuminating directive, which reflected his anxiety. He continued:

> The enemy's choice of time and place for landing operations will not be based solely on strategic considerations. Reverses in other theatres of operations, obligations towards his allies, and political motives may prompt the enemy to arrive at decisions that would be unlikely to result from purely military deliberations.
>
> Even enemy landing operations with limited objectives will — insofar as the enemy does establish himself on the coast at all — seriously affect our own plans in any case. They will disrupt our coastline shipping and tie down strong Army and *Luftwaffe* forces which thereby would become unavailable for commitment at critical points. Particularly grave dangers will arise if the enemy succeeds in taking our airfields, or in establishing air bases in the territory that he has captured.
>
> Moreover, our military installations and war industries that are in many instances along or close to the coast, and which in part have valuable equipment, invite local raids by the enemy.

Special attention must be paid to British preparations for landings on the open coast, for which numerous armoured landing craft suitable for the transportation of combat vehicles and heavy weapons are available. Large scale parachute and glider operations are likewise to be expected.

Thereafter the directive laid down Hitler's erroneous tactical doctrine of destruction of enemy invasion forces on the beaches, which was to be the rule henceforward for the German defence of occupied Europe. Five days later the heroic British raid on St. Nazaire gave a first taste of the difficulties of this doctrine in the defence of such an enormous coastline. It reinforced Hitler's invasion fears and sowed the seeds of the idea for 'Fortress Europe', behind walls of concrete fortifications.

After the departure of Marshall and Harry Hopkins, the British planners set to work to study the implication for them of both the SLEDGEHAMMER and ROUNDUP plans. On 8 May 1942 the Chiefs of Staff heard the force commanders (Vice-Admiral B.H. Ramsay, Lieut-Gen. K.A. Schreiber, Air Vice-Marshal T. Leigh-Mallory) express the view that the 1942 plan SLEDGEHAMMER, 'with the resources available is not a sound military operation'. It was agreed that it was feasible only if German morale broke. To launch it 'in the event of a Russian collapse would be courting disaster without materially aiding Russia.'

Brooke contended that the 'conditions which must obtain for SLEDGEHAMMER were unlikely to arise, therefore we should examine the possibility of a large scale raid in order to carry out our object. This raid might consist of two to four divisions and last from one to four weeks.'

More cautiously, General Paget, C-in-C Home Forces, argued cogently that 'one of the main difficulties is that to break the crust on a sufficiently wide front on the enemy occupied coast, it is necessary to employ considerable forces and might even lead to an operation of SLEDGEHAMMER size. The use of large forces made the problem of evacuation a difficult one.' Paget also warned that a large scale raid lasting for a week or two might easily 'lead to premature uprising of the French patriots, which was to be avoided.' After Air Chief Marshal Portal had called for the launching of this large-scale raid as soon as the German offensive in Russia had begun, the Chiefs of Staff agreed that a plan should be prepared for a major raid on the French coast about mid-July within the area of fighter protection.[17] This was to culminate in the Dieppe raid, in August 1942.

It was in the light of this firm British belief that a large-scale raid was the nearest approach possible to a 'second front' in 1942, that Soviet Foreign Minister Vyacheslav Molotov arrived in London on 20 May on his way to Washington at Roosevelt's invitation. The creation of a 'second front in 1942' was one of the main objectives of his visit as Stalin's closest henchman.

5 DEADLOCK

Vyacheslav Molotov, Soviet Foreign Minister, then regarded as the world's most frigid diplomat, arrived in London when Soviet troops in the south of Soviet Russia were in retreat and Timoshenko's troops, fighting a counter-offensive towards Kharkov, already faced encirclement. For Stalin's prim and unsmiling henchman the issue of a second fighting front in Europe was therefore critical, more important even than the recognition of Russia's 1941 frontiers based on military seizure, which Stalin sought as well.

At a meeting with Churchill on 22 May, Molotov said that the object of his visit 'was to learn how the British Government viewed the prospects of drawing off in 1942 at least 40 German divisions from the USSR, where it seemed that at the present time the balance of advantage in armed strength lay with the Germans.'

In the course of a long account of plans for future operations on the Continent, Churchill explained the problem of disembarking large forces under the conditions of modern warfare. These conditions restricted landings, he said to the Pas-de-Calais, the Cherbourg tip and part of the Brest area. 'The problem of landing a force this year in one or more of these areas is being studied, and preparations are being made. . . . The crucial point in making our plans and preparations is the availability of the special landing craft required for effecting an initial landing on the very heavily defended enemy coastline.'[1]

He added firmly the familiar argument that 'with the best will and endeavour' any move we were able to make in 1942 would be unlikely to draw off large numbers of German forces from the Eastern Front. In the air, however, we were already containing altogether about one half of the German fighter and one half of their bomber strength. 'If our plan for forcing air battles over the Continent proved successful, the Germans might face the choice of seeing the whole of their substantial fighter air force in the West destroyed in action, or of making withdrawals from their air strength in the East.'

With regard to Molotov's proposition that we should try to draw off not less than 40 divisions from Russia, Churchill pointed out: 'At the present time 11 Axis divisions face us in Libya, of which three are German, the equivalent of 8 German divisions in Norway and 25 German divisions in France and the Low Countries. These total 44 divisions.'

Molotov was obviously disappointed with Churchill's refusal to commit himself, but satisfied with the 20-year treaty of mutual aid he had negotiated with Eden, even though it left the issue of Russia's frontier with Poland unresolved. He flew off to Washington via Iceland and Labrador in a Soviet aircraft on 26 May to try to enlist Roosevelt's support.

Exploiting Molotov's visit, the campaign for a second front in Europe at this time had grown more strident than ever, both in Britain and the United States, where Beaverbrook was loud in his praise of Soviet generals and troops. In London, no less than 50,000 people attended a Trafalgar Square rally, mainly organised by the Communist Party, to demand the immediate launching of a second front to relieve Soviet Russia. Rather than condemn it, Churchill publicly called it evidence of 'the militant aggressive spirit of the British nation'. But with Molotov then on his way to force the issue in Washington, he decided to consider the possibilities yet once again in the light of his military planners' most recent studies.

At a War Cabinet meeting attended by the Chiefs of Staff at 5.30 pm on 26 May 1942, soon after Molotov's departure, he demanded what operations could be launched in Western Europe on the assumption that heavy fighting continued throughout the summer on the Russian front, without any decision.

Paget contended, and Mountbatten agreed, that the landing craft shortage limited operations to 4,300 men with 160 tanks in the first flight. 'This small assaulting force would have the greatest difficulty in establishing a bridgehead wide enough for the disembarkation of supporting forces, without serious interference from coast defence guns,' Paget said. 'There would not be enough airborne forces available this year to effect the capture of the coast defences from the rear.'

When Mountbatten declared that 21 days would be needed to put ashore a force of 6 divisions (100,000 men) and 18,000 vehicles, Churchill said bluntly that he was not prepared to accept this; Mountbatten should improve on it by the use of floating piers and other devices. 'It would however', Churchill agreed, 'be looking for trouble to attempt to force a bridgehead on the narrow frontage which is imposed by the shortage of armoured landing craft. The fact that we had made a gallant but fruitless attempt to open a second front in this area would be no consolation to the Russians.

'An assault in this area (Pas-de-Calais) would probably cause a patriot uprising in the north of France and failure on our part would result in terrible consequences. . . . In view of the authoritative arguments put forward he said he was not prepared to give way to the popular clamour for the opening of a second front in Europe in these circumstances.'[2]

Beaverbrook and the 'second front' propagandists at home and abroad were faced by a definite refusal.

Churchill then turned to the operation he had always favoured — a landing in northern Norway in late summer. He said it might be the prelude to the rolling up of German forces in Norway, and he asked the Chiefs of Staff to make a study of what was involved.

Although the War Cabinet agreed that planning for the 1942 cross-Channel operation SLEDGEHAMMER should go on, it was clear that this part of the plan for which Marshall had pushed so hard was now unlikely ever to take place. A hint of British feelings about it appeared in Churchill's ambiguous message of 28 May 1942 to Roosevelt, enclosing a report on Molotov's visit. 'We are working hard with all your officers, and all preparations are proceeding ceaselessly on the largest scale,' he said. 'Dickie [Mountbatten] will explain to you the difficulties of 1942 when he arrives. I have also told the Staffs to study a landing in the north of Norway, the occupation of which seems necessary to ensure the flow of our supplies next year to Russia. . . . We must never let GYMNAST [the landing in French North Africa] pass from our minds. All other preparations would help, if need be, towards that.'[3]

This message, announcing Mountbatten's mission to explain why it was impossible to launch a cross-Channel attack in 1942, was the first move by Churchill and Brooke to bring the American military chiefs round to favouring GYMNAST, in French North Africa, instead.

Molotov, his pince-nez glinting in the spring sunshine, met President Roosevelt in the White House at 4 pm on 29 May 1942 and, said Robert Sherwood, with humorous understatement, 'Roosevelt was by no means appalled by the new and strange problem in human relations that Molotov presented.' Bluntly Molotov again put the question that Churchill had already disposed of: could offensive action be undertaken to draw off 40 German divisions, which would be, to tell the truth, distinctly second-rate outfits? If the answer should be in the affirmative, the war would be decided in 1942; if negative, the Soviets would fight all alone, doing their best, and no man would expect more from them than that. Molotov said that he had not received any positive answer in London.

According to Harry Hopkins' report Molotov argued that the difficulties would not be any less in 1943. 'The chances of success are actually better at present while the Russians still have a solid front. If you postpone your decision', he said, 'you will eventually have to bear the brunt of the war, and if Hitler becomes the undisputed master of the Continent, next year will undoubtedly be tougher than this one.'[4]

Faced with this threatening statement, the President asked his Chief of Staff, Marshall, whether developments justified our saying to Stalin that a second front was being prepared. Marshall answered yes. Roosevelt then authorised Molotov to tell Stalin that 'we expect the formation of a second front this year'. Then, without any prior consultation with Churchill, although the burden of a 1942 second front would fall upon the British almost entirely, Roosevelt agreed with Molotov an official communiqué which included the statement: 'In the course of the conversations full understanding was reached with regard to the urgent tasks of creating a second front in Europe in 1942.'

Molotov left for London delighted with his achievement in winning this communiqué, which, vague and meaningless though it was, the British Government would have no alternative but to accept and agree to publish.

Roosevelt was in the throes of the first of his efforts, based on misjudgement and credulity, to ingratiate himself with Stalin. He believed that the brutal, realistic Stalin admired him and he felt he had to make a gesture. 'I'm especially anxious that Molotov shall carry back some real results of his mission and give a favourable report to Stalin,' he cabled Churchill enthusiastically on 31 May, and he went on to say that he was anxious that a Normandy landing should take place early in August — in about two months' time!

This startling proposal meant that a first-wave attack of 5,000 men, the maximum then possible, would be thrown against well-mined beaches defended by masses of artillery and by fighting troops drawn from the 25 enemy divisions then in France. If despite these formidable obstacles a beachhead was somehow established and held, 21 days, according to Mountbatten, would then be needed to disembark 6 divisions with which to overcome the enemy.

This was the suicidal prospect to which Roosevelt, in a mood of combined euphoria and self-delusion, had committed the British-American forces for Stalin's sake. He was ready, he had told Molotov with pride, to risk the sacrifice of 100,000 to 120,000 men 'even though that might lead to a second Dunkirk'.[5]

The effect upon Churchill, the War Cabinet, Brooke and the other Chiefs was predictable. Seriously alarmed, they dug themselves in and determined not to give way. And Churchill produced a paper for the

Chiefs of Staff proposing that there should be '(a) no substantial landing in France unless we are going to stay; and (b) no substantial landing in France unless the Germans are demoralised by another failure against Russia.' This meant, he added, 'that we should recognise that, if Russia is in dire straits, it would not help her for us to come a nasty cropper on our own.'[6] It also implied that SLEDGEHAMMER depended not on Russian failure, but on Russian success and proved German demoralisation in the West.

Molotov met Churchill and some members of the War Cabinet in London on 9 June 1942 after his return from Washington and produced the explosive communiqué that he had agreed with Roosevelt about the 'full understanding' concerning creating a second front in 1942. Perhaps, for once, Molotov's was the only smiling face round the conference table that day, hard as this is to imagine, for the War Cabinet was forced to authorise the comuniqué for publication on 11 June. Making a virtue of necessity, Churchill reflected that it might at least cause the enemy to hold the maximum possible of their forces in the West.

But so that there should be no doubt whatsoever, on the evening of 10 June Churchill handed Molotov an important *aide mémoire*, which stated:

> We are making preparations for a landing on the Continent in August or September 1942. As already explained, the main limiting factor to the size of the landing force is the availability of special landing-craft. Clearly, however, it would not further either the Russian cause or the Allies as a whole if, for the sake of action at any price, we embarked on some operation which ended in disaster and gave the enemy an opportunity for glorification at our discomfiture. It is impossible to say in advance whether the situation will be such as to make this operation feasible when the time comes. *We can therefore give no promise in the matter*, but provided that it appears sound and sensible we shall not hesitate to put our plans into effect.

The next day, 11 June, when the communiqué was published round the world, the War Cabinet approved the terms of the paper on conditions for a second front that Churchill had put to the Chiefs of Staff three days earlier. 'PM in good form and carried the Cabinet with him', Brooke noted in his diary that night, 'in the proposed policy that we do not move to France in strength except to stop there and we do not go there unless German morale is deteriorating.'[7]

With this firm decision taken, the British-American camp was now divided, for Roosevelt, Hopkins, Stimson and Marshall still strongly backed the SLEDGEHAMMER plan for a landing in 1942 at all

costs. A crisis in the development of British-American war strategy
had been reached. It would continue dangerously for weeks, to the
accompaniment of a resounding series of victories by Germany in
Libya, southern Soviet Russia and the Crimea.

The British War Cabinet and the Chiefs of Staff, the American
War Department chiefs, the Combined Chiefs of Staff — all these
august bodies argued their cases for and against the 1942 second front
interminably this summer. Reading through these official reports
today one is struck by the apparent waste of time and effort, for not
content with deciding firmly once, even twice, that the project was
impossible, the British War Cabinet and the Chiefs of Staff did so
repeatedly, so that on 6 July 1942, three months after their first 'no'
following the Hopkins-Marshall visit, the Prime Minister and the
Chiefs of Staff were still nodding heads sagely in unanimous agreement that 'operation SLEDGEHAMMER offered no hope of success
and would merely ruin all prospect of ROUNDUP in 1943'.[8]

Their predicament is clear, for many and loud were the voices in
America calling for an immediate second front. Stimson, Marshall and
the American War Department planners wanted to justify sending
their share of the men and equipment to Britain rather than to
MacArthur's command in the Pacific. Admiral King, grudgingly
accepting Roosevelt's 'Germany first' strategy, urged that the British
should be forced to agree to an immediate landing, in the hope that the
landing craft and other vessels would be available sooner for his
operations in the Pacific against the Japanese. Roosevelt was set upon
it because he faced the urgent need to get some of the three million
American troops in action against the Germans quickly; and because
he believed that this would be the best way to help Soviet Russia stay
in the war and strengthen friendly relations with Stalin.

Unfortunately, led by Churchill, Britain's war leaders believed
that they should handle the Americans with diplomacy, whereas blunt
and forceful argument was more effective with outspoken and tough
leaders like Stimson, Marshall and King. And so the issue meandered
on for week after week without progress. No wonder Lord Ismay
regretted in a subsequent talk with Eisenhower that the British failed
to speak more frankly.

Earlier, on 3 June, in Washington, Mountbatten had a long
discussion with Roosevelt on the subject. 'I had to try to persuade
Roosevelt and his advisers that our entire strategy needed re-think-
ing,' wrote the clear-sighted Mountbatten, who was beginning to
believe that ROUNDUP, the major invasion project, would have to be
put off even until 1944. But he found that Roosevelt was adamant.
There was a 'great need for American soldiers to be given an opportunity of fighting as soon as possible,' the President stressed. He coupled

this with a request that Mountbatten should remind the Prime Minister of their agreement 'that in the event of things going very badly for the Russians this summer, a sacrifice landing would be carried out in France to assist them'. Roosevelt was mistaken, for there was no such agreement.

Mountbatten argued pointedly that 'no landing that we could carry out could draw off any troops, since there were some 25 German divisions already in France and landing craft shortage prevented our putting ashore an adequate number. The chief German shortage', he added, 'lies in fighter aircraft and all our efforts are being bent towards provoking fighter battles in the West.'

At Roosevelt's request he gave an assurance that Britain would be ready to follow up a crack in German morale by a landing in France this autumn and that such an operation could be launched at two months' notice. Roosevelt remarked that he did not wish to send a million soldiers to England on the offchance of ROUNDUP being on in the spring of 1943 unless he could give a guarantee that they would be given a chance to fight whatever happened in Russia. Mountbatten noted particularly that Roosevelt, in connection with re-opening the Mediterranean, had been very struck with Churchill's recent remark about 'remembering GYMNAST'.[9]

Mountbatten's report, which Churchill studied on 12 June — while Rommel's Afrika Korps in Libya was destroying British armour and threatening the key port of Tobruk — caused him some additional anxiety. He told Brooke over the telephone next day in apparent reference to the President's mention of a 'sacrificial landing' that he considered Roosevelt 'was getting a little off the rails'. He therefore planned another visit to Washington on Thursday, 18 June 1942, to win the rejection of operation SLEDGEHAMMER and its replacement, if possible, by GYMNAST. That same day, 13 June, General Ritchie's 8th Army, defeated by Rommel in a tremendous tank battle, retreated forlornly to the Egyptian border, while the 2nd South African Division hung on desperately in Tobruk. It was hardly an encouraging situation.

In Washington, hearing of Churchill's impending visit, War Secretary Henry L. Stimson, aged 72, and General Marshall both sprang to the defence of the SLEDGEHAMMER and ROUNDUP operations, which they called BOLERO. In a long message to the President, Stimson, who had been an American infantry officer in World War 1, argued that all the reasons for agreement on BOLERO still held good — that Britain was the best jumping off base for US forces in an attack on Germany, that it should be done soon and that GYMNAST, an unnecessary diversion, would tie up shipping and aircraft carriers. Stimson overlooked both the crucial shortage of landing craft, without which the cross-Channel attack was impossible, and also the President's fervent wish to engage American troops against the Germans in 1942 — *somewhere*. Marshall opposed GYM-NAST for the same reasons, and because its success might depend on political factors like the reaction of the Vichy French Government.

So Churchill would face powerful adversaries in strongly prepared positions when he arrived in Washington with Brooke and General Ismay, Deputy Military Secretary to the War Cabinet, to press the case for GYMNAST, instead of SLEDGEHAMMER. Deciding to face the risk of an air journey he took off in the Boeing flying-boat in the night of 17 June 1942 as a full moon shone on the dark water. Sitting in the co-pilot's seat for some time he thought of the desperate fighting in the desert. Next day, travelling with the sun he found the day long, and had first one luncheon, six hours later another and then looked forward to a late dinner after touchdown in the evening on Washington's Potomac River.

The day after, he flew up to Hyde Park, Roosevelt's family home on the Hudson River in New York State, for private talks with him and Hopkins. In Washington, Field-Marshal Dill and Generals Brooke and Marshall engaged in the never-ending 'second front' argument against the alarming background of Rommel's threat to Egypt and the chance of a Soviet collapse under the German blows in southern Russia. Marshall and Brooke both agreed at that time on opposition to the North African (GYMNAST) venture and that while BOLERO (i.e., the build-up of troops in Britain) should continue, an invasion of Europe in 1942 should depend on the outcome of the fighting on the Eastern Front.

Churchill, meanwhile, had given Roosevelt a masterly document setting out his own emphatic views. In it he said that arrangements were being made for a landing of six or eight divisions on the coast of northern France early in September. He went on:

> However, the British Government do not favour an operation that is certain to lead to disaster, for this would not help the Russians whatever their plight, would compromise and expose to Nazi vengeance the French population involved, and would gravely delay the main operation in 1943. We hold strongly to the view that there should be no substantial landing in France this year unless we are going to stay.
>
> No responsible British military authority has so far been able to make a plan for September 1942 which had any chance of success unless the Germans became utterly demoralised, of which there is no likelihood. Have the American Staffs a plan? At what points would they strike? What landing craft and

shipping are available? Who is the officer prepared to command the enterprise? What British forces and assistance are required? If a plan can be found which offers a reasonable prospect of success His Majesty's Government will cordially welcome it, and will share to the full with their American comrades the risks and sacrifices. This remains our settled and agreed policy.

But in case no plan can be made in which any responsible authority has good confidence, and consequently no engagement on a substantial scale in France is possible in September 1942, what else are we going to do? Can we afford to stand idle in the Atlantic theatre? Ought we not to be preparing within the general structure of BOLERO some other operation by which we may gain positions of advantage, and also directly or indirectly take some of the weight off Russia? It is in this setting and on this background that the French North West Africa operation should be studied.[10]

While Churchill and Roosevelt also conferred privately on the top secret project of the construction of the world's first atomic bomb, upon which scientists of both nations were at work, Hopkins sent this controversial letter to Marshall and King. With it, he enclosed instructions drawn up by Roosevelt and himself that they should prepare a case for a British-American attack on German forces 'in the areas controlled by them' before 15 September 1942, on the assumption that the *Wehrmacht* would in August be threatening Moscow, Leningrad and the Caucasus.[11]

The crippling three months' discord between Great Britain and the United States about whether a cross-Channel invasion should be launched in 1942 now approached its first peak. For Marshall and his War Department planners had made ready a strong defence of SLEDGEHAMMER for a conference with Churchill and Roosevelt on 21 June.

Marshall proposed a force of up to four American infantry divisions and one armoured division with five British divisions, but unfortunately landing craft would be available for only 20,000 men with 1,000 heavy and 300 light vehicles, or, barely one division with supporting services. With his scanty knowledge of disembarkation on defended beaches, Marshall also proposed making do with whatever additional other small craft of various kinds could be found to carry more men.

The American planners agreed, however, that there was a possibility that the venture could lead 'to disaster' and that it did not comply with the agreed condition in Marshall's first plan, that there should be a strong chance of success. They argued, not very convincingly, that 'the power of the immense British Air Force [sic] in the UK alone in support of any operations within its effective range, would more than counterbalance any shortages in other means' — meaning presumably, shortages of landing craft. Referring to the North African project they argued, upon this unsound premise: 'If disaster is to be expected in an operation supported by the entire British Air Force based in the United Kingdom and a large increment of the United States Army Air Force, what chance can any operation without such support have?'[12]

These arguments ignored the key point Lord Louis Mountbatten had made to the President only a few days before — that there were already 25 enemy divisions in France, so that the Germans would have no need to take troops from the Russian front to oppose any attack the Allies could launch in 1942. Also there were no strong coastal defences in North Africa.

On the evening of 20 June Roosevelt and Churchill moved from Hyde Park to the White House, and on Sunday morning they met in the President's study to argue with Marshall and King the case against SLEDGEHAMMER. But Churchill then received a severe shock. The news came that Tobruk had fallen, with 25,000 men and vast quantities of supplies captured.

It was one of the sharpest knocks of the war for him. Egypt and the entire British position in the Middle East were now threatened. He made no attempt to conceal from Roosevelt and Hopkins the shock he had received. 'Nothing could exceed the sympathy and chivalry of my two friends,' he wrote later. Marshall came in and the President quickly arranged with him that the Prime Minister's plea for Sherman tanks should be met at once; arrangements were made for 300 of them plus a hundred 105-mm self-propelled guns, which were shipped to Egypt without delay.

Brooke and Ismay arrived, and Churchill, disregarding Tobruk for the moment, launched his attack on the lines of his letter to Roosevelt, depicting the cost of SLEDGEHAMMER in colourful figures of speech — a 'river of blood' in the Channel, loss of life on the scale of the batles of Passchendaele and the Somme; and now despite the American War Department arguments, put forward by Marshall, Roosevelt to some extent moved round to Churchill's point of view. Long and heated debate followed, and hours later, at the end of the meeting, Ismay drafted a final report agreed by both sides, which mainly reflected Churchill's views. This document stated:

> Plans and preparations for operations on the Continent of Europe in 1943 on as large a scale as possible are to be pushed forward with all speed and energy. It is, however, essential that

the United States and Great Britain should be prepared to act offensively in 1942.

Operations in Western Europe in 1942 would, if successful, yield greater political and strategic gains than operations in any other theatre. Plans and preparations for the operations in this theatre are to be pressed forward with all possible speed, energy and ingenuity. The most resolute effort must be made to overcome the obvious dangers and difficulties of the enterprise. If a sound and sensible plan can be contrived we should not hesitate to give effect to it. If on the other hand detailed examination shows that despite all efforts, success is improbable, we must be ready with an alternative.

The possibilities of French North Africa (operation GYMNAST) will be explored carefully and conscientiously, and plans will be completed in all details as soon as possible. Forces to be employed in GYMNAST would in the main be found from BOLERO units which have not yet left the United States. The possibility of operations in Norway and the Iberian Peninsula in the winter of 1942 will also be carefully considered by the Combined Chiefs of Staff.[13]

So the conference ended with no firm conclusion, although it paved the way for a North African, rather than a northern France invasion in 1942. No wonder that when General Eisenhower, appointed to command of ETOUSA (European Theatre of Operations, United States Army) arrived in London on 24 June, General Paget complained wearily to him: 'We constantly go over the same ground and no real progress has been made.'[14]

But Churchill had done his best. He arrived back in London on 27 June, the day that Rommel's *Afrika Korps* broke through the 8th Army's defences near Mersa Matrûh on the Egyptian coast but failed to stop it retreating in good order to El Alamein, 60 miles from Alexandria. He easily survived a vote of censure on the conduct of the war in the Commons on 1 July while in the desert General Auchinleck was preparing to counter-attack Rommel's overstretched forces.

Churchill was mainly concerned to settle once and for all the issue of a second front, or not, in 1942. 'During this month of July,' he wrote later, 'when I was politically at my weakest and without a gleam of military success, I had to procure from the United States the decision which, for good or ill, dominated the next two years of the war. This was the abandonment of all plans for crossing the Channel in 1942 and the occupation of French North Africa in the autumn or winter by a large Anglo-American expedition. I had made a careful study of the President's mind and his reactions for some time past and I was sure that he was powerfully attracted by the North African plan.'[15]

On 6 July he took the chair at a meeting of the Chiefs of Staff, where it was 'unanimously agreed that SLEDGEHAMMER offered no hope of success and would merely ruin all prospects of ROUNDUP in 1943.' The Prime Minister said that he was certain that Roosevelt intended to undertake the French North Africa invasion if SLEDGE-HAMMER was found impracticable.

The next day, when the War Cabinet considered this report on SLEDGEHAMMER by the Chiefs of Staff, with Churchill presiding, it was nevertheless decided that the right policy would be not to abandon SLEDGEHAMMER altogether, but only to make such preparations for it as would enable us to deceive the enemy, but not at the expense of interference with ROUNDUP; that it was desirable to go ahead with GYMNAST (French North Africa), which would absorb a force of about six American and two British divisions; and that they should undertake JUPITER (invasion of northern Norway) if 'a sound and sensible plan could be devised'. The Cabinet therefore invited the Prime Minister to inform Roosevelt 'that in view of the unlikelihood of SLEDGEHAMMER, it was assumed he would wish to proceed with GYMNAST.'[16]

And in a personal minute to the Chiefs of Staff, for use in dealing with their American counterparts, Churchill declared: 'No responsible British general, admiral or air marshal is prepared to recommend SLEDGEHAMMER as a desirable or even practicable operation in 1942. No confirmation of the hopes of additional landing craft from United States has been obtained. The three American divisions will not be here in time to be trained for the special amphibious work required. The chances of favourable conditions in the first part of September are dependent on the uncertain factors of wind and visibility during the limited period when moon and tide are suitable.'[17]

It was absurd to go on, and on, with this time-wasting debate that hampered production of specific weapons and in other vital ways slowed down the conduct of the war. Churchill now repeated his views as forcefully as possible to Roosevelt in his eloquent cable of 8 July 1942. 'In the event of a lodgement being effected and maintained it would have to be nourished and the bomber effort on Germany would have to be greatly curtailed,' he declared.

> All our energies would be involved in defending the bridge-head. The possibility of mounting a large scale operation in 1943 would be marred, if not ruined. All our resources would be absorbed piecemeal on the very narrow front which alone is open. It may therefore be said that premature action in 1942 while probably ending in disaster would decisively injure the prospect of well organised large-scale action in 1943. I am sure

myself that GYMNAST is by far the best chance of effecting relief to the Russian front in 1942. This has all along been in harmony with your ideas. In fact it is your commanding idea. Here is the true second front of 1942. I have consulted the Cabinet and Defence Committee and we all agree. Here is the safest and most fruitful stroke that can be delivered this autumn ... It seems to me that we ought not to throw away the so great strategic stroke open to us in the Western theatre during this cardinal year.[18]

Churchill followed this harangue with two more messages to the President. First, the War Cabinet having agreed that Roosevelt should be invited to appoint an American to command ROUNDUP owing to the proposed greater ratio of United States forces to British, he cabled this fateful decision, saying: 'It will be agreeable to us if General Marshall should undertake this supreme task in 1943.' Secondly, he tried to clarify the codewords for proposed operations, the use of which had grown meaningless, if not absurd. Blunt Henry Stimson, the United States War Secretary, called sometimes 'a New England conscience on legs', had even coined his own name, 'ROUNDHAMMER', for a cross-Channel attack, the precise meaning of which only he understood. 'Our codewords need clarification,' Churchill cabled desperately to Roosevelt, in an effort to dispel the fog.

By BOLERO we British mean the vast arrangements necessary both in 1942 and 1943 for the operations against the Continent. The Joint Anglo-American Staffs Committees are all working on this basis. They are not operational, but purely administrative. What you in conversation have called 'One-third Bolero' we have hitherto been calling SLEDGEHAMMER. The name ROUNDUP has been given to the 1942 operation. ... Please let me know whether you have any wishes about this. The GYMNAST you and I have in view is, I think, the variant called by your staffs 'Semi-Gymnast'. I also use the word JUPITER to describe an operation in the far north.

Roosevelt replied in a cable which summarised the code-words' meaning and stopped further confusion:

1. That the term BOLERO be used to designate the preparation for and movement of United States forces into the European theatre, preparations for their reception therein, and their production, assembly, transport, reception and storage of equipment and supplies for support of the United States forces in operation against the European Continent.
2. That the term SLEDGEHAMMER be used to designate an

offensive operation of the British and American troops against the European Continent in 1942, to be carried out in case of German internal collapse, or imminent Russian military collapse which necessitates an emergency attack in order to divert German forces from the Russian front.

3. That the term ROUNDUP, or any other name which you may desire, be used to designate an offensive operation against German dominated Europe, to be carried out by combined American and British forces in 1943 or later.[19]

The use of code words became a mania among the Americans, for Roosevelt and Hopkins, according to Robert Sherwood, also devised their own private code names of persons for cable use, some of them both comic and irreverent. Churchill was 'Moses Smith'; Marshall, 'Plog'; Brooke, 'Mister Bee'; Portal, 'Rev Wilson'; and Stafford Cripps, 'Mrs Johanson'. All of these code names derived from real people linked with the Roosevelt home at Hyde Park. Moses Smith was a tenant farmer there, William Plog an employee, the Reverend Wilson a local parson, Mr Bee a caretaker and Mrs Johanson the owner of a local petrol station and restaurant.

In Washington on 8 July, the same day that Churchill informed Roosevelt of British unwillingness to undertake SLEDGEHAMMER, the US War Department Operations Staff reached an important decision to the contrary. It was that a commitment to undertake emergency operations in Europe in 1942 should not be delayed any longer and certainly no later than 1 August.[20] Despite British expert opinion to the contrary, they held stubbornly to the desirability of SLEDGEHAMMER. Dill had a preliminary talk with Marshall in Washington about the decision, as set out in Brooke's cable on the same lines as Churchill's to the United States Chief of Staff. He was alarmed to find Marshall so hostile to what he saw as another change of plan that he was ready to recommend that the United States should divert all its forces away from the West to the Pacific.

And this is what Marshall then actually advised. Admiral King was absent from Washington, but when he came back on 10 July the US Chiefs of Staff foregathered and heard Marshall first read Brooke's refusal to launch SLEDGEHAMMER; and next raise two issues he thought it involved. These were, whether the United States should go along with the British wish to invade French North Africa; and secondly, whether the British really wished to invade Europe in 1943 at all. 'If the British position must be accepted,' the official report quotes Marshall as saying, 'he proposed that the United States should turn to the Pacific for decisive action against Japan.'[21]

King supported Marshall and after much discussion joined him in submitting to the President a memorandum the General had drafted opposing GYMNAST on the grounds that it would exclude SLEDGEHAMMER [*which in any case the British had declined to undertake*] and would 'curtail if not make impossible' ROUNDUP in 1943.

Marshall reinforced his views in a private and informal memorandum to the President which ended with a proposal that showed how stubborn he had become in defending his views about the issue. 'I believe that we must now put the proposition up to the British on a definite basis and leave the decision to them,' he declared. 'It must be made at once. My object is again to force the British into acceptance of a concentrated effort against Germany, and if this proves impossible, to turn immediately to the Pacific with strong forces and drive for a decision against Japan.'[22]

Marshall's memorandum now heralded the advent of a deadlock in war strategy that without Roosevelt's sane counsel and cool head could have split asunder the British-American partnership. Stimson was drawn into it. 'Marshall told me of a new and rather staggering crisis that is coming up in our war strategy,' he wrote in his diary on 10 July. 'I found Marshall very stirred up and emphatic over it.' Stimson 'cordially endorsed' Marshall's proposal of a 'showdown' with the British, although later he 'was not altogether pleased with his part' in the threat to leave Britain to cope as best she could with Germany.[23]

The President moved swiftly on receiving Marshall's memorandum at Hyde Park and telephoned him requesting 'a detailed comprehensive outline' of the plan to turn to the Pacific, *that very afternoon*. Marshall was put on the spot. In a reply signed by him and his two fellow Chiefs of Staff he admitted that there was no plan for the Pacific alternative yet; but that in short term it meant that parachute units and three amphibious divisions trained for cross-Channel operations would be diverted at once to the Pacific instead of being sent to Britain, while still other units would be sent to garrison areas from which the Japanese had been driven. In addition, two thirds of the air forces assigned to Britain for BOLERO, that is, 34 out of 52 Air Groups, would be re-allocated, while only two more divisions, which were earlier commitments of the ARCADIA conference, would be sent to Britain.[24]

It added up to a diversion of military strength that would have left Britain dangerously vulnerable to a sudden German *Blitzkrieg* against her, made possible by a Soviet collapse or by Germany going on to the defensive in Russia. On Stimson's part it was a bluff — 'absolutely essential to use it . . . if we expected to get through the hides of the British'. But Marshall, a man liable to take umbrage when strongly opposed, which for some time in the War Department he had never been, seems to have been determined on this course, but he failed dismally to persuade the President.

And Churchill, knowing of the stand Marshall was taking about SLEDGEHAMMER, wrote the President a short decisive note on the matter on 14 July. 'I am most anxious for you to know where I stand myself at the present time,' he said.

> I have found no one who regards SLEDGEHAMMER as possible. I should like to see you do GYMNAST as soon as possible, and that we in concert with the Russians should try for JUPITER. Meanwhile, all preparations for ROUNDUP in 1943 should proceed at full blast, thus holding the maximum enemy forces opposite England. All this seems to me as clear as noonday.[25]

Churchill knew that GYMNAST was 'the President's great secret baby'. On that same day, 14 July, Roosevelt made up his mind. He told Stimson that he 'did not like the manner of the memorandum'. It was a little like 'taking up your dishes and going away'. And to Marshall he sent an emphatic message: 'I have definitely decided to send you, King and Harry to London immediately. . . . I want you to know that I do not approve of the Pacific proposal.' Next day he told Marshall of his concern that it might seem that his memorandum 'had proposed what amounted to abandonment of the British'.[26] Nor did he think it was sound to defeat the Japanese first.

Roosevelt was a President in the grand style. Within 12 hours Marshall, with Hopkins and King, left hurriedly for London, bearing his emphatic instructions to make an agreement that would bring American forces into action somewhere in 1942.

6 'GYMNAST' INSTEAD

Hitler's *Wehrmacht* seemed on the crest of a wave of victory in July 1942 as the President's three envoys flew to Great Britain on their mission to try to break the deadlock in strategic planning that had arisen. Rommel's *Afrika Korps* was attacking desperately in the churned up desert sands 60 miles from Cairo. In southern Russia, Sebastopol had fallen, the Kharkov front had given way and the Soviet forces there had staged a general withdrawal in face of violent Nazi blows. Worse still, the U-boats were winning the battle of the Atlantic. Unless this was reversed starvation might bring Britain to her knees.

If Marshall's vehement defence of SLEDGEHAMMER arose to some extent out of his fear of a Soviet military defeat at this time, his inflexibility made him totally blind to the arguments against it. The main one of course, was that with 25 divisions in northern France already, the Germans would have no need to withdraw troops from the Russian front to meet the strongest British-American cross-Channel attack possible in 1942, which amounted to some seven divisions, five of them British.

Churchill and the Chiefs of Staff were resolute in the belief that SLEDGEHAMMER would be a military disaster which would not help the Soviets in any way. As Churchill argued in a letter to the chief of the British side on the Combined Chiefs of Staff in Washington, Field Marshal Sir John Dill, GYMNAST afforded 'the sole means by which United States forces can strike at Hitler in 1942,' and the letter went on:

> If GYMNAST were successful our resulting threat to Italy would draw important German air forces off Russia. GYM-NAST does not interrupt the vast preparations and training for ROUNDUP now proceeding on this side. It only means that six United States divisions will be drawn intact from ROUNDUP. These might surely be replaced by new United States divisions, which would be ready before the transportation schedule is accomplished.
>
> However, if the President decides against GYMNAST the

matter is settled. It can only be done by troops under the American flag. The opportunity will have been definitely rejected. Both countries will remain motionless in 1942, and all will be concentrated on ROUNDUP in 1943.

There could be no excuse in these circumstances for the switch of United States efforts [to the Pacific], and I cannot think that such an attitude would be adopted.[1]

What objections to GYMNAST, the North Africa operation, had the American Chiefs of Staff decided upon, as they flew high over the Atlantic to Great Britain in the first of the trans-Atlantic airliners, the Boeing Stratocruiser? Admiral King's objections were that it would cause withdrawal of warships, especially of aircraft carriers, from the Pacific, where they were urgently needed. And that it would mean the protection of a new line of sea communications, which would raise fresh problems having regard to the Atlantic and Pacific demands. But Churchill and Mountbatten had already dealt effectively with these arguments in the light of the distribution of British and American naval forces. Nor did the Combined Chiefs of Staff believe that the opposition, if any, from the French in North Africa would be worth much.

Marshall contended that GYMNAST would destroy any chance of launching the northern France operation, ROUNDUP, in 1943; but the President was demanding that American troops must go into action against the Germans in 1942. Marshall wanted this as well, but only according to his plan for the cross-Channel assault, SLEDGEHAMMER, whatever the cost. Field-Marshal Dill quoted him as believing that Germany 'will never again be so preoccupied in the East as she is today, and if we do not take advantage of her present preoccupation we shall find ourselves faced with a Germany so strong in the West that no invasion of the Continent would be possible.' It was a view, soon to be blown apart, based on sheer conjecture as to the real military strength of the Soviets.

Little account did it apparently take of the thousands of tanks, military aircraft, vehicles and guns which Great Britain and the United States had been pouring into Russia for the past 12 months. Neither Churchill nor Roosevelt had pressed Stalin to give in return a simple account of Soviet war production, and he had not volunteered it, so no sound assessment of how long the Soviets could go on fighting was possible. But as well as believing that a Soviet collapse was not far off, Marshall hoped that the United States War Department would take over entirely the strategic direction of the war. It seemed appropriate to him since the ultimate aim of Roosevelt and the U.S. Government was world supremacy, in place of Great Britain. He also had a low opinion of British strategic ability.

Marshall and the American War Department planners had drafted instructions to act as a guide in the London negotiations and had submitted them to the President. This document excluded GYM-NAST completely and insisted that SLEDGEHAMMER should be urged upon the British; but if this was impossible Marshall should inform the President, whose views, the document said, were that plans for ROUNDUP should be continued together with '*planned* activities and *present* commitments' elsewhere,[2] that is in the Far East. At the same time, Marshall had cabled Eisenhower, in London, to prepare a plan as to how SLEDGEHAMMER in 1942 could be carried out.

Marshall, stubbornly challenging the President's known views, was still pushing his ultimatum to the British, but Roosevelt again asserted his authority as C-in-C and after studying the document redrafted it so that it reflected his own opinion. The key points of it stated:

> In regard to 1942 you will carefully investigate the possibility of executing SLEDGEHAMMER. Such an operation would definitely sustain Russia this year. SLEDGEHAMMER is of such grave importance that every reason calls for the accomplishment of it. You should strongly urge immediate all-out preparations for it, that it be pushed with the utmost vigour, and that it be executed whether or not Russian collapse becomes imminent. In the event Russian collapse becomes probable, SLEDGEHAMMER becomes not merely advisable but imperative. The principal object of SLEDGEHAMMER is the positive diversion of German air forces from the Russian front . . .
>
> If SLEDGEHAMMER is finally and definitely out of the picture I want you to consider the world situation as it exists at that time and determine upon another place for the United States troops to fight in 1942.
>
> You will determine the best methods of holding the Middle East. These methods include definitely either or both of the following: a. sending aid and ground forces to the Persian Gulf, to Syria, and to Egypt. b. A new operation in Morocco and Algeria intended to drive in against the back door of Rommel's armies. The attitude of French colonial troops is still in doubt.[3]

The President added a blunt rebuttal of Marshall's Pacific alternative, expressing the belief that, 'Defeat of Germany means the defeat of Japan, probably without firing a shot,' and concluded: 'Please remember three cardinal principles — speed of decision on plans, unity of plans, attack combined with defence but not defence alone. This affects the immediate objective of United States ground forces fighting against Germans in 1942. I hope for total agreement within one week of your arrival.'

The cardinal point of the President's instructions was that American soldiers must be in action against German soldiers in 1942, somewhere.

The American envoys, Hopkins, Marshall and King, with several aides landed at Prestwick early on 18 July. Marshall and King considered essential a meeting first in London with General Eisenhower, Admiral Stark and other American commanders, as instructed by Roosevelt, to concert their tactics in the talks with the British. So orders were given for the train to carry on to London. General Brooke met the party at Euston at 7.50 am on Saturday morning. Declining Brooke's invitation from Churchill to proceed thence to Chequers, without even an explanation by telephone the party began their private talks that morning at Claridge's Hotel, in Brook Street, near their Grosvenor Square embassy.

Churchill, extremely sensitive where protocol was concerned, was deeeply offended that America's military leaders — leaders of a foreign power — should feel themselves free to disregard his invitation and proceed about their own business in Great Britain without at least the elementary courtesies. That morning, over the telephone, Hopkins bore the brunt of Churchill's wrath, and even though he pleaded Roosevelt's orders, and that rudeness had certainly not been intended, the Prime Minister was not pacified. Hopkins was obliged to go to Chequers personally next day, Sunday. It took all his psychological skill to restore Churchill's goodwill towards the American mission.

Churchill had still to persuade the British Chiefs of Staff, Brooke, Portal and Pound, to support fully the proposed North African action, GYMNAST. They were his dinner guests that night in the absence of the Americans and until 2 am on Sunday they argued the issue. That SLEDGEHAMMER offered no hope of success the Chiefs of Staff had agreed over and over during the last few months, and finally also on 6 July;[4] so GYMNAST was the only hope for an offensive in 1942. Furthermore, Auchinleck was at last holding on in Egypt and with reinforcements arriving might do better. Churchill's argument that GYMNAST would threaten Rommel's rear therefore had gained force. Cabinet records state that 'there was complete agreement between the Prime Minister on the one hand and the Chiefs of Staff on the other.' The record continued:

> In respect of action in 1942, the only feasible proposition appeared to be GYMNAST. It would be much to our advan-

tage to get a foot in North Africa cheaply, in the same way as the
Germans got Norway cheaply, by getting there first.

GYMNAST would in effect be the right wing of our
second front. And the American occupation of Casablanca and
district would not be sufficient. The operations would have to
extend to Algiers, Oran, and possibly farther east. If the
Americans could not supply the forces for all of these we might
undertake the more easterly operations with British troops
accompanied by small American contingents.[5]

This clear understanding united the British side in the talks that
began with Marshall and King at 3 pm on Monday, 20 July, at
Downing Street. That day and for the next three days the Americans
presented and argued Eisenhower's new plan — for a landing on the
Cotentin (Cherbourg) peninsula. 'They failed to realise', Brooke
scrawled tersely in his diary, 'that such action could only lead to the
loss of some six divisions without achieving any results.' The crux of
the issue was that the British Government, for political reasons,
insisted on permanent landings, but the American plea that the
Cherbourg operation would make this possible, Brooke and his
colleagues dismissed as impossible, owing to the winter weather and
the forces the enemy could bring to bear against them.

The main point of the 21 July meeting was the statement by
Marshall, that there was no chance of staging an offensive in Europe to
help the Soviets after September. Beyond this date, the weather and
the tides in the Channel would make a landing physically almost
impossible. 'We went on arguing for two hours during which King
remained with a face like a sphinx, and with one idea, to transfer
operations to the Pacific,' Brooke observed.

In the afternoon of the next day too, the Americans pushed this
same proposal, despite its acknowledged defects, but the British
Chiefs of Staff held their ground. Complete deadlock had now been
reached and Marshall said he would have to request the President for
instructions, but that he wished to see Churchill first. Agreeing with
this proposal, Churchill commented that nothing could be worse in
the war than disagreement between Great Britain and America.

Roosevelt told Marshall that he was not surprised at the failure to
implement SLEDGEHAMMER. He instructed his envoys to settle
as quickly as possible on one of five alternatives he listed, according to
preference. They were: 1. An American-British invasion of French
North Africa, i.e., in Algeria, Morocco, or both: 2. The original all-
American operation against French Morocco (GYMNAST): 3. The
landing in northern Norway by British-American forces: 4. Reinforcement of Egypt by American divisions: 5. American operations in
the Caucasus through Iran.[6]

So far in the talks Churchill and Brooke had carefully avoided any mention of GYMNAST. Now the initiative for it came from the President. And of all the alternatives listed Marshall and King favoured GYMNAST, with the reservation that it would push ROUNDUP forward into 1944. The issue was finally agreed in Conference Room B in the War Cabinet offices, Great George Street, Whitehall, on Friday 24 July at a Combined Chiefs of Staff meeting to consider the American memorandum on the subject. Marshall said that he believed very strongly 'that no unavoidable reduction in preparations for ROUNDUP should be considered so long as there remains any possibility of its successful execution before July 1943. After that date the odds were against ROUNDUP for the remainder of the year unless the German army showed unmistakable signs of rapid deterioration. If ROUNDUP becomes impracticable GYMNAST seems the best alternative.'

Now came the crucial point in the American memorandum. Marshall pointed out that if the situation on the Russian Front 'by 15 September, indicates such a collapse or weakening of Russian resistance as to make ROUNDUP appear impracticable of successful execution, the decision should be taken to launch a combined operation against the north-west coast of Africa at the earliest possible date before December 1942.'[7]

Marshall had side-stepped Roosevelt's clear French North Africa alternative to SLEDGEHAMMER, and instead had made it conditional upon the situation on the Russian Front by 15 September 1942. If by then Soviet military power had collapsed to the extent that ROUNDUP in 1943 seemed unlikely to succeed, then the French North Africa operation should be launched not later than 1 December 1942. Marshall thus offered a choice of ROUNDUP in 1943, or French North Africa in 1942, in that order.

Arguing that GYMNAST would pre-empt ROUNDUP, Marshall said: 'We consider that a commitment to GYMNAST implies the definite acceptance of a defensive encircling line of action for the continental European theatre except as to air and blockade operations against Germany.' He emphasised that in the meantime it was important that training for SLEDGEHAMMER as a deceptive measure should continue until October 1942 at least.

Air Chief Marshal Sir Charles Portal questioned whether GYMNAST could be correctly described as a purely defensive line of action. It would in fact, he argued, open up a second front and might commit Germany to the occupation of Italy and Spain. It was even conceivable, he said, that Germany might be so weakened by this that ROUNDUP might be undertaken in 1943.

Marshall bluntly contradicted him. 'Once large forces have been put into North Africa ROUNDUP is no longer practicable at all,' he said.

When Brooke declared that the British Chiefs of Staff 'were fully determined to go ahead with preparation for an invasion of the Continent on a large scale', King contended that 'once GYMNAST is undertaken with all the commitments it might involve, there is no possibility of carrying out ROUNDUP in its original form. An entirely new operation would have to be prepared.'[8]

The Americans hoped by using these tactics to trap the British into seeming to repudiate ROUNDUP in 1943 by accepting in 1942 the French North African operation, instead of the Cherbourg SLEDGEHAMMER, but Brooke and his colleagues had already agreed that it was likely now that ROUNDUP might be delayed. The memorandum was accepted 'as a Combined Chiefs of Staff document' for submission to the War Cabinet and to Roosevelt — with minor changes, chiefly re-allocation of 15 United States Air Groups from BOLERO to the Pacific. Churchill accepted the document without question; but later, in the War Cabinet, the criticism was raised that since all depended on hypothetical events in Russia, it was not clear whether TORCH, as the North African operation was now renamed, or ROUNDUP would take place. But to avoid even more delay the War Cabinet finally accepted it.

If TORCH were to be launched, landings on the Atlantic coast of Africa at Casablanca were to be entirely American; those in the Mediterranean at Oran and Algiers, would be British, 'under a United States veneer' for political reasons linked with French hostility over British action against the French at Mers-el-Kebir, Syria and Madagascar. With reference to ROUNDUP, which the document agreed was unlikely to take place in 1943, it said that 'the organisation, planning, and training, for eventual entry in the Continent should continue so that this operation can be staged should a marked deterioration in German military strength become apparent . . .'

It seemed that Marshall had been successful in avoiding a final decision for TORCH, despite Roosevelt's wishes. But Hopkins, uneasy at the way the President's demand for an early and definite date for the operation had been flouted, now warned Roosevelt by cable that unless he named a day for the actual landings for TORCH there might be 'procrastinations and delay'. The President at once cabled to London that the landing should take place no later than 30 October 1942, a date Hopkins had proposed. He asked his aide also to tell Churchill he was 'delighted' that the decision was made and that orders had been given for 'full speed ahead'.

The President had thus asserted his power as Commander-in-Chief and had simply overruled the Combined Chiefs of Staff document on TORCH. He told War Secretary Stimson, Admiral Leahy and Generals Arnold and McNarney, that 'he desired action and that he could see no reason that the withdrawal of a few troops in 1942 would prevent BOLERO [i.e. ROUNDUP] in 1943.'[9]

It seemed now that so far as the British and American war leaders were concerned the unwise plan for a second front in Europe in 1942 was dead, and instead TORCH in North Africa held the field. 'This was a great joy to me, especially as it came in what seemed to be the darkest hour,' Churchill confessed later. But in his reply to Roosevelt on 27 July, hinting at Marshall's obduracy, he said: 'I doubt if success would have been achieved without Harry's aid.' He continued: 'We must establish a second front this year and attack at the earliest moment. As I see it this second front consists of a main body holding the enemy pinned opposite SLEDGEHAMMER and a wide flanking movement called TORCH (hitherto called GYMNAST). Now everything is decided we can, as you say, go full speed ahead.'[10]

But Marshall thought otherwise. Game to the end, he now at the Combined Chiefs of Staff meeting in Washington on 30 July after his return from London made a determined last-ditch stand against the President's decision for an immediate TORCH. Admiral Leahy, senior American member, proposed that since the President and the Prime Minister both believed 'that the decision to undertake TORCH has already been reached', the launch of it should be brought forward as far as possible. Sir John Dill, for Great Britain, agreed, but General Marshall said he considered that the final decision had not been made, and he argued that it still depended upon whether they should agree 'to undertake TORCH and as a corollary to abandon ROUNDUP.'

Admiral King, with his eyes still on the Pacific, supported him, declaring that he believed 'that the President and Prime Minister had not yet reached an agreement to abandon ROUNDUP in favour of TORCH'. Linking the issue with the defence of Great Britain against invasion, he proposed that it should be put before the President and the Prime Minister once more. Leahy was obliged to agree that he would 'now tell the President that a definite decision was yet to be made'.[11]

It seemed that Marshall had won the day. The deadlock which had plagued British-American strategy for three valuable months, far from having been resolved, was now to be raised in terms involving the basic security of Great Britain — an ultimatum, if ever there was one. Little wonder that Churchill had warned Brooke that 'Marshall was trying to assume the powers of Commander-in-Chief of American troops, which was the President's prerogative'.

But swiftly Roosevelt surmounted the challenge to his authority that Marshall's attempt to sidetrack the North African venture implied. That same day in an announcement from the White House he declared that 'the President stated very definitely that he, as Commander-in-Chief, had made the decision that TORCH would be undertaken at the earliest possible date. He considered that this operation was now our principal objective and the assembly of means to carry it out would take precedence over other operations, as for instance BOLERO.'[12]

So at last the deadlock was overcome, a deadlock that had arisen almost entirely through Marshall's evident ambition to take into his own hands the direction of the combined British-American war strategy. On 27 July 1942 General Eisenhower was appointed Allied Commander in North Africa, with headquarters temporarily in London. Planning now went ahead 'at full speed', or at least, as fast as the different British and American views as to the times, places and strengths of the landings allowed. Not until 5 September was this agreed, so that the actual operational planning could start.

Meanwhile, on 27 July 1942 the Chiefs of Staff authorised a new directive for the Dieppe raid, the so-called 'reconnaissance in force' now to be launched on 19 August. Its heavy losses would teach the second front propagandists a few home truths about the kind of military disaster likely if the War Cabinet had heeded the popular clamour for it that they were raising. Towards the end of July, when Rostov-on-Don had fallen and Hitler's armies threatened the Caucasus, this was considerable. At a War Cabinet meeting on 22 July fears were even expressed that 'public opinion might get out of hand in regard to the starting of a second front should the position on the Russian front continue to deteriorate.' It was therefore proposed that the Prime Minister should see the press to give a clear off-record outline of the dangers involved in such an undertaking; but instead it was decided that Brendan Bracken, Minister of Information, should be told of the views expressed, presumably so that the second front propaganda could be discreetly counteracted.[13]

A problem with Stalin now raised again the inevitable fears that Soviet Russia might possibly make separate terms with her German enemy. A message to him from Churchill on 18 July, before the TORCH agreement with the Americans, had implied that a second front in Europe in 1942 was unlikely. In a blunt, undiplomatic reply on 23 July Stalin wrote: 'I gather from your message that despite the agreed Anglo-Soviet communiqué on the adoption of urgent measures to open a second front in 1942, the British Government is putting off the operation till 1943 . . . I fear the matter is taking an improper turn. In view of the situation on the Soviet-German front I state most emphatically that the Soviet Government cannot tolerate the second front in Europe being postponed till 1943.'[14]

The threatening tone of Stalin's letter persuaded Churchill that he should combine his forthcoming trip to Cairo — to make changes in the Middle East High Command and the 8th Army Command — with a visit to Stalin. The Soviet dictator answered his proposals with the suggestion that the meeting should be in Moscow, together with General Brooke, 'to consider jointly the urgent question of the war against Hitler . . .'

On 4 August 1942, 'in the pale, glimmering dawn the endless, winding silver ribbon of the Nile stretched joyously before us' Churchill noted as the American Liberator aircraft came in to land. Six days later, when he left for Moscow, on the night of 10 August 1942, with an entourage that filled three aircraft, he had appointed General Alexander to be Commander of Middle East forces, in succession to General Auchinleck; and General Montgomery to be 8th Army Commander, replacing General Ritchie.

It was a disquieting and unrewarding task, with which Churchill was now confronted — to persuade the leader of the 'sullen and sinister Bolshevik state' that a cross-Channel attack in 1942 would be a disaster, and that TORCH, instead, offered great hopes of hurting the enemy and eventually knocking Italy out of the war altogether. Churchill did not relish it. 'I should greatly like to have your aid and countenance in my talks with Joe,' he cabled to Roosevelt. 'Would you be able to let Averell [Harriman] come with me? I feel that things would be easier if we all seem to be together. I have a somewhat raw job.'

The story of the famous interview between Churchill and Stalin about the second front has been told and retold many times, by Churchill, Brooke, Sherwood and others — how Churchill in the first 'black and sombre meeting' on 12 August confirmed, to Stalin's dismay, that there would indeed be no second front in Europe that year — how Stalin taunted Churchill about the British fear of the Germans — how at the right moment Churchill revealed Operation TORCH, sketching the outline of a crocodile and explaining with it the plan to attack its soft belly — and how Stalin, allegedly, muttered: 'May God prosper this undertaking,' and summed up its likely strategic gains — how the first meeting ended with Churchill believing that human contact had been made, only to be faced next day with insults and abuse on the lines of 'When are you going to start fighting?'; 'You won't find it too bad once you start' — and how Churchill crashed his fist down on the table and declared at the start of a long oration that he pardoned such remarks only on account of the

Red Army's bravery — and how Stalin finally, with ill grace, said he must accept his Allies' decision. 'It is my considered opinion', Churchill reported to the War Cabinet next day, 'that in his heart, so far as he has one, Stalin knows we are right, and that six divisions on SLEDGEHAMMER would do him no good this year.

'Moreover, I am certain that his surefooted and quick military judgement makes him a strong supporter of TORCH. I think it not impossible that he will make amends ... Anyhow I am sure it was better to have it out this way than any other. There was never at any time the slightest suggestion of their not fighting on, and I think myself that Stalin has good confidence that he will win.'[15]

On their homeward journey Churchill and his colleagues stopped again at Cairo for further military talks. While they were there the costly raid on Dieppe was launched on 19 August 1942. This SLEDGEHAMMER in miniature had for its objectives the seizure of the port for a day, then successful withdrawal and re-embarkation, with information needful for a major landing in the future. Since its postponement in July, Montgomery, who was then to command it, had advised against it on security grounds, but to satisfy the Americans and Russians Churchill felt obliged to go on with it.

Misfortune began when the small armada was detected crossing the Channel and although the British Commando forces stormed a coastal defence battery and captured valuable radar equipment, the Canadian armoured division was pinned down by murderous artillery fire and lost 3,000 men killed or captured. The RAF lost no less than 106 fighters, the enemy only 48.

This revelation of the heavy losses that even a minor assault on Hitler's Fortress Europe could involve was to quieten those enthusiasts in the United States War Department and in London who had been calling for a major cross-Channel assault that year. Useful lessons learned from Dieppe included the need for heavy blows by naval artillery against hostile defences prior to landings, as well as improvement in aerial bombardment techniques, and teamwork in the organisation of combined operations. All of this information was vital to the planning for a major cross-Channel assault of the future.

Although the President had instructed the United States War Department that TORCH should be undertaken as soon as possible, another deadlock had arisen between the British and American Chiefs of Staff over the question of where and when it should be done. It threatened anew the entire operation. Thorny indeed was the path of the British-American alliance.

TORCH, as finally launched, affected the date of the final cross-Channel assault in 1944, so it must be examined. Briefly, the British plan involved the speedy occupation of Tunis and Bizerta and the main North African airfields, as the fruits of surprise landings at Oran, Algiers, Bône and Philippeville on the Algerian coast. Eisenhower, recently made Commander-in-Chief of the Allied Expeditionary Force, supported this plan, with minor reservations. Marshall, who was so eager to risk everything with a cross-Channel assault against Hitler's Western Wall, opposed this lesser enterprise because he believed it to be a risky operation in which failure could mean a disaster for American forces.

Gibraltar, he argued, was the sole base for protecting the flank and rear of the great amphibious TORCH force from enemy attack; but the Spaniards might decide to end their neutrality, attack Gibraltar's airfield and, with their guns at Ceuta opposite, in Morocco, close the Straits, thus leaving the British-American forces cut off in the Mediterranean. In addition, anti-British French officers in Algeria might obey Vichy commands and oppose the invaders with their 200,000 troops, mainly colonial, as might the French Air Force, also a power to be reckoned with there.

Marshall and the United States War Department therefore proposed making a major landing of 50,000 men at Casablanca, on the Atlantic coast, some 1,100 miles west of Tunisia; and a similar landing at Oran, about 500 west of it in the Mediterranean, leaving Algiers and Bône out of the operation altogether. A cautious plan, it would give them a secure Atlantic base, but throw away every advantage of surprise, for the communications between Tunis and Morocco were poor indeed.

A shocked Churchill informed Roosevelt on 27 August that he was 'profoundly disconcerted' at this — 'the whole pith of the operation will be lost if we do not take Algiers as well as Oran on the first day . . . not to go east to Oran is making the enemy a present not only of Tunis but of Algiers. . . .

'If it came to choosing between Algiers and Casablanca it cannot be doubted that the former is incomparably the more hopeful and fruitful objective.'[16]

Roosevelt however, felt unable to overrule his military advisers on this issue. He and Churchill therefore compromised. Casablanca would be included as a safe port outside the Mediterranean. Two American regimental combat teams of 5,000 men each would be assigned to the Algerian landing from Casablanca and Oran to combine with the larger British force there, while the entire operation would still be carried out behind an American façade, for political reasons. It was the best agreement Churchill could get, but he had to accept the fact that it would slow down the rate of advance and create the risk that the Germans would forestall them into Tunisia, thus losing the whole point of the operation. And this is precisely what took place.

On 5 September 1942 at top speed began the assembly of the armada of 400 ships on both sides of the Atlantic to transport in secret the force of 90,000 assault troops and 100,000 follow-up units for the landings on 8 November. The day before this had come the first glimmer of pale light at the end of the long tunnel which the British people entered with the fall of France in June 1940 — the battle of Alam el Halfa, 30 August to 4 September 1942. Attacking in the sandstorms which swept the deserts around Halfa Ridge, the Germans ran into concentrated British artillery fire and lost heavily in tanks for three days running. On the fourth day they began to retreat, knowing that their last desperate hope of reaching Cairo had gone. Montgomery had successfully exploited Auchinleck's plans, and British morale soared.

On 22 October the first TORCH transports steamed in darkness down the Clyde for Gibraltar. Significantly the next day, with the crash of nearly 1,000 guns, began the famed second battle of El Alamein amid the minefields and the rutted desert sands. Not until 4 November 1942, after days of suspense, was the outcome certain. 'After 12 days of heavy and violent fighting the 8th Army has inflicted a severe defeat on the German and Italian forces under Rommel's command,' General Alexander cabled Churchill. But it was only the beginning of the end for the *Afrika Korps*.

Four days later, soon after 1 am on 8 November, followed the TORCH landings at Algiers, Oran and, amid the Atlantic surf, Casablanca. They were succeeded three days later by the seizure by British parachutists of airfields in eastern Algeria and the advance of the British 30th Brigade into Tunisia itself.

But the Germans reacted swiftly, occupying the free zone of France, and within 24 hours dropping into Tunis their first reinforcements of two parachute regiments, then four battalions of infantry units of the 10th Panzer Division and six battalions of Italian infantry. These reinforcements, designed to protect the rear of the hard-pressed *Afrika Korps*, were increased rapidly, until by the end of November 15,000 troops with 100 tanks supported by 60 field guns, 30 anti-tank guns and squadrons of dive-bombers operating from the Tunisian airfields confronted General Anderson's British-American armies.

By early December German forces about 20,000 strong had attacked and forced back advanced British units only 14 miles from Tunis, while Hitler, in a major strategical error — for the Soviet counter-offensive at Stalingrad had begun — flew in more and more troops, until by Christmas 50,000 of them were holding the Tunisian peninsula; and the total was soon to rise to 100,000.

Then the North African rains fell. With the RAF handicapped by lack of reliable air strips, roads churned up into deep mud, so that fuel, ammunition and provisions often ran short, General Anderson's poorly co-ordinated force of British, American, French and French colonial troops was held in the Tunisian highlands by the battle-tried Germans.

Gone now were the hopes of a speedy victory on which the campaign was based. General Brooke, CIGS, was admitting nervously that to dislodge the Germans from Bizerta, the French naval and military base, and Tunis, would take a great deal of hard fighting.

Eisenhower, as C-in-C, was now forced to stop the offensive until the spring, and in the rain-sodden hills the troops dug in and waited. Eventually, in June 1943, the campaign in North Africa was fought to a victorious end with great losses to the Germans. But this cannot disguise the fact that from the standpoint of its strategic conception — a quick victory to reopen the eastern Mediterranean and knock out Italy — it was a failure.

Mainly, the cause was Marshall's stubborn caution and pedestrian attitude. His rigid insistence on the wasteful Casablanca landing and his unwillingness to support bold airborne landings near the Tunisian frontier had thrown away the surprise element in the operation and kept the door open for the Germans. And with this went the hope of a major cross-Channel attack in 1943.

Having imposed the American plan for TORCH, Marshall and the United States War Department made a series of studies to count its cost in terms of the cross-Channel operation ROUNDUP, and of BOLERO, which was the code-name for the build-up of troops and air power in Great Britain for ROUNDUP.

First results of this were decisions to cut by 15 the number of air groups destined for Great Britain and drastically to reduce to 427,000 the proposed future strength of American BOLERO forces in Great Britain. No date for reaching this figure was decided, owing to the shortage of shipping, but the strength of United States ground forces there by 30 November, including the 29th Infantry Division, was already as low as 23,260. By 1 December the flow of troops across the Atlantic had fallen to 8,500 a month.

Having decided that ROUNDUP was unlikely in 1943 Marshall and King felt free to send more troops to the Pacific. Towards the end of 1942 about 100,000 more had gone there than had been agreed in the BOLERO plan. In terms of both the army and the air force 50,000 more men were fighting the Japanese than the Germans — and this despite the agreed strategy that Germany must be defeated first. It was a blow for the British War Cabinet and Chiefs of Staff.

In late November Churchill hoped that a quick victory in North Africa would allow ROUNDUP to go on as planned in 1943. Although he knew the Americans had slowed down the BOLERO build-up, he made no protest until in a letter from General Hartle, United States deputy-commander ETOUSA, he read with astonishment the abrupt statement that construction of accommodation for United States troops in the United Kingdom must be limited to 427,000 and that lend-lease materials for anything in excess of this would not be provided.

It was the first official indication of any American change in the BOLERO build-up and Churchill reacted swiftly. 'We have been preparing under BOLERO for 1,100,000 men, and this is the first intimation we have had that this target is to be abandoned,' he told the President in a letter on 24 November that made clear his hope of a cross-Channel assault in 1943. TORCH, he emphasised 'is no substitute for ROUNDUP, and only engages 13 divisions as against the 48 contemplated for ROUNDUP ... Only by the building up of a ROUNDUP force here as rapidly and regularly as other urgent demands on shipping allow can we have the means of coming to grips with the main strength of the enemy and liberating the European nations.'[17]

In his reply two days later Roosevelt denied any intention of abandoning ROUNDUP, and asserted that 'no one can know' whether a cross-Channel attack was possible in 1943, but 'if the opportunity comes we must obviously grasp it'. Echoing Marshall's by then groundless fears of the danger of Spain's closing the Straits of Gibraltar he went on: 'Until we have provided adequately against the possible reactions from Spanish Morocco and are clear as to the situation in Tunisia, North Africa must naturally take precedence. We are far more heavily engaged in the south-west Pacific than I anticipated a few months ago, nevertheless we shall continue with BOLERO as rapidly as our shipping and other resources will permit....'[18]

Churchill's main concern however was the effect on the Soviets of what he called 'lying down in 1943, content with descents on Sicily and Sardinia ...' In a paper to the Chiefs of Staff he stressed that only 13 American and British divisions were fighting in North Africa, compared with 48 divisions earlier earmarked for action against the enemy in 1943, a reduction of 35 divisions. Yet he had told Stalin that 1943 would see a great cross-Channel attack on Europe. 'I feel that we have got to get much closer to grips with this whole business,' he went on. 'I fear I shall have to go to the United States in the near future ... We have in fact pulled in our horns to an almost extraordinary extent, and

I cannot imagine what the Russians will say or do when they realise. My own position is that I am aiming at a ROUNDUP retarded till August . . . I never meant the Anglo-American army to be stuck in North Africa. It is a springboard and not a sofa . . .'[19]

The issue then, was: where should British-American armies be launched in battle against the Germans in 1943, after crushing them and their Italian allies in North Africa? Roosevelt proposed to Churchill in November that Sicily and Sardinia were suitable stepping-stones in the move to invade and knock out Italy, and then possibly win Turkish aid for a flank attack through the Black Sea against Germany.

Marshall, however, opposed launching any more Mediterranean operations. He wanted a short sharp spring campaign to clear the North African shore from Egypt to the Gibraltar Straits. Then, except for well-armed garrison troops, he wished to ship the 13 divisions there back to Great Britain to build up a powerful force ready to launch a major cross-Channel invasion in 1943. Some of Marshall's army planners in Washington, however, shaken and sobered by the losses in the August attack on Dieppe, had come round to the view of the British Chiefs of Staff. This was that it would be impossible in 1943 to mount an assault of the weight needed to storm Hitler's western wall, owing to shortage of both troops, landing craft and almost every other kind of equipment.

Of the three alternatives for 1943 — victory by strategic bombing of enemy industrial centres: launching a European second front through an invasion of Sicily and Italy: or a cross-Channel invasion, they reluctantly concluded that only the second offered an effective operation within their grasp.[20]

At this time indecision was rampant among the Americans. It was worsened by the system of autonomous rivalry between the United States Army, represented by Marshall, and the Navy, represented by King, described by General Sir Ian Jacob as a man 'angular and stiff' who 'finds it difficult if not impossible really to unbend'. King was at all times eager to push ahead with the war against Japan as hard and fast as possible; and despite policy agreements to the contrary to lay hold of all the troops and equipment he could for this purpose.

In December 1942, while Roosevelt tried vainly to persuade Stalin to join him and Churchill soon in a new meeting about war strategy, Churchill was pushing hard for a cross-Channel invasion in 1943. 'It should be assumed', he wrote to the Chiefs of Staff on 3 December 1942, 'that all landing craft, etc., needed for ROUNDUP will be back in Great Britain by the end of June; that July will be devoted to preparation and rehearsal; and that August, or, if the weather is adverse, September, should be taken as the striking target.'

He was therefore glad, when on 14 December, Dill wrote from Washington to say that, during a private talk, he had noted that Marshall was also 'getting more and more convinced that we should be in a position to undertake a modified ROUNDUP before the summer, if, as soon as Africa is cleared of Axis forces, we start pouring American forces into England instead of sending them to Africa for the exploitation of TORCH.'[21]

Brooke, the stern and prudent CIGS, who never put one foot forward, in the military sense, till he knew precisely what the consequence would be, now saw the danger that at the forthcoming conference Churchill and Marshall would join forces and enlist the President's backing for a major assault in 1943 across the Channel. And he believed strongly the Allies had not yet the strength for this, bogged down as they were in North Africa.

But at a meeting on 16 December, the Chiefs of Staff tabled a paper for the War Cabinet that Brooke believed convinced Churchill that the policy for 1945 should be: to exploit TORCH as vigorously as possible with a view to (a) knocking Italy out of the war, (b) bringing Turkey into it, and (c) giving the Axis no respite. (2) Increased bombing of Germany. (3) Maintaining supplies to Russia. (4) Building-up BOLERO as much as possible so as to be able to be ready to re-enter the Continent with about twenty-one divisions in August or September 1945 . . .[22]

For Brooke, who was to play so decisive a role at Casablanca, this was a success. He had high hopes that the conference, due to begin on 14 January 1943, would afford him a chance of persuading the American Chiefs of Staff too as to the soundness of this policy.

The British Chiefs of Staff and their planners had, in readiness for this policy confrontation at Casablanca, prepared every possible statistic and fact, with arguments based upon them, to support their case. Apart from the Prime Minister and the Chiefs of Staff, they took with them a formidable array of military planners and their aides, in marked contrast to the much smaller ill-prepared American party, headed by the President. For despite his warning — 'the British will have a plan and stick to it' — the Americans and their planners failed to work out a united position on the next move.

When at a meeting in Washington on 7 January 1943 the President asked his Chiefs of Staff whether it was agreed that they should go to Casablanca 'united in advocating a cross-Channel operation', Marshall admitted that they were divided over the issue. The Chiefs of

Staff wanted a cross-Channel operation, but some of the planners preferred action in the Mediterranean.[23] And at Casablanca this disunity was as obvious as a threadbare patch on a well-brushed military uniform.

7 CONFLICT AT CASABLANCA

General Sir Ian Jacob, Assistant Military Secretary to the British War Cabinet, had served the two war leaders and their staffs well in choosing the Anfa Hotel, about five miles outside Casablanca, as the locale for the Conference. One each of the comfortable villas in the grounds of the hotel — which, on high land, overlooked the rolling Atlantic Ocean — were reserved for Roosevelt and Churchill. The military staffs occupied the hotel itself and the whole enclave was secure behind a wire barrier patrolled by American soldiers. The distant white buildings of Casablanca gleamed in the sunshine against the sparkling blue sea, a picture of beauty and serenity in stark contrast to the grim issues of war.

At that time, Montgomery's 8th Army, still pursuing the retreating *Afrika Korps*, expected soon to capture the Libyan port of Tripoli; General von Paulus's 6th Army, encircled at Stalingrad, was under massed bombardment by 7,000 Russian guns, while in the Pacific United States forces had again checked and defeated the Japanese at Guadalcanal. Only in the Atlantic was the enemy making gains, with shipping losses mainly from U-boat attacks exceeding new launchings in 1942 by nearly a million tons and a total of 1,664 ships sunk, 1,160 by torpedo. Hence Brooke's grave warning to the Combined Chiefs of Staff at Casablanca in a survey of the world war scene in the morning of 14 January 1943: 'The shortage of shipping is a stranglehold on all offensive operations and unless we can effectively combat the U-boat menace we might not be able to win the war.'[1]

From the start of the conference American disunity was clear in their failure to assert with confidence any definite policy themselves, instead half-heartedly if stubbornly questioning the British arguments. At a meeting at 2.30 pm on 15 January Brooke first defined the two broad alternative policies for 1943. These were first, to close down in the Mediterranean as soon as the North African theatre was cleared and the sea route through the Mediterranean had been opened. At the same time devote every effort to building up in the United Kingdom for an invasion of Northern France at the earliest possible moment.

Brooke said that the British Chiefs of Staff calculated that up to 23 divisions could be made available for this purpose by September. Shipping would allow nine or twelve United States divisions to be transported to the United Kingdom by September, but the number of troops able to be transported to France was still limited by landing craft.

One of the objections to operations against the north of France was the excellent railway connection across Europe, which would enable the Germans rapidly to reinforce the invaded area, while only one division at a time could be moved from north to south to meet the Allied attack in the Mediterraean. And since it was impossible to begin until the early autumn, no help could be given to Soviet Russia during the vital summer period. In any case, Brooke explained, it was unlikely that the relatively small force· they could land would force the Germans to withdraw troops from Soviet Russia to oppose it.

The other broad possibility, Brooke said, was to 'maintain activity in the Mediterranean while building up the maximum air offensive against Germany from the United Kingdom and putting as many troops as could be spared with a view to undertaking a comparatively small operation such as seizing the Cherbourg peninsula.' The Mediterranean, he stressed, offered a choice of Sardinia, Sicily, Crete and the Dodecanese. . . .

'If Italy could be knocked out, Germany would be involved in large new commitments in an attempt to bolster her up . . . The British Chiefs of Staff consider the best policy would be to threaten Germany everywhere in the Mediterranean, to try to knock out Italy and to bring in Turkey on our side . . . With Turkey as a base we could attack the Rumanian oilfields and open up the Black Sea route to Russia.'[2]

Admiral King responded that the more we concentrated our forces in the Mediterranean the more likely it was that the Germans would invade Spain, but Brooke countered with the argument that the British Chiefs of Staff did not think Spain would allow free passage to German forces. 'It is calculated', he said, 'that some 20 divisions would be necessary to occupy the country if Spain resisted at all. This would be a very large commitment for Germany. In any event we would be able to secure the south side of the Straits of Gibraltar by occupying Spanish Morocco and this would prevent the complete closure of the sea route.' He did not think it possible for Germany to seize Spanish airfields in the south by parachute troops. The problem of supplying them by air would be very difficult.

Air Chief Marshal Portal, cool and clear-sighted as ever, then pointed out:

'If the Spaniards allow the Germans free passage we would declare war on Spain, which is depending on us for many of the necessities of life. Even if the Germans did go in we would be better able to afford aircraft for the protection of shipping through the Straits of Gibraltar than could Germany for its attack.

'It would be much more advantageous for the Germans if we built up against France and left the Mediterranean alone. They would then be able to withdraw large numbers of air forces from the Mediterranean and reinforce the Russian front, relying on the strong defences of Northern France to resist invasion.

'On the other hand, if we keep the Mediterranean active, they will be compelled to keep large air forces there the whole time. This is of the greatest importance, since Germany's main shortages are air forces and oil.'[3]

Even the stubborn Admiral King could not deny the force of Portal's lucid analysis.

The next day, 16 January, Marshall and King brought the debate round to the question of basic strategy. The United States Chiefs of Staff, Marshall said, were anxious to learn the British concept as to how Germany is to be defeated. 'Is an operation against Sicily', he asked, 'merely a means towards an end or an end in itself? Is it to be part of an integrated plan to win the war or simply taking advantage of an opportunity?'[4]

King said he too thought it most important to determine how the war was to be conducted. He wanted to know whether the United Nations were to invade the Continent, and when? Should we adopt a planned step by step policy or rely on opportunities?

Marshall argued that we should reorientate ourselves and decide what the main plot was to be. 'Every diversion on a side issue from the main plot acts as a "suction pump",' he said. But he added that operations against Sicily appeared to be advantageous because of the excess number of troops in North Africa brought about by the splendid efforts of the British 8th Army. But before deciding on it we should decide what part it should play in the overall strategic plan.

An argument developed. Brooke said that ground operations by the United States and the United Kingdom would not exert any great influence on the Continent until there were definite signs that Germany was weakening. Marshall replied that if a bridgehead were to be established in Northern France, and Germany did not attempt to meet our air superiority, the bridgehead could be expanded. On the other hand, if they did meet our air superiority, it would necessitate withdrawing large air forces from the Russian front.

Brooke retorted that with limited ground forces he did not believe they could constitute a sufficient threat in northern France to force the Germans to withdraw much of their air forces from the Russian front. He continued:

> The Germans have 40 divisions in France, some of which have been moved south as a result of operation TORCH. However, the Germans still have sufficient strength to overwhelm us on the ground and perhaps hem us in with wire or concrete to such an extent that any expansion of the bridgehead would be extremely difficult. Moreover we cannot undertake any operation in northern France until very late in the summer of 1943. Since therefore we cannot go into the Continent until Germany weakens, we should try to make the Germans disperse their forces as much as possible. This can be accomplished by attacking Germany's allies, Italy in particular.
>
> This would result in a considerable shortage of troops on the Russian front. An effort should be made to put Italy out of the war ... If Italy were out of the war Germany would be forced to occupy that country with a considerable number of divisions and also would be forced to replace Italian divisions in other Axis occupied countries, such as Yugoslavia and Greece.

Emphasising that in the Mediterranean the Germans would have to be prepared to meet us in Sardinia, Sicily, Crete, Greece and the Dodecanese, Brooke then said that this would cause a much greater withdrawal of strength from the Russian front than any operations which we might undertake across the Channel. At the same time, he contended, there must be a continuous build up of the United Nations' forces in the United Kingdom. These must be prepared to undertake the final action of the war as soon as Germany showed definite signs of weakness.

Pound added weight to the argument for action in the Mediterranean by pointing out that the capture of Sicily would enable us to move troop convoys as well as cargo convoys through the Mediterranean with relative safety. Portal again joined in with the argument that once we were committed in northern France the Germans would quickly bring up air forces from the Mediterranean, realising that we could not undertake amphibious operations on a considerable scale both across the Channel and in the Mediterranean. On the other hand, by threatening in the Mediterranean we would cause a far greater dispersion of German forces. He added that in his view it was impossible to make out a detailed plan for winning the war, but Germany's position if we knocked out Italy would undoubtedly be most serious. 'Her ability to continue to fight depends on possession of the necessary resources and the will to fight on. As regards resources, her main shortages at present are oil and air power.'

Reinforcing the British argument about the relatively small forces available for a continental invasion in 1943, Brooke then pointed out that the number of divisions which the British Chiefs of Staff calculated could be available for operations into northern France were: 21–24 if the North African Mediterranean theatre were closed down; and 16–18 if additional Mediterranean operations were undertaken.

Major-General Somervell, United States Assistant Chief of Staff, raised the issue of the availability of landing craft. LSTs (landing ship, tank) carried 150 infantry as well as tanks, and the LCI (landing craft, infantry) carried 250 infantry. Referring to the possible invasion of Sicily, he calculated that if all the available landing craft were concentrated in North Africa we should be able to lift 30,000 men by April. Allowing for the use of 105-foot and 50-foot craft as well, the lift would probably increase to 90,000 in June. If this force of landing craft were used for a second and third flight on a short sea crossing their lift would probably be about 60,000 and 45,000 in the third crossing, allowing for casualties.

He considered that the use of these landing craft working beaches a sounder proposition than the risking of large ships under air attack, but to transfer these landing craft from the Mediterranean to the United Kingdom presented considerable problems.

Mountbatten intervened to say that this would take about three months. But the assault force to lift three brigade groups with transport for an assault against heavy opposition would always be ready. This spearhead in the United Kingdom was not affected by Mediterranean operations and would always be kept intact.

When Dill said that there was a possibility of beating Germany this year, King, always a realist, said he doubted whether it could be done before 1944, and then only by direct military action rather than a failure in German morale. Was it necessary, he asked, to accept that we could do nothing in northern France before April 1944?

Portal argued that it depended entirely on Germany's resistance. 'If we concentrate everything on Germany this year, it is possible we might cause her to crumble and thus be able to move in with comparatively small forces, but until this condition had occurred 20 divisions would get us nowhere on the Continent.'

Upon this indefinite note the 16 January Casablanca meeting ended. 'It is a slow and tedious process, as all matters have to be carefully explained and re-explained before they can be absorbed,' Brooke noted wearily in his diary that night.[5]

On 17 January, described by Brooke as 'a desperate day', agreement between the two sides seemed far away. Even the concept of defeating Germany first was at one time in question by the American Joint Planners.

Soviet Russia was criticised during a discussion about maintaining convoys of war weapons to Murmansk. Pound revealed that the Admiralty had pressed the Soviets to help with escorts and air attack. He complained that they had helped with air attack but they always found some reason for not sending their surface ships out as far as Bear Island, where the danger was greatest.

It would be quite unsafe, he insisted, to rely on their promises and reduce the scale of our own protection. Two RAF squadrons of Hampden bombers had been sent up to North Russia in 1942. After the withdrawal of RAF personnel they were manned by the Soviets. Recently however, when the German cruisers *Hipper* and *Lutzow* came out, the Russians failed to take any action against them, although they were asked to do so.[6]

As Brooke had noted, the arguments at Casablanca tended to go round and round without regard for what had been agreed earlier. On 18 January, despite the careful analysis put forward by both Brooke and Pound in the preceding days, Marshall began by saying all over again that he wanted to go into France. He was most anxious not to become committed to interim operations in the Mediterranean. He wished northern France to be the scene of the main effort against the Germans — that had always been his conception.[7]

Portal's answer showed the wide measure of disagreement that still existed between the two sides. It was impossible, he argued, to say where we should stop in the Mediterranean, since it was hoped to knock out Italy altogether. 'This action would give the greatest support to Russia and might open the door to an invasion of France.'

The issue of the attack on Germany was seen in the light of the offensive in the Pacific, when Marshall reminded the British that pressure must be maintained against the Japanese by mounting attacks. King said ominously that he thought these would demand twice as many United States troops in the Pacific as at present.

The British Chiefs of Staff retorted that this could mean weakening the offensive against Germany, and Brooke said it called in question 'the correctness of our basic strategic concept which calls for the defeat of Germany first'. Marshall, in this heated exchange, argued that if the United States waited until Germany was defeated before deploying for the final offensive against Japan it would only prolong the war. King, firmly asserting the right of the United States to act independently in the Pacific, argued that the American Chiefs of Staff alone must be responsible for details of operations there and that these would not affect what could be done from the United Kingdom.

Portal responded that the British Chiefs of Staff would be satisfied if they could be assured of this point. Their fear was that operations in the Pacific might cause an insufficient concentration in the United Kingdom to take advantage of the collapse of Germany The 18 January Casablanca meeting then ended with Marshall declaring that a further meeting of the Combined Chiefs of Staff might be necessary in the summer to decide these questions.

Despite these closely argued differences of opinion, Brooke, with the help of Dill, Portal and Air Marshal Sir John Slessor, managed that afternoon to outline a document, 'Conduct of the War in 1943', which was accepted by both sides. On the basis of this, it was agreed that the defeat of the U-boats must remain a first charge on the resources of the United Nations. Soviet forces must be sustained by the greatest volume of supplies that could be transported to Russia.

> Operations to defeat Germany in the shortest possible time with the maximum forces that can be brought to bear will be concerned first with efforts to force them to withdraw ground and air forces from the Russian front. The main targets in the Mediterranean for 1943 are the invasion of Sicily, strengthening of Mediterranean communications and the increasing pressure on Italy.
>
> Forces and landing craft will be at the same time prepared and assembled in England for a cross-Channel attack as soon as German resistance is weakened enough, while the maximum combined air offensive will be launched against Germany from the United Kingdom. Every effort will be made to bring Turkey into the war as an active ally.[8]

To this document the President and the Prime Minister added a note to the Chiefs of Staff which included reference to the need to build up United States forces in England fast enough to undertake a SLEDGEHAMMER attack in August 1943.

In the Casablanca meetings that followed, the Combined Chiefs made an attempt to decide how to put these policies into effect. At the 21 January meeting Brooke spelt out carefully his logical approach to the cross-Channel assault to which Marshall was so strongly wedded. There are, he said, 'two types of planning involved. One is for a limited offensive operation which might be expected in 1943, and the other is for the larger task of all-out invasion of the Continent.[9]

'In the latter case the decision must be made as to the direction of the attack once the landing is effected. It must be decided whether such an attack would be aimed at Germany or at occupied France. Plans might be made for both contingencies.' Brooke added that any operation in 1943 would be limited, since an all-out offensive across the Channel could hardly be undertaken till 1944. It was the first time the British had revealed doubts about the 1943 operation.

General Somervell said it would be possible to bring the strength of United States forces in the United Kingdom to 400,000 by the first of July. About 172,000 would be air corps troops, plus five or six ground divisions.

It was then agreed that representatives of the Chiefs of Staff should prepare and submit recommendations at once for the Combined Chiefs of Staff, to be ready not later than 1 pm on 22 January, relative to the command, organisation, planning and training set-up necessary for entry into continental Europe from the United Kingdom in 1943 and '44. They resolved to attack Sicily in 1943, with the favourable July moon as the target date, and agreed to appoint Eisenhower as Supreme Commander in the Mediterranean with General Alexander as his deputy. Alexander was to be responsible for the detailed planning, preparation and execution of the actual operation, the invasion of Sicily, when launched.

Meeting next day the Combined Chiefs of Staff took a historic decision. It was to appoint at once a British Chief of Staff, together with an independent United States-British staff, for the control, planning and training of cross-Channel operations in 1943 under condition of German disintegration: a limited operation to seize a bridgehead for exploitation later, and finally an invasion in force in 1944.[10] At last, some clarity and agreement had been reached.

Looking ahead to this great event, the Combined Chiefs discussed the appointment of a supreme commander. Brooke argued that it would be premature to designate a supreme commander for large scale operations on the Continent at present, in view of the limited operations which could be carried out with the available resources in 1943. A special staff was however, necessary for the cross-Channel operations and should, he thought, be set up without delay.

Marshall agreed that a supreme commander would make a top-heavy organisation at present, but thought that it was desirable to put a special staff under a selected Chief of Staff of sufficient standing; such an officer should perhaps suffice for the command of limited operations during the summer. The Committee therefore agreed that a supreme commander would ultimately be necessary for the re-entry to the Continent, but that he should not be appointed at the present time.[11]

It was a decision that was soon to lead to the appointment of the Chief of Staff to the Supreme Allied Commander (COSSAC). Although the supreme commander did not yet exist, this decision was a clear break-through in the tangled planning for the second front.

Initially, at Casablanca, Roosevelt had actually proposed a British supreme commander, but Churchill, putting forward the principle that 'the command of operations should, as a general rule, be held by an officer of the nation which furnishes the majority of the force', argued that this decision should be postponed and that it would suffice to appoint a British officer for planning. At the final meeting on 23 January, Roosevelt sensibly asked if 'sufficient drive would be applied if only a Chief of Staff were appointed'. Brooke, who had great hopes that he himself eventually would be made supreme commander, argued that, 'A man with the right qualities ... could do what was necessary in the early stages.'[12]

And so it was agreed. After discussion and argument lasting ten days, mainly because both sides had clung so desperately to convictions that arose mainly from national interests, the most productive decision of all had been made fairly quickly. Planning for OVERLORD, as the 1944 cross-Channel invasion came to be called, would now begin, with the selection of the British COSSAC (Chief of Staff Supreme Allied Command), who would set to work to make what was then still a hopeful ambition into a feasible military operation.

Roosevelt and Churchill's message to Stalin of 25 January about the Casablanca decisions, avoiding the mention of a definite date for the promised cross-Channel attack, caused Stalin to demand information about the date of the planned operations, which it was of course impossible to give.

In a joint reply, Roosevelt and Churchill on 12 February 1943 said vaguely that they were 'pushing preparations to the limit of our resources for a cross-Channel operation in August ... Here again shipping and assault landing craft will be limiting factors. If the operation is delayed by weather or other reasons it will be prepared with stronger forces in September. The timing of this attack must of course be dependent upon the condition of German defensive possibilities across the Channel at that time.'[13]

The last two sentences left the date more uncertain than ever and the Soviet leader didn't like it. Relations with him began to worsen. On 16 February 1943 he complained that already, owing to the slow-down in the Tunis operations, which gave relief to Hitler, the Germans had transferred 27 divisions from the West to the Soviet front. Observing that having rallied their forces the Germans might recover, he called for a speeding-up of the date of the second front to the spring or early summer.

Churchill answered stoutly with a summary of the demands upon the American and British forces at sea, in the air and on land in the Mediterranean, the Far East and the Pacific, as well as in the transport of supplies by the Arctic route to Russia. A premature attack, he argued, would lead simply to 'a bloody repulse, Nazi vengeance on the local population if they rose and a great triumph for the enemy', and he rammed the message home with a statement that this 'declaration of our intentions ... must not be understood to limit our freedom of decision.'

Stalin, of course, could only see the Soviet end of the argument. The first Communist state in the world was losing the flower of its armies while the capitalist states of the West held off, refused risks and conserved their troops. He therefore refused to play any part in the war against Japan and in his reply of 15 March, alluding to past Allied promises to launch a second front in 1942 or the spring of 1943 at latest, he ended: 'I recognise these difficulties. Nevertheless, I deem it my duty to warn you in the strongest possible manner, in the interest of our common cause, how dangerous would be from the view-point of our common cause further delay in opening a Second Front in France. This is the reason why the uncertainty of your statements about the contemplated Anglo-American offensive across the Channel arouses grave anxiety in me about which I feel I cannot be silent.'[14]

What was the 'danger' to which Stalin rather ambiguously referred? Was he hinting that he might be forced to make a separate peace with Germany? This, in view of the surrender of General von Paulus and 200,000 troops at Stalingrad in February, and the subsequent great victories over the Germans in the Ukraine, was unlikely. But Stalin knew of the British-American fear that he might do so, and cleverly he played upon it in his unceasing efforts to engineer a cross-Channel invasion at once.

The Casablanca plans to assemble the OVERLORD force began now to make headway, but Stalin's great expectations were soon due to be blighted again.

8 'COSSAC' PLANS FOR 1944

Upon Lieutenant-General Sir Frederick Morgan fell the mantle of glory, or, perhaps, the crown of thorns, of the appointment of Chief of Staff to the Supreme Allied Commander, on General Brooke's recommendation. Morgan, a remarkable professional soldier who had served on the Western Front as a young officer throughout the First World War, was commanding British First Corps at the time. But before approving the recommendation, Churchill studied the Staff College's years old confidential report on Morgan: 'Character: strong and exceptional personality. Professional knowledge: good and backed by considerable experience. Mental and physical characteristics: quick and above average, possessing originality combined with soundness; energetic and active.'

This, from a source usually sparing with praise, sounded good enough, but after such conventional remarks as 'works hard', 'keen to learn', the report ended on a human note in stressing what was clearly Morgan's outstanding characteristic — 'a keen but kindly sense of humour which should prove a great asset to him.'[1]

It could have added one more: that Morgan was emphatically not given to undue respect for great reputations; but in a military context this might well have undone its aim, which was to underline his best qualities. The prediction that his sense of humour should 'prove a great asset', might almost have been written for the COSSAC period of Morgan's life, when it went through a fiery furnace of experience, and emerged undimmed.

Morgan tells how he first heard of his impending switch away from First Corps to COSSAC, on 12 March 1943, when ascending in the lift at the Combined Operations New Scotland Yard Headquarters. Admiral Lord Louis Mountbatten jumped in straight from a meeting with the British Chiefs of Staff and loudly congratulated him in front of a full load of all ranks. Morgan pretended that it was of no consequence, or in any case a mistake. The order appointing him from command of First Corps to COSSAC came through about three weeks later on 1 April, confirmed appropriately on 13 April, which wryly he thought ominous.

Morgan's first directive, drawn up by the British Chiefs of Staff, said that he would be responsible to them and would have the command responsibilities of the Supreme Commander until that officer was appointed. The Americans, however, opposed what seemed a one sided arrangement and changed the directive to make COSSAC responsible instead to the Combined Commanders in Washington, at the same time limiting his powers to planning only. They also made the ETOUSA Commanding General — then General Frank M. Andrews — representative of the United States Chiefs of Staff on COSSAC's staff.

Meantime planning for cross-Channel operations had become a little tangled. Marshall had made it clear that there would be no shipping available for transport to the United Kingdom in March and April, while even that for May was uncertain. This, combined with the needs for North Africa and the forthcoming invasion of Sicily, ruled out any cross-Channel attack at all in 1943.

The issue came to a head in April when the American General John M. Lee sought Churchill's aid in obtaining nevertheless an order to take over an area of the United Kingdom, clear out the British population and train divisions for SLEDGEHAMMER. Churchill said he would look into it, but that day he expressed doubts as to whether 'anything of this drastic character should be enforced,' in a letter to Major-General 'Pug' Ismay, his Deputy Military Secretary:

> Here you have these very keen men trying their utmost to mount an operation which we have all decided cannot physically take place. . . . We really must come to some clear cut decision and issue the necessary orders to prevent dissipation of effort. We must reach a decision with the American Chiefs of Staff and the President. The question of camouflaging the decision should be considered later. I shall be glad therefore to know what the Chiefs of Staff wish done about BOLERO. Is it to mark time or is it to be stopped altogether? Surely, a steady build-up should go on for 1944 so as to take advantage of any collapse on the part of the enemy . . . I do not propose to inform Stalin about these developments . . ..[2]

The next day, 15 April 1943, Churchill informed the CIGS, General Brooke, that since nearly all landing craft were needed for Sicily and hardly any American troops would arrive this year and be trained before the weather breaks, they 'must recognise that no important cross-Channel enterprise is possible this year. This is the fact that dominates action.'

Churchill emphasised that this should not become widely known; that there should be no sudden stop to BOLERO preparations and that powerful camouflage and cover operations should continue. But they should not use money and effort for projects 'which are impossible in 1943, and about which there is no fixed plan for 1944.' A precise plan should be made to slow down BOLERO so as to ensure steady progress for a target date not in 1943, but in 1944.

He concluded that the impression must be given that 'American troops were continuing to arrive in large numbers', and nothing should be said or done to the contrary.[3]

American troops in the United Kingdom were involved in this change of plan, so on 23 April 1943 Brooke made the American General Andrews a party to it. It was essential, he explained in a letter, to keep enemy forces pinned down in the West by a constant threat of invasion from the United Kingdom, preventing their withdrawal to the Russian front or to reinforce the Mediterranean. 'So long as no actual attack could be launched against the Continent in 1943,' he said, 'we must continue to exercise that threat by false preparations and feint assaults.[4]

> Moreover, since a large air force is now gathered in the United Kingdom, we should also endeavour to regulate our feint, possibly supported by landings of small parties of men, so as to bring about an air battle on the largest scale . . . in an area within operational range of our fighter airfields. Meanwhile, the evidence of our preparations might induce the Germans to attempt to bomb landing barges and bases, and would afford us further opportunities for inflicting on the German air force heavy wastage which the air battle was designed to bring about.

But Andrews was not altogether convinced. He asked Brooke whether these feint assaults would assist our preparation for the invasion in 1944. He feared lest this additional task would divert General Morgan's staff from the main task, but Brooke brushed his fears aside. He said that he believed Morgan's staff could easily take on this additional commitment.

Events proved that he was right. Morgan's task was nothing less than the creation of the military cornerstone of the great British-American victory arch. It is impossible to exaggerate its importance. Upon it depended the future direction of world history, the Anglo-American alliance, the fate of Great Britain and millions of people in occupied Europe and as well the lives of several hundred thousand soldiers.

All of this hung upon the time, the place, the manner and the weight of the assault upon Hitler's Western Wall that Morgan was to plan. There was a likelihood that in doing it he would be crushed between the sometimes divergent interests and the rivalries of the

British Empire and the United States of America. There was the chance too that the then un-named Supremo, American or British, would when chosen, march into his headquarters at Norfolk House in London and blow sky-high the plan that he, COSSAC, had produced.

Morgan neither quailed nor lost his ironical sense of humour at the immensities and the dangers of his task. Nor did he forget the omnipotent ghost at the table in the empty office. 'We were serving generalissimo x, not merely producing ideas and papers,' he wrote ruefully. 'Which was a grand idea for internal consumption at COSSAC, but didn't seem to go so well in contact, and often conflict, with other outside bodies of greater reputation and stature who were sufficiently fortunate to possess high-ranking commanders in the flesh. We were forced to take what comfort we could derive from the last, pithy, verbal directive issued to me by the CIGS: "Well, there it is; it won't work, but you must bloody well make it." '[5]

For Morgan, this modest man who had avoided the limelight even to the point of declining to supply biographical details to *Who's Who*, all this involved some psychological readjustment. From the start he had to be totally certain in his own mind that in embryo he had actually become the Supreme Headquarters of the Allied Expeditionary Force (SHAEF), that would fight its way into Fortress Europe and destroy the *Wehrmacht*; and nothing less.

And from this standpoint he assembled his staff, for which task he was well qualified. In the late '30s as a member of the Staff Duties Directorate in the War Office, he had acquired knowledge of the records of all British officers up to the rank of major-general eligible for a staff job. He was thus able to assemble the British Army part of the staff more or less overnight and, as he said, 'it was able to hit its stride in amazingly quick time'.

But around April 1943 came fresh Anglo-American discord. It threatened the whole future of COSSAC and therefore of any cross-Channel operation. Despite British protests General Marshall had failed to carry out the Casablanca agreements for the build-up of American troops in Britain. Fierce fighting against the Japanese was drawing more and more United States armed forces out to the Pacific.

Brooke had already reminded the War Cabinet that Eisenhower's deputy, General Somervell, had assured them that at least seven American divisions would be in the United Kingdom by September 1943, whereas now it was clear that one or two at the most would be here. The forces employed in a 1943 cross-Channel operation would therefore be largely British. 'This is a very different situation to that envisaged at Casablanca,' he protested.[6]

Brooke and his colleagues on the Chiefs of Staff committee had to decide their course of action in view of this changed situation.

Gloomily they began to consider whether or not they should call off
the establishment of COSSAC entirely. If the Americans did not
intend or could not be relied upon to fulfil their part of the bargain
there seemed little point in going ahead.

For some weeks the fate of COSSAC — the entire cross-Channel
operation — hung in the balance. Two factors finally persuaded
Brooke and his colleagues that they should not advise this radical
change of policy to Churchill and the War Cabinet.

First was the fear, rightly stressed by the British 'staff in
Washington, that the Americans might lose all interest in operations in
Europe if the COSSAC plans were halted. The second was the very
clear memorandum on the subject that Morgan put forward.

The main point of this document was a warning that delay could
not be tolerated because action might be forced on them in 1943 owing
to a German collapse. Morgan therefore asked for the appointment of
a Chief of Staff 'invested with plenary powers, temporarily to imper-
sonate the commander-to-be. Such an officer could launch the
organisation and maintain impetus until the arrival of the Supreme
Commander.'[7]

He proposed that planning and execution should go hand-in-hand
in this organisation and that there should be prepared forthwith 'the
nucleus of the eventual Allied GHQ in the field'. Boldly, he continued:
'It is of prime importance that the highest possible degree of
autonomy, at least in the operational sphere, be granted to all concerned in this enterprise. . . .' He recommended that there should be
created forthwith 'the nucleus of an Allied GHQ and the HQ of the
Second British Army and an American army in the United Kingdom.
At the earliest possible stage the Allied GHQ should assume direction
of all offensive enterprises of whatever kind initiated from the United
Kingdom.'

Morgan's memorandum, with its emphasis both on urgency and
on freedom to plan and execute relevant operations in the future,
seems to have cleared away British doubts. Brooke privately informed
Dill, in Washington, that the British Chiefs of Staff had decided to
keep to the plan adopted at Casablanca; that Morgan would after all be
appointed COSSAC, and that with some reservations his proposals
would be accepted.

Shorn only of power to initiate operations, Morgan now went
ahead at full speed. He established five main staff branches, navy,
army, air, intelligence and administration, which included logistics.
Each of them was headed jointly by a British-American principal staff
officer with the rank of major-general, except for Intelligence, which a
British officer only would head, because of the scarcity of American
officers trained in this field.

Subordinate to the principal staff officers were three main departments, Intelligence, Operations and Administration, each divided again into navy, army and air force. Once again these were headed jointly by a British and an American officer, assigned to the task of planning for the three elements of Morgan's directive: a return to the Continent under conditions of a German collapse (RANKIN); holding German forces in the West by deception to invade (COCKADE), and the invasion in 1944 as soon as possible (OVERLORD). Later in 1943 division by nationality was ended and the departments functioned as single units.

Soon after the setting up of COSSAC, Morgan's deputy, the American Major-General Ray Barker; and Major-General C.N.D. Brownjohn, in charge of administration, joined him. Admiral Sir Charles Little, C-in-C Portsmouth, was appointed Naval C-in-C (designate) for COSSAC's cross-Channel operations; and at the same time, early in May, Commodore J. Hughes Hallet, Commander of the seaborne force at Dieppe, joined as his representative until August, when Rear-Admiral G.E. Creasey succeeded him. Air-Marshal Sir Trafford Leigh-Mallory, C-in-C Fighter Command, was in June temporarily made commander of air operations.

Morgan held his first meeting with some of his staff at Norfolk House, St. James's Square, London on 17 April 1943, and at once emphasised his view that COSSAC's function was not merely that of planning but was operational too, despite the confining terms of his directive. 'The term "planning staff" has come to have a most sinister meaning — it implies the production of nothing but paper,' he declared. 'What we must contrive to do somehow is to produce not only paper; but action,' and he went on: 'We differ from the ordinary planning staff in that we are . . . the embryo of the future Supreme Headquarters Staff.'[8]

Morgan praised the work that he inherited from the earlier cross-Channel attack planners, but he also fired a few of his own barbed darts of irreverent humour at them. 'Planners are most irreverently compared at times to the jesters of the Middle Ages,' he noted. 'Just as no nobleman of olden times was apparently a nobleman unless he employed his tame jester, so, in 1943, no commander was alleged to be worth his place in the field unless he retained his own planner.'[9]

Morgan's sense of humour was his best armour in his thankless task.

Studying the terms of the first directive they received from the Combined Chiefs of Staff, Morgan and his planners found that its meaning needed most careful analysis. As defined in it, the object of the COSSAC enterprise was 'to defeat the German fighting forces in north-west Europe'. Here was the nub of the matter. From the outset they had serious doubts as to whether the sole object of the invasion could, in fact, be simply that. Were there not, for example, they asked themselves, political aims with regard to post-war Europe, and Germany in particular, which would have important bearing on the assault they were planning? Military and political aims should surely march hand in hand, they sensibly, but vainly argued. 'In this present instance we tried, but in vain, to obtain some such statement of a long-term political object,' Morgan lamented later.

It goes without saying that the Soviet leadership pushed their political aims hand-in-hand with military action to try to shape the future of post-war Europe as they wanted it. Churchill and Eden were also, though to a lesser degree, aware of this need, but their views were unfortunately stifled by Roosevelt's and Marshall's intense suspicion of political ideology of any kind: hence Marshall's stern demand that the war should be fought solely on 'sound strategic principles'.

Churchill's aim was to keep the Soviets fighting the Germans by one means or another, and to keep intact the Anglo-American agreement to defeat Hitler first. While these objects were being accomplished his voice was perforce stilled in this regard for fear of the consequences of airing his views. As a result the war on the Anglo-American side was fought in negative terms — simply the destruction of Hitlerism with its declared aim of tearing apart the already well-worn values of Western civilisation. There were on the Allied side no banners to raise, inscribed with the symbols of an inspiring new Western ideology.

Morgan was clearly concerned over this lack in Anglo-American policy, though with reservations over what was desirable and what was possible. Later, he put the transcendent question: 'What should have been the true object of the Western allies and how should their object have been expressed in written words at the time when the fighting forces of these allies set about the invasion of north-west Europe in 1944?'[10]

If the objective was Berlin, he questioned, what was the object, or political aim? The overthrow of the Government, the system or the nation? Ruination and devastation, followed by limited or permanent occupation? Or partial ruin, succeeded by the building of a new Germany and the setting up of a new Government? Morgan could, of course, make no answer, beyond hopefully putting forward the issue as a 'fruitful study for future generations', and lamenting that sometimes the COSSAC staff wistfully envied Genghis Khan the crude simplicity of his war aims. Today we still lament and pay for the lack of an inspiring answer.

But Morgan was also faced by another set of, this time, soluble problems, when he and his staff analysed the directive's proposed three operations for which he was ordered to prepare. These were: (1) an elaborate camouflage and deception scheme with a view to pinning the enemy in the West in the summer of 1943, including at least one amphibious feint with the object of bringing on an air battle: (2) the return to the Continent speedily in the event of German disintegration: (3) a full-scale cross-Channel assault in 1944, as early as possible.[11]

It was as he noted later 'a deceptively simple-looking directive', but when he and his staff took it apart and sought its meaning, problems arose on all sides. First, there were not in fact three different plans but one only, with three elements. The 1943 deception plan inevitably impinged on the 1944 main assault, which it must not affect adversely in any way. And the 'reverse Dunkirk plan' — as Brooke sometimes called it — for a speedy splashback across the Channel to the Continent if Germany collapsed, was simply the 1944 plan in quick time without any severe opposition. Each of them had therefore to be set up with due regard for its effect upon the other two.

Pressure of time had also to be considered, for there was literally not a day to be lost. The 1943 deception scheme needed to be first drawn up and then scrutinised by the Combined Chiefs of Staff in time for the operation to be launched by September. For after this, according to the Navy, the Channel could become a bad enemy of all amphibious enterprises. This left something less than five months up to the word 'go'.

Equally, haste was vital for the 'Reverse Dunkirk' plan, for COSSAC discerned similarities between Germany's 1943 and her 1918 situation, when after a victorious Spring she collapsed to her knees in November. (They overlooked the power of Himmler's death-dealing SS to prevent disintegration and hold both army and state together.)

Though last in time, work on the main cross-Channel assault in 1944 — the 'second front' for which Left-wing propaganda continued to bay — had to be started more or less instantly, if the plan was to be completed in July as directed by the Combined Chiefs of Staff. For prior to the assembly of its great array of force, it would need to be studied, analysed, weighed in the balance, faulted, re-written and finally approved by all from the highest to the lowest military authorities.

The questions Morgan raised were argued at some length. Finally, it was decided to co-ordinate the planning of the three separate operations; and to defer defining more precisely the objective of the main cross-Channel assault until the mid-May Combined Chiefs of Staff meeting with Roosevelt and Churchill in Washington. The worst problem, of the non-existent Supreme Allied Commander for whom

Morgan was Chief of Staff, would continue while Roosevelt wrestled with the question of whom among his military chiefs he could spare.

How did Morgan begin work on a military enterprise of this magnitude, and while bedevilled by an acute shortage of time? There was, of course, the vast mass of data built up by the earlier planners, the Combined Commanders, for SLEDGEHAMMER and ROUN-DUP, as well as for Dieppe and St. Nazaire. 'The more we became aware of what had been done, the more we came to realise that we were heirs to a considerable fortune,' he observed.

Most thorough of the earlier studies for the whereabouts of the cross-Channel assault — one can imagine how the COSSAC staff sighed with relief when it was brought to their attention — was 'Selection of Assault Areas in a Major Operation in North-West Europe.'[12] This study was undertaken from November 1942 to February 1943 by the American General Ray Barker and Major-General J.A. Sinclair, Chief British Planner. Barker and Sinclair made a clean break with the earlier schemes advocating several separate assaults at once, as proposed by Churchill, and instead adopted the well-tried military principle of a concentrated blow in one carefully chosen area.

The Combined Commanders approved this study in February, and it was agreed, as recommended in it, that the Cotentin, Caen and Seine sectors of the coast of northern France should be taken as target areas against strong opposition; and the Belgian sector as the target if there was very little opposition. Since this study established permanent signposts regarding the question of where the assault should be made, it is worth while taking a close look at it.

First, Generals Barker and Sinclair pointed out that the invasion would depend on good air cover for beaches and shipping. Bombers and fighter-bombers, which need fighter escort, would have to provide tactical air support in the initial stages. In 1944 the range of Spitfire and Hurricane fighters extended only to Cherbourg, and to Knokke, near the Belgian–Dutch frontier. This therefore limited the possible areas of assault to between these two places.

This condition also called for the selection of an assault area containing airfields which could be captured for use by our own aircraft. Bombing operations outside the limits of land-based fighter cover should only be staged, the report said, if the *Luftwaffe* was very weak and if the airfields it needed to attack over the assault area were denied to it. The greatest concentration of airfields was south and south-east of Calais; there was another important group at Caen, but west of it there were only isolated airfields.

From the naval point of view, Barker and Sinclair noted, it would be best to attack between Calais and Cherbourg. An operation east of Calais would call for much more mine-sweeping, while enemy ships from Germany would have an advantage in knowing their own swept channels. An operation against the north coast of Brittany would involve prior capture of Guernsey, and ocean-going ships would be needed for a Biscay operation.

Regarding enemy defences, Barker and Sinclair observed that the only sectors of the coast where these were comparatively weak, but within reasonable fighter cover, were the east and west beaches of the Cotentin and the Caen sector. Enemy beach and coastal defences should be able to be destroyed by every possible means, including airborne troops and special support vessels. A combination of probable extensive flooding and demolition by the enemy ruled out Holland; in Belgium and the Pas-de-Calais widespread demolition could hamper operations. South-east of the Cotentin peninsula flooding could create an obstacle.

In any chosen assault area our possible rate of build-up and progress must compare with the rate at which the enemy could engage his reserves. If shortage of landing craft or other resources prevented our forces reinforcing enough to defeat the German reserves likely to be brought up, the only practicable operation was the capture of the bridgehead able to be held.

Considering the question of maintaining a force, Barker and Sinclair pointed out that two groups of ports would be needed for the enterprise if a large force undertook it, and at least one major port with good facilities must be captured very soon. Since about three months were needed to make captured ports workable again, ammunition, fuel and supplies would need to be brought ashore over beaches, so that suitability for this was a factor in selecting the main assault area. The beaches must therefore be sheltered from prevailing winds, which could hamper maintenance operations and they should have the capacity to pass vehicles inland rapidly through exits — a paramount factor.

Of all the beaches considered, from Belgium to Brittany, Barker and Sinclair reported that only those between the Cotentin peninsula and the River Seine, were reasonably sheltered and had a large capacity. Those in the Belgian sector, for instance, were exposed to prevailing winds, backed by extensive obstacles in the form of sand dunes and overlooked by high ground inland. The Dutch beaches were exposed, had limited exits, were beyond the range of suitable fighter cover and could easily be flooded.

In the Belgian sector a force could be maintained for a limited period in fine weather, but it could not succeed against any considerable enemy force. Defences here were very strong, so success could be counted on only if enemy morale had fallen.

The Pas-de-Calais area, proposed by some of the ROUNDUP planners, was turned down because most of the beaches were exposed to the prevailing winds, were strongly defended and were overlooked by high ground from which field artillery commanded the beaches and heavy coast defence guns the sea. Sand dunes able to hamper exits surrounded the bigger beaches, while none of the nearby ports were big enough to handle the supplies for a large force. Small, exposed beaches overlooked by cliffs, and exits blocked by towns ruled out the Seine area too, and in any case the defences there were very strong. Brittany, apart from its port capacity, failed to meet any of the chief needs and was also a long way from Germany.

The Caen and Cotentin peninsula sectors were suitable in every respect. The large beaches in the Caen sector, sheltered from westerly and south-westerly winds, would enable a big force to be put ashore rapidly and maintained across them. Barker and Sinclair were not put off by the fact that the beaches west of Cabourg were made unusable by being under fire from coastal defence guns in the Havre area.

The Caen group of airfields would provide the necessary fighter bases, and, denied to the enemy, would hamper their activity over the Cotentin and Havre areas, while the Seine river would help to protect the east flank of an assault force. The disadvantage of the Caen sector was a lack of suitable ports, so that Barker and Sinclair proposed that Caen should be the main assault area, with a subsidiary assault on the Cotentin peninsula's east coast in order to bring about the speedy seizure of Cherbourg.

Even so, port capacity would not be great enough for a large force. It was therefore suggested that either the Seine or the Breton group of ports should be taken. The first involved crossing the Seine river; the latter long vulnerable lines of communication, justified only if it was believed essential to build up a large force west of and protected by the Seine river.

Concluding their remarkable analysis, the two Generals reported soberly that the Caen sector would be suitable for an assault provided that at the same time the east beaches of the Cotentin peninsula were also seized in order that the port of Cherbourg could quickly be captured. In the Seine sector a second assault should be undertaken in support of the main one.

Before the advent of COSSAC the Combined Commanders had used the data study to draw up a plan called SKYSCRAPER based on a 10-division assault and an advance north-east towards Antwerp and the Ruhr. The British Chiefs of Staff, however, turned down the plan because the cost in resources was far beyond anticipated means.

The Barker-Sinclair study provided Morgan with vital data as to the best and safest places to stage a landing, but this was hardly enough. As he noted later, 'It wasn't just the beaches we were looking for. The landing beaches were just one x in an algebraic expression that contained half the alphabet.' Other vital unknowns were the size of the anticipated forces, the strength of air cover and the number of landing craft and ships available.

A planning impasse arose when further analysis by the COSSAC planners produced unexpected British support for an assault in the Pas-de-Calais, instead of Normandy. To try to decide this basic issue, the American members of COSSAC's army operations staff were directed to draft a plan for an assault against the Normandy beaches; and the British against Pas-de-Calais. The exercise evolved as a hard-fought contest. 'It was tough going and feeling ran high,' Morgan wrote later. 'We, the deputy Chief of Staff and I, knew that the moment was approaching when we should have to make up our minds not only as to which of the two alternatives being worked out would prove to be the less inviting, but, even worse, whether or not the thing was possible at all.'[13]

Opposition to any kind of cross-Channel assault whatsoever was now located and moreover among several senior officers of British Home Forces Headquarters. They held that with the available resources the project was far too risky; but that if it came to an order, Pas-de-Calais should be chosen. To Morgan this impasse was 'an appalling quandary'. He hardly knew where to turn. But Lord Louis Mountbatten intervened to transport the entire staff to Combined Operations Scottish headquarters at Largs, on the Ayrshire coast, to find inspiration away from London, in a new and stimulating atmosphere.

After a full day's argument there between the sea and the hills, the chances of agreement as to whether or not to assault, and if so, where, still seemed hopeless. No less than Mountbatten, Morgan himself wanted to undertake the operation but he had to respect the strong convictions of highly experienced senior officers on the planning staff. As he wrote later: 'The prospect of launching an invasion out of England was little short of appalling. There was no precedent in all history for any such thing on the scale that must of necessity be achieved here. If it was to be undertaken, every chance of failure that could be eliminated beforehand would have to be eliminated.'

Aware now that they had reached an alarming crisis, Mountbatten and Morgan strolled together in the evening over the lawns above the Firth of Clyde, assessed the strength of those opposing the operation and questioned whether or not they themselves would have to agree to give up the project entirely. They decided on one more day's effort,

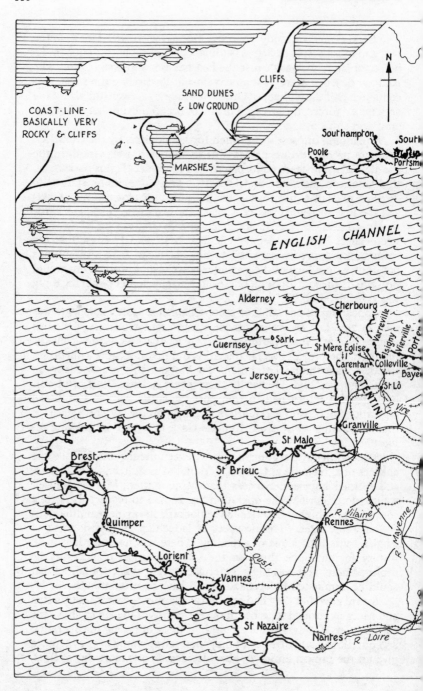

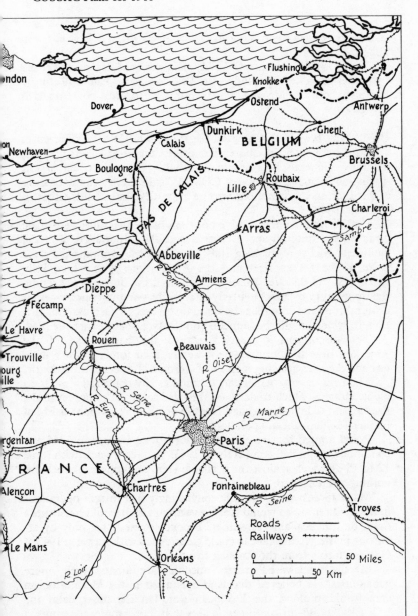

Lieut-General Sir Frederick Morgan and his team studied the entire French and Belgian Channel coasts for suitable landing areas for the invasion fleet before recommending the Baie de la Seine to the Chiefs of Staff. Only this particular stretch of coast fulfilled all the essentials.

and that next day's argument in favour of OVERLORD at last won unanimous approval.[14]

For COSSAC, at least, OVERLORD was on. But the issue of the two alternatives, Normandy, or Pas-de-Calais, had still to be hammered out and Morgan, who favoured Normandy, now turned to this task.

On 12 May 1943 in Washington began the TRIDENT Conference, attended by Roosevelt, Churchill and the Combined Chiefs of Staff, including Generals Brooke and Marshall. The subjects for urgent discussion included revision of COSSAC's directive and the bearing of Mediterranean operations upon a cross-Channel assault either in 1943 or 1944.

On this first day the relative positions of the two sides were made clear when Churchill spoke first to urge the importance, after the capture of Sicily, of pushing Italy out of the war, winning the great prize of the Italian fleet and the 26 divisions with which Italy garrisoned the Balkans. Roosevelt approved the question of keeping the troops busy by attacking Italy after Sicily, but questioned whether or not this might prejudice the build up of forces for a cross-Channel assault, which should be launched on the largest scale early in 1944.

The discussions proceeded against the background of the American urge to continue strengthening their forces in the Pacific war and the ever-growing menace of German U-boats in the Atlantic.

The next day the American Admiral Leahy delivered a paper on global strategy which underlined the need to divert resources to the Pacific, and to launch a second front in north-west Europe instead of further Mediterranean operations.

Portal argued that re-entry into north-west Europe in 1944 was conditional upon defeating Italy in 1943. 'A re-entry now with some 12 to 15 divisions against the available German forces could achieve nothing,' he declared.[15]

Marshall answered not very convincingly that further operations in the Mediterranean would create a vacuum which would constitute a drain on our available resources. Brooke retorted that only by attacking in the Mediterranean could we achieve a withdrawal in 1943 of German forces from the Russian front.

Marshall answered these specific arguments with more generalities. He believed that land operations in the Mediterranean area would prolong the European war. On the other hand the BOLERO build-up of forces in Great Britain would constitute a threat which would demand a German reaction. Brooke did not agree. The reduction in BOLERO caused by Mediterranean operations would only be some three to four divisions in 1943 and none at all in

1944. 'We must take advantage of the deterioration in Italian morale,' he contended.

Persistently, the British side stressed the view that the main task in 1943 was the elimination of Italy from the war. 'If we could achieve this . . . we should have gone a very long way towards defeating Germany,' Brooke declared. 'We do not believe that there is any method of giving effectual help to the Russian front this year other than a continuance of Mediterranean operations and the intensification of our bomber offensive.'

The two sides were deeply divided. Brooke records an informal talk with Marshall as they were walking together to one of the meetings which sheds light on this and their somewhat soured personal relations. Marshall had said: 'I find it hard even now not to look on your North Africa strategy with a jaundiced eye.' Brooke answered: 'What strategy would you have preferred?' Marshall: 'Cross-Channel operations for the liberation of France and advance on Germany; we would finish the war quicker.' Brooke countered: 'Yes, probably, but not the way we hope to finish it.'[16]

In face of this impasse on 15 May the Combined Chiefs tried to find a way out by the old method of inviting each side to produce a paper on how it proposed to go about the war in Europe. The British would report on how it should be done in concert with Mediterranean operations to defeat Italy; the Americans on how they would do it by concentrating entirely on BOLERO, or the build-up of forces in the United Kingdom. This was done. The British paper was entitled: 'Defeat of the Axis powers in Europe (Elimination of Italy first).' And the American: 'Defeat of the Axis Powers in Europe (Concentration of the Largest Possible Force in U.K.)'.

The British presented their arguments for defeating Italy first, and declared: 'This calamity would immediately prove for Germany a military disaster of the first magnitude . . .' It argued that the Italian defeat would also cause 'a reduction from some 1,480 to 950 aircraft in the potential ability of Germany to resist our cross-Channel operations. Only some unknown and incalculable weakness on the part of Russia could ease this situation for Germany.'

The impetus of the 'powerful and seasoned forces' in the Mediterranean must be sustained 'till we have reaped the great advantages in weakening Germany which it promises. Not to do so would be to cast away an unrivalled opportunity of inflicting on Germany a mortal injury and, instead, give her a chance to parry the final blow and delay her defeat by at least a year. This final blow can only be struck across the Channel; it cannot be delivered from the Mediterranean, but the peculiar nature of the cross-Channel operation sets limits to the weight of this blow.'

The paper proposed 8,500 landing craft to transport a force of 10 divisions, equally British and American, four for the assault and six for immediate follow-up, to be ashore by D-day plus 7, then 20 by D-day plus 90; 25 by D-day plus 125. It estimated that 10 to 14 British divisions would be available in the United Kingdom by 1 April 1944, according to whether or not 'cannibalisation' occurred owing to shortages of men and equipment.[17]

Suspiciously viewing their British opposite numbers across the table in the unfriendly atmosphere between the two allies that had developed, the American Chiefs of Staff questioned whether the impossibly high figure of 8,500 landing craft was not a ploy to side-step a cross-Channel assault altogether. In tough old Admiral King's hard words, having no intention at all of launching the invasion in the spring of 1944, the British sought to sink the plan through 'the matter of the number of landing craft'.[18] It was brutally candid.

The American paper was based on the assumptions that no amphibious operations would be carried out in the Mediterranean after the capture of Sicily, and that all operations should end there by 31 August 1943 so that landing craft could be released by 15 August for movement to other areas for further operations.

It was also assumed that the bombing offensive against Germany would continue as planned and that air operations in the Mediterranean area would be limited to the bombing of Italy. The elimination of Italy, the Americans argued, could possibly be brought about without the need for further amphibious operations in the Mediterranean by the successful invasion of Sicily and the intensification of bombing. The advantages to be gained in eliminating Italy by conducting further amphibious operations were not worth the cost in forces, shipping, amphibious equipment and time, and would have a drastic effect upon BOLERO and ROUNDUP in terms of using great additional forces.

The American paper proposed, like the British one, an assault force for the cross-Channel assault of 10 divisions, and estimated that enough landing craft would be available provided that no other Mediterranean operations after Sicily were undertaken. The landing craft were estimated at 4,657 of all types.

The paper argued that major operations in the Mediterranean after the capture of Sicily would prevent the release of forces for ROUNDUP, and that diversion of shipping to the Mediterranean would hamper the BOLERO build-up. It estimated that another amphibious operation after Sicily would reduce the available landing craft to 3,540 and a second one to 2,461. The paper said that it was probable that landing craft remaining after Sicily would not be sufficient, so any lesser number would be entirely inadequate.

Concluding, it contended that operations in the Mediterranean after Sicily should be limited to an air offensive, because any other operations would use resources vital to ROUNDUP and present the risk of a limitless commitment of resources to the Mediterranean vacuum, thus needlessly prolonging the war.[19]

By no means as closely reasoned as the British one, the American paper mainly asserted their point of view without any statistical or logistical backing. Marshall, in particular, seemed at this stage to express emotional dislike of the Mediterranean operations as such. On the other hand it is fair to say that, Italy apart, control over additional operations there was wise in the light of hopes of a cross-Channel assault in 1944.

At last the Combined Chiefs compromised. Their paper — 'Overall Strategic Concept for the Prosecution of the War' — limited Mediterranean operations in favour of the BOLERO operation in Great Britain for the 1944 cross-Channel assault. It did, however, point to an Italian invasion after the capture of Sicily, although not so clearly as Churchill wished. Eisenhower was to be directed to plan urgently 'operations . . . as are best calculated to eliminate Italy from the war and to contain the maximum number of German forces'. As well as any other Mediterranean operation it was to be subject to the approval of the Combined Chiefs. In addition, only forces already allocated to the Mediterranean could be used for the project.

Finally, seven combat-trained divisions, three British and four American from the Mediterranean were to be held in readiness after 1 November to transfer to England as part of the 1944 cross-Channel forces — even though they would be surplus to the available landing craft capacity. It was one of the provisions favouring cross-Channel operations that Churchill later believed ruined Alexander's campaign in Italy.

The TRIDENT Conference decision led to a supplementary directive for Morgan on 25 May which gave him, as he noted, 'a more tangible object'. He was instructed to 'secure a lodgement on the Continent from which further offensive operations could be carried out'. For this purpose he was to plan for the seizure and development of Continental ports after the initial assault, in order that the build-up of forces could be augmented by shipments from the United States or elsewhere of additional formations, at the rate of three to five divisions per month.

The target date for the operation was 1 May 1944, while outline plans were to be ready for the Combined Chiefs by 1 August 1943, a mere nine weeks four days' time. A total of 29 divisions would be available, five for the assault, two for the immediate follow-up, all seven loaded simultaneously; two airborne divisions, and another 20 ready for the advance into the lodgement area.[20]

When Morgan received his supplementary directive on 26 May 1943, his staff still debated daily as fresh intelligence about the enemy situation arrived whether to assault in Normandy, or the Pas-de-Calais. Two factors were eventually decisive.

First, the poor defences on the Normandy coast compared with Pas-de-Calais, where massive concrete fortifications signalled where Hitler's fears lay. Secondly, although fighter aircraft duration in the air was greatly cut by the longer distance from British airfields to Normandy than to the Pas-de-Calais, this was a drawback which hit the *Luftwaffe* even worse. For the bomber offensive had drawn much of the enemy's fighter strength in France into the air battle over Germany. It could be redeployed in Normandy to counter an invasion, of course, but those best informed considered that its present activity in Germany was worth gambling on.

So in June 1943 the final decision was made for Normandy.

It was a round-the-clock job for the COSSAC staff, analysing the evidence upon which they came to their decision. Nothing relevant was left out of the vast mass of information. Finally came the certainty that the best answer had been found; and, as history showed, it was the best answer. 'Once our attention was focused on Normandy it was satisfactory to see work going on in the Pas-de-Calais,' Morgan noted blithely. 'Our hopes would be fulfilled so long as work stood still in Normandy.'[21]

COSSAC's deception and camouflage operations played a significant part in this for work on operation STARKEY, the plan to persuade Hitler that the Allied assault was pointed at Pas-de-Calais, went on at the same time as the Normandy plan, at a furious pace.

The equation Morgan and his staff needed to solve before they could complete the plan was complex. First, their sparse allocation of landing craft and shipping forced them to prune the assault from the Combined Chiefs' optimistic allocation of seven divisions, five for the assault, two for the immediate follow-up, to three divisions for the assault and two for the immediate follow-up — two British tank brigades or American tank regiments and an American Regimental Combat Team. While two airborne regiments were still available it seemed then that lack of air transport could make them doubtful starters.

Morgan and his planners began with the premise that in order to seize the vital port of Cherbourg during the invasion they would need somehow to divide their initial assault force of three divisions into a main one against the beaches to Bayeux; and a smaller one against the east side of the Cotentin, north of the estuary of the Vire river (see map).

But they were stopped taking this short cut to Cherbourg, which avoided a long detour south-west around the marshy Vire estuary, towards the Cotentin, by the total impracticality of splitting up three assault divisions between main and auxiliary landings. All these problems arose out of their hopelessly small share of landing craft.

Sometimes, Morgan wondered desperately whether COSSAC really counted for anything, at least in the American mind in Washington. Could there be any significance in their having been charged with the responsibility of creating a plan for the assault without the appropriate hardware? He even asked himself sometimes if he and his staff were 'really only taking part in a gigantic cover plan or hoax, with the object of hoaxing among others, ourselves'.[22]

But despite these fleeting doubts, entertained while Eisenhower prepared his Anglo-American force for the Sicily invasion, and Hitler made desperate plans to revive his failing fortunes by an attack soon on the key Soviet city of Kursk, Morgan pressed ahead with his job of fulfilling his directives.

Soon, with all the probabilities surrounding this vast enterprise, it became clear to him and his staff that in fact they could not submit 'a clear and unqualified affirmative report'. So, with the OVERLORD Outline Plan, faithfully delivered to General Ismay on 15 July 1943, went a memorandum outlining the governing circumstances.

First, referring to the need to maintain forces over the beaches for two or three months in variable weather while port facilities were being restored, Morgan emphasised that improvisation of sheltered anchorages off the beaches was vital, and that the operation should not be launched unless the problem had been solved. The chances of success, he went on, would be increased 'in proportion as additional shipping, landing craft and transport aircraft can be made available'. A reasonable chance of success depended also on concentrating an assault across the Norman beaches about Bayeux.

Pleading that conditions both inland in France and in the air above it should be, so far as they were controllable, 'such as to render the assault as little hazardous as may be, so far as it is humanly possible to calculate', he warned: 'The essential discrepancy in value between the enemy troops, highly organised, armed and battle-trained, who await us in their much-vaunted impregnable defences, and our troops, who must of necessity launch their assault at the end of a cross-Channel voyage with all its attendant risks, must be reduced to the narrowest possible margin. . . .'[23]

The OVERLORD plan itself, which COSSAC and his staff drafted in about six weeks, consisted of a digest and three sections: (1) selection of a lodgement area; (2) appreciation of outline plan for the opening phase up to the capture of Cherbourg; (3) the development of operations after the capture of Cherbourg. A number of highly technical appendixes with maps and tables covered alternative operations and special details.

These included: port capacities; naval forces required; attainment of the necessary air situation; planning data for landing craft and shipping; rate of build-up; landing forces available; airborne forces; enemy defence system; German flak system; beaches; meteorological conditions; topography of the Caen sector; administrative considerations and methods of improving discharge facilities on the French coast.

COSSAC first re-stated the object as defined in his 25 May directive — to secure a lodgement on the Continent from which further offensive operations can be developed, and he added that the lodgement area 'must contain sufficient port facilities to maintain a force of some 26 to 30 divisions and enable that force to be augmented by follow-up shipments . . . at the rate of three to five divisions per month'.

Proposals for selecting the lodgement area covered the ground already analysed by Barker and Sinclair, and recommended again the Caen-Cotentin area, rather than Pas-de-Calais. Morgan turned down a main attack on the Caen beaches together with a subsidiary one in the Cotentin: 'An attack with part of our forces in the Cotentin and part on the Caen beaches, is, however, considered to be unsound. It would entail dividing our limited forces by the low-lying marshy ground and intricate river system at the neck of the Cotentin peninsula; thus exposing them to defeat in detail.'

In proposing the weakly defended Caen beaches (Lion-sur-mer/Courseulles; Courseulles/Arromanches-Les Bain; Colleville-sur-mer/Vierville-sur-mer) for the assault landings, Morgan emphasised again that the beaches were of high capacity and sheltered from the prevailing winds. Inland, the terrain was suitable for airfield development while much of it was unfavourable for Panzer division counter-attacks. 'Maximum enemy air opposition', he noted approvingly, 'can only be brought to bear at the expense of the enemy air defence screen covering the approaches to Germany; and the limited number of enemy airfields within range of the Caen area facilitates local neutralisations of the German fighter force.'

He recommended seizure of the Brittany ports between Cherbourg and Nantes for the creation of a base for the final advance eastwards. 'To seize the Seine ports would entail forcing a crossing of the Seine, which is likely to require greater forces than we can build up through the Caen beaches and the port of Cherbourg.'

Emphasising the importance of the air situation, he declared that the first objectives after the landing in the Caen sector were the early capture and development of airfields there, and of the port of Cherbourg. Main limiting factors affecting this were doubts about imposing our air superiority, enemy fighting strength in terms of the number of divisions he could make available, the shortage of landing craft and transport aircraft, and, most important, the capacity of beaches and ports there.

One necessary condition was the reduction in the effectiveness of the *Luftwaffe* in the Caen sector and the prevention of air reinforcements coming from the Mediterranean. From the present to D-day the overall strength of the *Luftwaffe* needed to be reduced by all means.

Between 26 and 30 divisions were likely to be available in Great Britain for OVERLORD on 1 May 1944. Landing craft and ships were being provided to transport three assault divisions and two follow-up divisions across the water. Transport of the two airborne divisions would be limited, it seemed then, to two-thirds of one division.

Vehicle exits from the Caen beaches confined the landing to the equivalent of the three assault and the two follow-up divisions, because 12,100 vehicles, which were the transport for the three assault divisions, were the maximum that could go through the beach exits in 24 hours. Morgan proposed solving the problem of passing through the two follow-up divisions and subsequent ones by enlarging the bridgehead and the exits. The airborne forces would aid this by dropping inland to seize Caen and certain strongpoints.

He called for an all-round increase in landing ships and landing craft of at least 10 per cent to provide for contingencies, and said he would like another division for an additional landing on the east side of the Cotentin. Assuming 'optimum weather' and the provision of artificially sheltered waters so that the forces could be maintained over the beaches, he said it 'should be possible to build up the force . . . to a total by D+6 to the equivalent of some 11 divisions and five tank brigades and thereafter to land one division a day until about D+24.'

The preliminary phase of OVERLORD should start forthwith. 'All possible means including air and sea action, propaganda, political and economic pressure, and sabotage must be integrated into a combined offensive aimed at softening the German resistance. In particular, air action should be directed towards the reduction of the German air forces on the Western front, the progressive destruction of the German economic system and the undermining of German morale.

'In order to contain the maximum German forces away from the Caen area diversionary operations should be staged against areas such as the Pas-de-Calais and the Mediterranean coast of France.'

Before the assault air action was to be intensified against the *Luftwaffe* in northern France and against road and rail links necessary for the movement of German reserves to the Caen area. 'Three naval assault forces will be assembled with the naval escorts and loaded at ports along the south coast of England. Two naval assault forces carrying the follow-up forces will also be assembled and loaded, one in the Thames estuary and one on the west coast.'

A few hours immediately before the assault there should be a very short, heavy air bombardment of the beach defences, followed immediately by a simultaneous landing by the three assault divisions, and the same day by the equivalent of two tank brigades (US regiment) and a brigade group (US regimental combat team). The objective was the seizure of the general line Grandcamp-Bayeux-Caen on D-day.

Within 14 days the assault forces should capture Cherbourg, extend the bridgehead to include the line Trouville-Alençon-Mont St. Michel, have landed 18 divisions and be operating up to 33 fighter-type squadrons from 14 airfields they would have developed.

After the capture of Cherbourg, COSSAC considered that the enemy would retire with the major part of his forces to defend Paris and the line of the Seine, possibly with reinforcements taken from Russia. It would probably be necessary to seize the Brittany ports first, so as to build up a force strong enough to force the crossing of the Seine. To secure the left flank during this operation and to seize more airfields, the enemy should be forced eastwards and the line of the river Eure, seized from Dreux to Rouen, thence along the line of the Seine to the sea. Chartres, Orléans and Tours should be seized at the same time. The Brittany ports of Nantes and St. Nazaire should then be captured, followed by Brest and various small ports.

By this time, about D+50, COSSAC calculated there should be enough ports to maintain at least 30 divisions, while about 62 fighter squadrons should be operating from 27 airfields in the lodgement area. Operations would then begin to capture Paris and the Seine ports.

Concentration and surprise were the two main principles upon which the landing was to be based, and during the preliminary period every effort was to be made to dissipate and divert German formations by diversionary operations staged against areas such as Pas-de-Calais and the Mediterranean coast of France.

Morgan named three conditions which were essential for success. First, there should be an over-all reduction in the German fighter force by the time of the beach assaults, and this condition would dictate the date by which the amphibious assault could be launched.

Next, German reserves in France and the Low Countries should not exceed 12 full strength, first quality mobile fighting divisions; nor should the enemy be able to transfer more than 15 first quality divisions from Russia during the first two months. Moreover, on the target date the location of the enemy's first class reserve divisions should be such that he could not deploy to reinforce the coastal divisions by more than three of them on D-day, five on D+2 or nine by D+8. Finally, the provision of artificial port facilities was essential and immediate action was necessary to produce them in time.

Given these conditions, General Morgan believed Operation OVERLORD had a reasonable chance of success.[24]

Having submitted the OVERLORD Plan to the British Chiefs of Staff with some qualms on 15 July 1943, Morgan and his Staff awaited the verdict with eager optimism. 'This, the first acid test of our work . . . was good for all of us,' he noted. 'When one has lived by day and by night, slept, woken, eaten, drunk with one idea, breathed it in and talked it out for months, there is a danger that one may lose judgement and balance and no longer be able to retain a proper sense of perspective. Having to make our case before this august court, being able to watch the play of fresh minds upon the whole project, was a new and invigorating experience.'[25]

A critical point had been reached in planning the strategy of this war that was convulsing Europe and Russia, and raging across the wide Pacific spaces.

9 OVERLORD APPROVED

American and British forces of General Alexander's 15th Army Group had invaded Sicily on 9 July 1943 and seized the naval base of Syracuse three days later, but by 15 July had run into stiff enemy opposition to the north. At the same time Soviet forces were counter-attacking General von Kluge's army group centred around Kursk, 400 miles south of Moscow. By 13 July, in the war's biggest tank battle the Germans were defeated with 70,000 men killed and 2,900 tanks lost. Two days later the Soviet General Popov attacked the German defences at Orel, a hundred miles north, in a move which led to the recapture of the city on 5 August.

Against this background of the war, while the Chiefs of Staff studied the OVERLORD plan, Admiral Lord Louis Mountbatten completed a study code-named Conference Rattle[1] on the problems of the combined operations involved in OVERLORD. Its findings supplied valuable details for the assaulting forces. Notable was the emphasis that 'the critical period will be that between the lifting of naval and air bombardment before the first troops get ashore, and the time when the army can get its own guns into action on land ...' Mountbatten's memorandum declared that the answer could be in the combination of a number of measures.

These were: 'A carefully co-ordinated fire plan from the guns of surface ships and from a variety of weapons mounted in landing craft; the development of a highly trained force fully equipped to deal with special weapons and machines to enable them to overcome the obstacles they are bound to meet on the beach; the landing of the maximum possible number of airborne troops in the rear of the enemy defences and landing of a large number of commandos probably under the cloak of darkness at difficult and therefore undefended landing points.'

Mountbatten noted that the army was inclined to the view that it would be necessary to assault in the darkness, or at least first light, while the naval commander-in-chief was doubtful whether it would be possible to assemble a large number of mixed groups of craft at sea in the dark. Mountbatten said that it was possible that if the army could not evolve a more simple plan, naval considerations would force us to set about the landing in daylight. 'Therefore it may be all the more necessary to soften the landing area before the assault by an intense bombardment beforehand mainly by the Royal Air Force.'

Meanwhile, the British Joint Planning Staff, composed of senior planning officers of the three services, had scrutinised Morgan's plan with great care during the second half of July. On 2 August they sent their commentary on it to the British Chiefs of Staff, who were extremely critical of some aspects of it, although they did not turn it down. The notes of the Joint Planning Staff are worth giving in detail. Noting the three main conditions that Morgan said should be created before the operation could be launched, they declared:[2]

> We agree that conditions must be created which will limit the scale of the land operations with which the Germans can oppose our attack. In view of the difficulty of building up and maintaining our forces over the beaches, we feel that the land opposition General Morgan is prepared to accept is too great. We cannot rely on the Russians or on our own bomber offensive to reduce this for us, and must ourselves force the maximum possible dispersion on the Germans by operations elsewhere.
>
> If the conditions required by General Morgan are to be fulfilled, the essentials are that we should: (1) press on with our policy of eliminating Italy in order to impose the maximum possible dispersion on German land and air forces. (2) establish ourselves as far north as we can in Italy, and press home our attack on the German fighter industry with a view still further to reducing and extending the German fighter force. (3) stage the maximum possible diversion against southern France at the appropriate moment. We consider that we should pursue this policy in the Mediterranean theatre even if it means that OVERLORD has to be postponed until June, or even July, 1944.
>
> We recommend that pending approval by the Combined Chiefs of Staff, the Chiefs of Staff should give general covering approval to the outline plan and instruct General Morgan to proceed at once to determined planning in order to avoid delay.

They then proposed that General Morgan should be instructed to examine their attached comments and pursue all preparation with the utmost vigour so that the operation could take place on the target date. In a more detailed annexe to their commentary the Joint Planning Staff, agreeing with the choice of the Caen area, noted that the crowding of so many ships on a narrow front, the need to blast the beaches before the landing and also tidal limitations dictated a daylight assault, which in turn would call for an intense concentration of fire support.

Having compared the Allied estimated rate of build-up with the German one, they did not consider it likely that the opposition which General Morgan was prepared to accept would be exceeded. 'Our margin of superiority over the maximum acceptable rate of German build-up particularly during the first two critical days is small,' they noted cautiously. 'We feel therefore that our own rate of build-up will not be sufficient if the Germans succeed in disposing the maximum number of first quality divisions which General Morgan considers he will be prepared to take on.'

They believed that the estimated capacity of the artificial ports of 6,000 tons a day might turn out to be somewhat optimistic. They also regarded as optimistic the rate of advance indicated in the plan, of D+2:10 miles; D+8:24 miles; D+12:45 miles; D+14:60 miles; D+24:90 miles and D+40:140 miles.

They warned that the right flank of the 8th army in Sicily was prevented by maintenance factors from advancing more than 30 miles in three weeks against less serious opposition than that envisaged in this plan. They also called for a more definite strategic role for resistance groups in France, such as the staging of diversions in southern France.

Finally, they proposed that action should be taken to overcome the shortage of 370 out of the 1,004 transport aircraft agreed for the assault at the TRIDENT Conference. They agreed that Morgan should plan an assault against the east side of the Cotentin peninsula if landing craft for a further assault division could be found, but they noted that there was a shortage even of the TRIDENT allocation of landing craft and proposed that if necessary the target date of the operation should be postponed so that new production of landing ships and craft could be absorbed.

An even more critical paper than this was submitted by Colonel J.M. Macdonald of the Planning Staff[3]. Macdonald pointed out that the plan depended on a reduction of the existing *Luftwaffe* fighter strength; the provision of adequate air cover over the Caen sector; present enemy strength and coastal defences not being materially increased, and the provision of artificial facilities for beach maintenance. He considered the fulfilment of these conditions 'rather doubtful' and said that it was unsound to base our strategy on a plan of so many large imponderable factors.

He was not satisfied, considering the estimated German rate of build-up, that Morgan would have ashore enough forces between the initial assault and D+5 to 'ensure the retention of his initial bridgehead'. He therefore proposed that a defensive line should be established on the River Orne and that a bigger lift should be provided for airborne forces, which should be more generally emphasised in the assault plan. Finally, he remarked that he considered Morgan's plan for operations after D+8 to be 'a first class effort of clairvoyancy'. Morgan and his staff sometimes called it, more simply, 'educated guesswork'.

On 4 August 1943, the day before General Brooke was to sail for Quebec with Winston Churchill and the Chiefs of Staff for the QUADRANT Conference with the Americans, Morgan was called in by them for a hasty cross-examination about the plan. In a short summary of it, he explained to those present that in assessing the number of enemy divisions in the Caen area he had excluded non-mobile coastal defence divisions, and that in the areas proposed for the assault there was at present, only one enemy regiment.

The Chiefs of Staff had time at this meeting only to criticise the plan's weak points, not to approve its good ones. Brooke objected that the country round Caen (the *bocage*, with its high banks and deep ditches) was very broken and unfavourable to the attack. He therefore felt that the estimated rates of advance were too optimistic. 'We did not achieve so high a rate of advance in Sicily where circumstances, particularly port facilities, were more favourable,' he said. With regard to the airborne forces used, Morgan argued that the assault itself did not depend upon them but that the capture of Caen, which was a vital part of the plan, did.

Portal then drew attention to the long delay which might occur in waiting for the needful air and sea conditions to coincide. Ideal sea conditions were often accompanied by low cloud which would seriously affect glider operations. He asked whether it would not be possible to arrange matters so that the whole plan did not depend on the timely arrival of glider-borne forces.

Brooke said that he assumed from figures given in the plan for the rate of the arrival of German divisions, that some allowance had been made for our air interference. Otherwise, the estimates seemed to be too optimistic. Portal also argued that the construction of 27 airfields in 24 days envisaged in the plan seemed somewhat 'sanguine'. Morgan answered that he thought this could be achieved and referred to a recent exercise in South Wales, where an airfield had been constructed in 48 hours from which aircraft had operated. He stressed that two artificial ports were indispensable to his plan and that General Sir Harold Wernher had been charged with the task of co-ordinating work on this problem.

Portal said that if air action had been unable completely to stop German reinforcements to the north-east corner of Sicily, it was most unlikely that such action could be made effective in the far less favourable circumstances of OVERLORD.

The Chiefs of Staff accordingly instructed Morgan to consider the suggestions put forward and agree to give detailed consideration to the Joint Planning Staff's commentary on the plan. They ruled that pending approval of the plan by the Combined Chiefs of Staff further action to implement it should not be held up.[4]

Brooke and the Chiefs of Staff departed with the plan next day for Quebec, where, during the conference, the Combined Chiefs of Staff would spend some time dissecting it.

The Quebec QUADRANT Conference on future strategy began on 14 August 1943 in Room 2208 of the Chateau Frontenac Hotel with meetings of the Combined Chiefs of Staff while Roosevelt and Churchill met privately at the President's home, Hyde Park. This time the Americans were determined to enforce their view of war strategy, and were fully prepared. 'I believe that the time has come for you to decide that your Government must assume the responsibility of leadership in this great final movement of the European war which is now confronting us,' War Secretary Stimson had declared in an important memorandum to Roosevelt that urged the appointment of an American as Supreme Allied Commander, on the grounds that the British were half-hearted about the cross-Channel assault.[5]

And Marshall told his colleagues: 'We must go into this argument in the spirit of winning.'[6] So the American Joint Chiefs of Staff prepared in earnest to impose their policy on the British, who, they still believed, had beguiled them at Casablanca into Mediterranean operations that delayed launching a second front in north-west France in 1943. They studied British strategy and debating tactics and, even, how many specialists they would need to field to meet their Allies on equal terms. They had acquired a deep respect for the abilities of the team headed by the agreeable, but unbending CIGS, General Brooke.

The American Joint Chiefs of Staff made plain their attitude in a paper named 'Strategic Concept for the Defeat of the Axis Forces in Europe,' which the British Chiefs debated privately on 13 August, the day before their first talk with the Americans. It was a clarion call for an end to 'opportunistic strategy' and 'secondary operations', in favour of an all-out effort to 'reach the heart of Germany' through OVERLORD and the bomber offensive. 'The present rapidly improving position of the United Nations . . . requires the adoption of an adherence to sound strategic plans which envisage decisive military operations conducted at times and places of our own choosing — not the enemy's,'[7] it said, echoing Marshall's thinking.

With this attitude the British agreed, and indeed, it was what they were doing already, but the American paper went on: 'We must not jeopardise our sound overall strategy simply to exploit local successes in a generally accepted secondary theatre, the Mediterranean, where logistical and terrain difficulties preclude decisive and final operations designed to reach the heart of Germany.'

Believing that OVERLORD would bring about an earlier decisive victory over the Germans, the U.S. Chiefs agreed that operations should continue to cause the collapse of Italy, and that air bases should be established at least as far north as the Rome area. But, and here lay the difference in strategic thinking between the two sides: 'As between the operation OVERLORD and operations in the Mediterranean, when there is a shortage of resources OVERLORD will have an overriding priority.'[8]

These few words meant in effect that the Italian campaign could be starved of resources and effectively stopped at Rome, which was certainly not in line with the British thinking.

The British Chief of Air Staff, Air Chief Marshal Sir Charles Portal, with the big pointed nose and gleaming eyes, opened the counter-attack against the American position, arguing: 'The key to the situation from the air point of view would be the placing of strong offensive air forces in northern Italy. From there all south Germany would be within comfortable range and above all two of the largest German aircraft factories, which between them produce 60 per cent of German fighters ... If we could place a strong force of heavy and medium bombers there in the near future, Germany would be faced with a problem that seems insoluble.

'It is estimated that to protect their southern front against a similar scale of attack to that being made from the United Kingdom, they would require half the fighter force now on the Western front. The Alps would render the German radio warning system relatively ineffective. I regard the possession of northern Italy as the key to the situation.'

Portal went on to say in his incisive way that the withdrawal of German air forces to the West, and particularly withdrawal of experienced fighters, was making itself felt. 'The battle against German fighter forces is a vital battle,' he said. 'It must be watched, not only with hope and enthusiasm, but with the determination of providing reinforcements from wherever possible. If the German fighter strength is not checked in the next three months, the battle may be lost, since it is impossible to judge the strength which the German fighter forces may attain next spring if our attack is not pressed home.'[9]

But Admiral King warned of a possible German move to Spain aimed at cutting our vital lines of communication through the Straits of Gibraltar. They might wait, he said, till the United Nations were further committed in the Mediterranean, then flood the approaches to the Straits with U-boats.

Brooke said that at present there was no German threat to Spain. 'The necessary forces are not available, nor could they be made available unless Germany shortens her line in the East.'

Adopting a conciliatory approach during next day's meeting, 15 August 1943, Brooke pointed out that there was a great similarity of outlook and the differences between them did not seem to be fundamental. With reference to Morgan's OVERLORD plan, he repeated its three main conditions: a reduction of German fighter strength; the enemy ability to reinforce must be kept within limits; and the question of beach maintenance. He added that the plan envisaged a too rapid rate of advance and too small a margin of superiority. The enemy rate of reinforcement must be as slow as possible.

Operations in Italy therefore must have as their main objective the creation of a situation favourable to a successful OVERLORD by reducing German fighter strength through bombing fighter factories in south Germany from Italian aerodromes. He therefore considered the statement in the United States Chiefs of Staff memorandum that, as between OVERLORD and Mediterranean operations, when there is a shortage of resources OVERLORD will have the overriding priority, too binding. Sufficient forces must be used in Italy to make OVERLORD a possibility.

How far north was it proposed our forces should go in Italy? If the Milan-Turin area were taken, then the seven divisions earmarked for OVERLORD might be required in Italy until June or July, he admitted.

General Arnold, Chief of American Air Staff, argued very pointedly that the advantage of having the airfields in northern Italy was outweighed by the disadvantage of the additional forces required to gain and hold them. But Portal countered that there were many airfields in the Turin and Milan areas which would be capable of handling 1,000 heavy and 1,000 medium bombers, of which the Germans would make good use.

King heaped fuel on to the fires of dissension with the remark that as he understood it the British Chiefs of Staff had serious doubts as to the possibility of OVERLORD, but Brooke insisted that the British view was that OVERLORD would be a success if the three conditions laid down in Morgan's paper were brought about. It was essential to take the necessary steps. Bluntly, King said that he did not believe that a successful cross-Channel assault was dependent solely on operations in Italy.

Ignoring these arguments of the British to justify extended operations in Italy, Marshall then contended that unless over-riding priority was given to OVERLORD and unless a decision was taken to remove the seven battle-hardened divisions from the Mediterranean for the cross-Channel assault, OVERLORD would become only a subsidiary operation. If OVERLORD were not given priority, in his opinion it was doomed and our whole strategic concept would have to be re-cast.

'The United States forces in Britain might well be reduced to the reinforced army corps necessary for an opportunist cross-Channel operation,' he declared.

In face of the serious turn the debate was taking, Brooke pointed out that in the British view OVERLORD was the main operation and all operations in Italy must be aimed at assisting OVERLORD. The American General Barker, COSSAC deputy, perceived that the American Chiefs of Staff feared that Morgan's conditions for the attack might lead to the indefinite postponement of OVERLORD. He now sought to calm their fears with the explanation that the required conditions for the German build-up did not imply that the operation became impracticable if the conditions were not achieved. Rather that more extensive use would have to be made of available means to reduce the enemy's ability to concentrate his forces. But Barker agreed that unless OVERLORD were given over-riding priority it would become a minor operation in which we would depend for defeating Germany on bombing alone.

Admiral Lord Louis Mountbatten, General Barker and Brigadier Maclean then expounded the main features of Morgan's plan to the American Chiefs, whose planning staff had already made a favourable report on it. So there was at least one positive outcome of the day's meeting — approval by the Combined Chiefs of Staff of the OVERLORD plan, with endorsement of the British Chiefs' action in authorising Morgan to proceed with the detailed planning and full preparation for the cross-Channel assault in 1944.[10]

This apart, the deadlock on European strategy between the British and American sides was complete. And Brooke had nearly lost patience with Marshall. 'I have entirely failed to get Marshall to realise the relation between cross-Channel and Italian operations and the repercussions which one exercises on the other,' he lamented in his diary on the night of 15 August. 'It is quite impossible to argue with him as he does not begin to understand a strategic problem. He had not even read the plan worked out by Morgan for the cross-Channel operation and consequently was not even in a position to begin to appreciate its difficulties and requirements.'[11]

August 15 was a black day for Brooke. In the evening Churchill told him that despite his earlier promise to him he had agreed with the President's wish that the Supreme Allied Commander should be not him, but an American instead, and most likely Marshall. Brooke soldiered on, repressing his sorrow at being deprived of this great task he believed himself to be better equipped than any other Allied general to carry out.

The next day the Anglo-American debate on strategy continued in a far from friendly atmosphere behind closed doors and without either secretaries or planners present, just the six Chiefs of Staff alone, able to express themselves as forcefully as they wished.

It was a dramatic meeting, held in the light of the impending surrender of Italy. Brooke opened it with the frank statement that the cause of their failure to agree was that neither side trusted the other. It was an astonishing, but true admission.

During the argument behind closed doors that day, with King expressing himself in what is politely called 'undiplomatic language', Brooke tried hard again to make the American side understand his belief in the close link between the Italian campaign and the proposed cross-Channel assault in 1944, but vainly. The American Chiefs of Staff refused to budge from the stand they had taken that day based on a stiff memorandum that amounted to an ultimatum to the British, in the light of their threat to disregard the agreement to defeat Hitler first.

In it they proposed that the British should agree to a rigid formula assigning to OVERLORD 'an over-riding priority over all other preparations in the European theatre'. It concluded in dictatorial tone: 'The United States Chiefs of Staff believe that the acceptance of this decision must be without conditions and without mental reservations. They accept the fact that a grave emergency will always call for appropriate action to meet it. However, long range decisions for the conduct of the war must not be dominated by possible eventualities.'[12]

It looked as if the British would have to forget their Mediterranean strategy, for there was no hiding the fact that the Americans were in earnest about the Pacific threat.

But next day, 17 August, events took place that justified the Mediterranean strategy. The Sicilian campaign had ended the day before with a loss to the Axis of 250,000 troops killed, wounded and captured, among them a large proportion of Germans, compared with Allied losses of only 31,000, mainly wounded. Even more important, an Italian envoy, General Castellano, meeting Allied representatives in Lisbon, had stated that Italy wished not only to surrender, but to break her alliance with Germany and fight the war henceforward on the Allied side.

It was a dramatic turnabout and the proposed British-American landing in Italy at once grew more urgent. The Combined Chiefs instructed Eisenhower to order Montgomery's Eighth Army to land at Reggio Calabria and elsewhere along the toe of Italy by 1 September, after it had completed re-equipping. Seven days later two American and two British divisions of General Mark Clark's Fifth Army were to land at Salerno in a bid to seize Naples.

In the light of these events Brooke and the British Chiefs, one can imagine, hoped fervently that Marshall and his colleagues would ease a little their tough stand on giving unqualified priority in military resources to the cross-Channel assault. That day's talks started at 2.30 pm, again in closed session and quite soon Brooke secured agreement. In place of 'over-riding priority' for OVERLORD, the two sides agreed that: 'As between operation OVERLORD and operations in the Mediterranean, where there is a shortage of resources, available resources will be distributed with the main object of ensuring the success of OVERLORD. Operations in the Mediterranean theatre will be carried out with the forces allotted at TRIDENT except as these may be varied by decision of the Combined Chiefs of Staff.'[13]

The deadlock was broken, for at least there was now a chance for the campaign in Italy. Churchill, in the first plenary meeting, on 17 August, attended by the President and him, did not disguise the fact that he still had reservations about OVERLORD. He was, he avowed, in favour of the plan but it must be understood that it depended on there being not more than 12 mobile German divisions in northern France at the time the operation was mounted; and that the Germans would not be capable of a build-up of more than 15 divisions in the succeeding two months. If the German strength proved to be considerably greater than this the plan would be subject to revision by the Combined Chiefs of Staff.

When Harry Hopkins, Roosevelt's special adviser, said that he did not think the Allies would take a rigid view of these limitations, Churchill agreed that there should be elasticity in deciding whether or not the operation should be mounted. He wished to emphasise that he strongly favoured OVERLORD for 1944. He was not in favour of SLEDGEHAMMER in 1942 or ROUNDUP in 1943. Every effort, he said, should be made to add at least 25 per cent strength to the initial assault in OVERLORD. It would mean an increase in landing craft. He thought that the beaches selected in the plan were good, but it would be better to have at the same time a landing plan made on the east side beaches of the Cotentin peninsula. The initial lodgement must be strong, as it so largely affected later operations. Marshall also agreed that an increase in the initial assault was necessary.

The Quebec planners also directed that Morgan's proposal for a diversion against the south of France, timed to coincide with OVERLORD, should be launched instead as an offensive to establish a lodgement in the Toulon-Marseilles area, to be exploited northwards. Churchill questioned whether the dropping of arms to the French *maquis* might not be equally effective, but the directive went through.[14] A squeeze on the Italian campaign thus became inevitable, for Eisenhower was instructed to plan for the South France landing with his present resources in the Mediterranean, insufficient though they were already. It was a directive that would still further strain British-American harmony.

Morgan meanwhile was involved with operation COCKADE, the diversionary operation designed to hold enemy forces in north-west France, and especially in the Pas-de-Calais region, in expectation of an invasion there. By means of an amphibious feint called operation STARKEY, it was hoped to bring about an air battle so as to prune severely the *Luftwaffe* and to launch a landing exercise called HARLEQUIN. The object of this was to persuade the Germans that the target area was in the Pas-de-Calais instead of in Normandy.

At the same time, to try to hoodwink them into believing that the strength of the British and American forces in the United Kingdom was much greater than it was, British and Allied forces in Scotland made a great show of preparations for an attack against Norway — about which Hitler was particularly sensitive — while the Americans in Devon and Cornwall simulated the hatching out of an operation against the Brest peninsula.

Landing craft being as scarce as always, imitation ones built mainly of wood and canvas, named 'big bobs' and 'wet bobs', were moored in suitable estuaries and festooned with troops' laundry drying in the wind to deceive aerial reconnaissance. Meantime, while the army was obtaining practice in the discreet assembly of large forces, the RAF and the USAF made ready for the clash it was hoped to provoke against the *Luftwaffe*, and the Navy assembled a small fleet ready for the amphibious feint.

Finally, during the several weeks leading up to the event, civilian movement in and out of the areas, from Felixstowe to Southampton especially, was strictly controlled. Although both troops and civilians were told that all the fuss was simply the outcome of an exercise, measures were taken to suggest that in fact it was the real thing. These included arrangements for the billeting of a hypothetical influx of hundreds of thousands of troops, the actual arrival of anti-aircraft forces, the build-up of military supplies, attention to fire services, military surveys of bridges. An atmosphere of tension and expectation was thus created.

But months before D-day for STARKEY, 8 September 1943, it was clear that there would be no actual landing during the amphibious feint owing to the acute shortage of landing craft and unwillingness to risk any of them. Yet the rest of the plan went ahead. Troops and vehicles were marshalled through Southampton and other embarkation points, while flotillas of minesweepers finished early in a day of brilliant sunshine clearing channels 'practically to the muzzles of the German coast defence batteries, which had displayed little interest beyond a few fortunately badly-laid rounds.' As Morgan noted:

> Up Channel, in full view from both coasts came an impressive convoy of merchantmen that might well have been carrying the infantry of our invasion force, instead of merely anti-aircraft armaments ... Down to the hards all along the coast marched streams of troops of which the main bodies turned about on arrival at the beach while their anti-aircraft armament embarked in the waiting landing craft and put to sea ... The sky reverberated with the roar of great formations of American and British fighters racing for the battle that they failed to find. We were told that a German coast artillery subaltern on the far shore had been overheard calling his captain on the radio to ask if anybody knew what all this fuss was about. Were our faces red?[15]

The question has often been asked since, whether this feint was worthwhile. For although an increasing state of alert may have resulted there was no observable enemy expectation of imminent invasion in the form of troop movements at the time. Most likely Hitler and the *Wehrmacht* High Command were persuaded that this was a rehearsal in the Pas-de-Calais area for the real thing in 1944, because they kept valuable reserve formations there in June of that year for weeks after the actual landings in Normandy. Therefore it would seem to have been a military feint that even the feudal Japanese *samurai*, great experts in this tactic, would have agreed was perhaps decisive in its effect upon the impact of the actual blow in June 1944.

But from the late summer and the autumn of 1943 onwards, real problems central to mounting OVERLORD in reality, held Morgan's attention. These were, the very urgent need that the Supreme Allied Commander, for whom he had been planning the cross-Channel assault, should be appointed without delay; or that, meantime, Morgan should be given executive power; also that the linked question of command and control of the British-American forces should be decided; and that somehow or other the alarming shortage of landing craft for the cross-Channel operations should be overcome.

The Combined Chiefs had stated in their report to the President and the Prime Minister after QUADRANT that they 'have approved the outline plan of General Morgan for operation OVERLORD and have authorised him to proceed with the detailed planning and with full preparations.'[16] It went beyond Morgan's original May 1943 directive. This May directive authorised him, as Chief of Staff to the non-existent Supreme Allied Commander, to plan to secure a lodgement on the Continent by May 1944 from which further offensive operations could be carried out with certain forces; and to draw up an outline plan for the seizure and development of Continental ports. His plan having been approved, subject to recommendations to increase the strength of the assaults, Morgan was now in this revised directive authorised to undertake the whole executive undertaking for the entire mammoth enterprise from tactical planning to administration.

But this was clearly beyond the authority and scope of the COSSAC group, and belonged to the tactical headquarters concerned, First United States Army on the right front, and the Second British Army on the left. The Combined Chiefs were therefore in effect instructing COSSAC to make arrangements to put the plan into effect.

Morgan and his deputy, General Barker, realised at once that this implied command responsibility, which they lacked, and that therefore in the absence of the Supreme Allied Commander they must somehow be invested with 'adequate authority over seniors, should necessity for its use arise'.

It was a knotty problem, finding a way of giving a staff officer authority over commanders, senior in rank. In the end an attempt to solve the problem was made by tacking a short cautious sentence on to Morgan's original directive in the hope that it would have magical effect. 'Pending the appointment of the Supreme Allied Commander or his deputy,' he was informed, 'you will be responsible for carrying out the above planning duties of the Supreme Allied Commander and for taking the necessary executive action to implement those plans approved by the Combined Chiefs of Staff.'

Thus in terms of command Morgan was still tied hand and foot, still lacking the real powers he believed he needed to make any progress. That the illusion of command had been fobbed off on him, he was painfully aware. 'While I hate the sight of this whole business I am completely at a loss to suggest anything better, short, of course, of appointing the great man himself, which appears to be utterly impossible,' he wrote in September to General Denvers, who commanded United States troops in Europe.[17]

The obstacle to appointing at once the Supreme Allied Commander, who, it had been agreed, would be an American, arose out of

Roosevelt's hesitation over the choice of Marshall for the post. While the President and the American War Department agreed that he was the one man specially suitable for it, American pride was wounded at the suggestion that Marshall should, as it were, descend from the heights of his appointment as United States Chief of Staff to that of a mere theatre commander, even if this did involve so momentous an issue as the future of Great Britain and Europe, if not the world.

Such vaunting self-esteem may be hard to understand, but there it was, a barrier for months to fruitful and efficient Allied planning for the second front. A second factor, only slightly less comprehensible in its confusion of values, was a reluctance to move Marshall because of the good relations he had established with Congress.

Morgan made his feelings about this absurd situation plain during the meeting of the British Chiefs of Staff on 3 September, where he was told that he had been granted putative command. He first asked if the nationality of the Supreme Allied Commander had been decided, since 'it would have an effect on the command and control organisation of OVERLORD which now had to be set up. Would he be British?' Could he further assume, he asked, 'that the detailed recommendation made in his OVERLORD plan as to the command and control of land forces had been approved in detail?'[18]

In reply Air Chief Marshal Portal, told him that it was quite impossible to give an assurance as to the nationality of the Supreme Allied Commander, because no decision had yet been made. Of course, Churchill had already on 15 August told Brooke that an American, most likely Marshall, would be appointed, but Portal would not have been authorised to speak of this until President Roosevelt had actually made the appointment. Portal's following remark, that although Morgan's plan had been approved by the Combined Chiefs of Staff, this would not preclude the Supreme Allied Commander making alterations, merely served to underline the uncertainty and the difficulties that Morgan would experience in trying to carry out the Quebec instruction to go ahead with 'detailed planning and full preparations'.

But on 10 September, first exercising his new power, Morgan crisply informed the British Chiefs of Staff that too many independent reconnaissances across the Channel had been carried out, leading to waste of effort. He therefore requested first, a clear definition of COSSAC's operational area: and second, that COSSAC should be given authority to co-ordinate requests and priorities of all reconnaissance agencies in this operational area. He also asked that the system of command and control for OVERLORD recommended in his plan should be settled at the earliest date and once approved should not be altered.

Then on 16 September Morgan returned to the attack, pointing out that 'detailed planning can only be carried out by the Commander concerned' and it was for this reason that he requested approval now of his recommendations for command and control in this operation.

The Chiefs of Staff were finally persuaded. The operation, they agreed, should be carried out by one British, one Canadian and one American army, 'under the command of the British Commander of 21 Army Group until such time as a US Army Group is established on the Continent'.[19]

They also established that COSSAC's operational area should comprise the whole of France, Luxembourg, Belgium, Holland, Denmark, Norway, the Rhine and the Ruhr valleys and north-west Germany. No raiding or reconnaissance operations, it was also agreed, should be carried out against the coasts of north-west Europe without prior consultation and agreement with COSSAC. That same day Field Marshal Dill was instructed to seek the views of the Combined Chiefs in Washington on this arrangement. The message to him added: 'The establishment on the Continent of headquarters United States Army Group will depend on the time the Second United States Army is introduced. This is considered to be unlikely until the Brittany peninsula is captured, but the course of operations may make it desirable for headquarters United States Army Group to take over control of United States forces at an earlier date.'[20]

A few days later however, the British Chiefs of Staff requested that a decision on this issue should be postponed until Morgan's visit to Washington in October, at General Marshall's invitation, to discuss this among other issues, including the availability of landing craft, and of United States forces ready for the cross-Channel assault in May 1944.

Morgan's reason for seeking control of raiding and reconnaissance was important, for without this control evidence might pile up on the French coast to suggest to the watchful Germans that the British were now more interested in Normandy than the Pas-de-Calais.

Morgan flew from Prestwick to Washington on 7 October 1943. It is worth noting that one of his main reasons for going was not on the official agenda. His putative command had been far from satisfactory. It had not enabled him, for example, to plan for the bigger cross-Channel assault recommended at Quebec. 'We had gone about as far as our limited means and limited authority permitted,' he noted later. 'What was now needed was more means and more authority. The place to get them was right here in the States. Our object must be to get the United States Army rolling eastward and to insist upon having the body of the Supreme Commander or a competent deputy.'

Short of this, he believed that he himself should be invested with these miraculous powers.[21]

Rather than ambitious, Morgan was a determined realist anxious to complete his assignment; but now he met unexpected obstacles. The British Chiefs of Staff had already urged the Combined Chiefs to issue a directive combining the British and United States tactical air forces under the command of Air Marshal Leigh-Mallory, who, it had been agreed at Quebec, should be C-in-C Allied Expeditionary Air Force. On 12 October they had submitted to the United States Chiefs a draft directive laying down his responsibilities. On 19 October the American Chiefs refused their assent both to this proposal and to Morgan's earlier one regarding command and control of the assault forces.

'It is the view of the United States Chiefs of Staff that the issuance by the Chiefs of Staff of directives to subordinates of the Supreme Allied Commander is unsound,' they declared, with reference to the proposed directive to the C-in-C Allied Expeditionary Air Force. And they argued that to lay down the organisation of command in the field for the still unappointed Supreme Allied Commander, as Morgan had proposed, would encroach on his prerogative.[22]

By 21 October Morgan had talked a great deal with Marshall, the British planners, the American planners, the Combined Planners and even that august body the Combined Chiefs, too. The outcome was that there was still no Supreme Allied Commander, no deputy and outright rejection of his recommendations for command and control of OVERLORD. Even worse, a new impasse had arisen over the demand by Marshall that the Supreme Allied Commander, an American, should have control over the strategic bombing offensive, which meant control of the United States Air Force and RAF Bomber Command.

Next day, 22 October, Morgan tried desperately to cut this Gordian knot. At a meeting with the Combined Chiefs of Staff, he asked 'straight out' for the full powers for himself of the Supreme Allied Commander until the great man was appointed. This was the proposal that was not on the agenda, and from the astonished British side he received an outright refusal. A staff officer could not give orders, and that was that.

Admiral King then added to the confusion by remarking that he disagreed with Morgan in respect to his inability to plan in the absence of a Supreme Allied Commander. 'Morgan has received instruction from the Combined Chiefs of Staff to proceed with implementation of his plan and therefore has ample authority,[23] he said simply.

But this, of course, contradicted the assertion of the American Chiefs that Morgan must not encroach on the prerogatives of the

Supreme Allied Commander in the planning field. So when Marshall argued that co-ordination of the strategic bombing policy under the Supreme Allied Commander was essential, 'owing to the mobility of the air weapon', Morgan replied that this disagreement too arose from there being no Supreme Allied Commander. He added: 'I have produced the plan for OVERLORD which has been approved, and I have been instructed to put the plan into operation, but it is impossible for a Chief of Staff to exercise full authority in the absence of the Commander.

'I had hoped that the Combined Chiefs of Staff would give me the authority, but from the discussion it appears that this is not going to be the case. No progress will be possible until the Supreme Commander is appointed and if the Supreme Commander is not appointed within a very short time it will be impossible to meet the agreed target date for OVERLORD.'[24]

Nothing came of that argument and Morgan's hopes were again dashed next day, when the United States Chiefs submitted a memorandum to the Combined Chiefs stating that Morgan's proposal for 'successive' command of OVERLORD ground forces should be left to the Supreme Allied Commander, and therefore deferred until he had been appointed. They agreed, in principle, that the Supreme Commander should assume command of all forces in France as soon as he was in a position to do so. He should also be given authority to determine, subject to the Combined Chiefs' approval, the general scheme for operations in southern France.

Regarding air operations, they argued that the sphere of responsibility of the Supreme Commander should include the whole of Germany for this purpose, instead of the Rhine and Ruhr valleys only. They argued also that the strategic bomber offensive whether from United Kingdom or Italy . . . should come under the general direction of the Supreme Allied Commander for three or four months before the target date for OVERLORD, since this was part of creating successful conditions for OVERLORD.[25]

An impasse arose over this issue. The British opposed direction by the Supreme Allied Commander of the strategic bomber offensive because it was 'too highly specialised' and not suitable for control more detailed than that exercised by the Combined Chiefs. They held that 'an analogy is provided by control of the war at sea against Germany which, though directed towards producing conditions required for OVERLORD, cannot be exercised even in the most general way by one theatre commander'.[26]

Marshall, stiffening his long upper lip with vexation, added that 'the dominant factor in my opinion . . . is in the use of the term "command". Any other relationship in a military operation appears fundamentally unsound, and from the American point of view, unacceptable. The air forces of the Allied Strategic Air Force should be detailed to operate under the "command" of the Supreme Allied Commander. In my opinion a committee can not fight a battle.'[27]

It was over this point that the supremely sceptical Portal would soon join issue with Marshall, but meantime since the British objected so firmly to the American proposal action was postponed in the hope of a solution at the forthcoming Cairo conference. But on 26 October the British Chiefs again urged the Combined Chiefs to issue a directive to the Air C-in-C (designate) of the British and US Tactical Air Forces, giving him authority to 'initiate preliminary action' to prepare his forces for OVERLORD. 'All the necessary arrangements have been made here for setting up the command of the Allied Expeditionary Air Force here, which only now awaits the necessary authority,' the British Chiefs said, in a message that, in American eyes, pointed at underhand arrangements prejudicial to the sacred authority of the Supreme Allied Command.[28]

Nevertheless a directive was at last issued to Air Marshal Leigh-Mallory, appointing him Commander-in-Chief of the Allied Expeditionary Air Force and instructing him to take over command of the RAF Tactical Air Force on 15 November 1943 and the 9th United States Air Force on 15 December. Admiral Sir Bertram Ramsay was at the same time appointed Allied Naval C-in-C, Expeditionary Force. So at least something was achieved.

While Morgan was still in Washington, with the command and control issue still unresolved, the British Chiefs on 15 November prepared an important Draft Directive to C-in-C (designate) Army Group Allied Expeditionary Force. It stated:

> The land forces will be divided into an army group designated to undertake the early stage of the invasion and a reserve army group to come into operation later. You have been appointed C-in-C — Army Group, in which capacity you will command all the land forces allotted to take part in the early stage of the invasion. You will be assisted by a combined staff of United States and of British officers. You will be responsible for the organisation of the necessary headquarters and staff. You will have under your operational command the 1st (US) Army, 2nd British Army and 1st Canadian Army and such other land forces, if any, as will be allotted. You will be responsible under the Supreme Allied Commander for ensuring co-ordination of plans and preparations for these operations with those of the naval and air commanders-in-chief. You will also be responsible for the training by their respective commanders of these forces.[29]

Later, on 29 November, after his return from Washington, Morgan issued a revised directive on these lines to the Commander (designate) of British 21 Army Group, which was the formation of five armoured and ten infantry divisions set up by Brooke in July especially for the cross-Channel assault. It stated that the Commander would be 'jointly responsible with the Allied Naval Commander-in-Chief and the Air Commander-in-Chief, Allied Expeditionary Force, for the planning of the operation, and, when so ordered, for its execution until such time as the Supreme Allied Commander allocates an area of responsibility to the Commanding General, 1st Army Group.'[30]

Thus, under the Supreme Allied Commander, the Commander of 21 Army Group was on a par in terms of responsibility and authority with the naval and air commanders-in-chief during the opening phase of the assault, and until General Omar Bradley, appointed on 23 October Commander of the United States 1st Army, was allocated an area of responsibility.

A few days earlier, on 22 November, the Cairo conference (SEXTANT) between Roosevelt and Churchill and their military staffs, opened with many vital policy disagreements with regard to the cross-Channel assault still unresolved.

10 OVERLORD REVISED

The Cairo Conference (SEXTANT) between President Roosevelt and Prime Minister Churchill and their staffs, with Chiang Kai-Shek's Chinese delegation in attendance, lasted from 22 to 26 November 1943. The Americans and British then flew to Teheran for talks with Stalin and the Soviet delegation from 28 November to 1 December, returning to Cairo from 3 to 7 December to complete the SEXTANT talks. They were designed to reach final decisions on world strategy and to dovetail plans for the war against Germany with Soviet strategy.

We are concerned with the decision of the talks as they affected plans for the cross-Channel assault in 1944. Preferring to await the attitude of the Soviets at Teheran, the Americans avoided committing themselves at Cairo to Churchill's plea to postpone the cross-Channel assault until 1 July 1944. His objects in asking for this were that landing craft would then be available for: (1) a seaborne attack on the west coast of Italy in December, with a view to taking Rome in January; (2) the capture of Rhodes and the possible opening of the Aegean in February, and (3) the attack in March on the Andaman Islands, in the Bay of Bengal, that Roosevelt had privately promised to Chiang Kai-Shek. At this Cairo stage of the talks the Americans were readier to postpone OVERLORD than the Andaman attack, and inclined, if the British would approve their south-east Asian strategy, to approve that of the British for Europe.[1]

At Teheran, the situation was different. The war had reached a critical phase, and Stalin had been depicted by Soviet propaganda, absurdly as we now know, as a military leader of genius who personally directed his troops at the front, though in fact, Soviet historians reveal today, he rarely, if ever, went far from his Kremlin office. Because of his great prestige the Americans in particular were impressed when Stalin dismissed further operations in Italy as 'of no further importance as regards the defeat of Germany'.

Stalin pressed instead for the cross-Channel invasion in 1944, backed by an invasion in the south of France. 'Marshal Stalin thought it would be a mistake to disperse forces by sending part to Turkey and elsewhere, and part to southern France,' Churchill later reported about their first plenary meeting on 28 November. According to Churchill he went on:

> The best course would be to make OVERLORD the basic operation for 1944 and, once Rome had been captured, to send all available forces in Italy to southern France. These forces could then join hands with the OVERLORD forces when the invasion was launched. France was the weakest spot on the German front. He did not expect Turkey to enter the war.[2]

At the second plenary meeting on 29 November, Stalin urged that the date for OVERLORD should finally be decided and, secondly, that it should be supported by a landing in southern France, either two or three months earlier, or at the same time. The capture of Rome and other Mediterranean operations could only be regarded as diversions. The third matter to be decided, he declared, was the appointment of a commander-in-chief for OVERLORD, either during the conference or within a week.

Roosevelt supported Stalin's proposals, but Churchill questioned where the landing craft for the two operations could be found. It was agreed that the Combined Chiefs of Staff should make recommendations on the issues raised. Meeting on 30 December 1943 they proposed:

> That we should continue to advance in Italy to the Pisa-Rimini line. (This means that the 68 LST which are due to be sent from the Mediterranean to the United Kingdom for OVERLORD must be kept in the Mediterranean until 15 January.)
>
> (b) that an operation shall be mounted against the south of France on as big a scale as landing-craft permit. For planning purposes D-day to be the same as OVERLORD D-day.
>
> (c) to recommend to the President and Prime Minister respectively that we should inform Marshal Stalin that we will launch OVERLORD during May, in conjunction with a supporting operation against the south of France on the largest scale that is permitted by the landing craft available at the time.[3]

Churchill and Roosevelt accepted these recommendations and Stalin was told of this decision the same day. He answered that Soviet forces would launch an offensive about the same time to help. Thus the British and Americans had committed themselves both to the cross-Channel assault in May and the supporting southern France landing (ANVIL) at the same time, an impossible schedule, as they were soon to be reminded.

In Cairo on 3 December 1943 the Combined Chiefs met to decide where to find the landing craft for both operations at once. To Brooke's argument that ANVIL must be a two-division assault, King correctly replied that no decision had been taken at Teheran as to the strength of the assaulting force, but Brooke insisted that two divisions were the least possible. 'The attack must be planned with sufficient strength to be successful.' It was agreed at this meeting that the Combined Planners should be instructed to examine the operation from the basis 'that it should be carried out with the minimum of two divisions and that the resources for it were not to be found at the expense of OVERLORD.'[4]

Portal then asserted that 'in order to carry out a successful operation in the south of France other operations would have to suffer'. He thought that this should be the Andaman Islands operation. Finally, the Combined Chiefs, agreeing that both OVERLORD and a southern France landing of two divisions were planned without a sufficient margin of safety, recommended priority for operations in Europe at the expense of the Andaman Islands assault. Roosevelt finally agreed that it should be cancelled, though 'much distressed', Churchill observed, in view of his promise to Chiang Kai-Shek.

Marshall's wish to co-ordinate the command of the Strategic Air Forces was taken up again on 4 December, when it met with powerful and eloquent opposition from Portal, who argued that it was impossible to co-ordinate bombing operations from two different theatres of war. 'The technical difficulties in getting some 2,000 aircraft in the air at the same time require days of planning by a committee which has brought together all the best technical knowledge,' he said. 'The insertion of an overall air commander would merely insert another link in the chain of air command.' This assertion was in direct conflict with Marshall's belief that 'a committee cannot fight a war'.[5]

General Arnold argued, for the Americans, that closer co-ordination was necessary to organise heavier attacks from different quarters so as to lessen the present high losses in bombing Germany, but a decision was deferred until 7 December, three days later. The Americans then put forward a plan to which Portal felt himself obliged to agree. The United States Strategic Air Forces' Chief, General Carl Spaatz, was to be put temporarily under the command of the RAF Chief of Staff, Portal himself, together with RAF Bomber Command, until the operations of both were transferred to the Supreme Allied Commander.

But the most important decision of all was made two days earlier on 5 December. The President at last announced that his choice for the post of Supreme Allied Commander was General Eisenhower: Marshall was to stay on in Washington as American Chief of Staff. It apeared that Churchill's refusal to agree to making Marshall Commander of both OVERLORD and the Mediterranean, which in American eyes would not appear a lesser appointment than his present one, was a factor in the decision.

Air Marshal Sir Arthur Tedder, formerly Air Officer Commanding-in-Chief, RAF Middle East, was appointed Deputy Supreme Commander; General Sir Harold Alexander, Commander-in-Chief Italy, to replace General Montgomery, who would return home to command 21 Army Group and the United States 1st Army in the cross-Channel assault until General Bradley was allocated an area of command in France. And so at last, with prodding from Stalin, Roosevelt had cut the knot of indecision that had stopped progress for so long.

General Eisenhower's appointment as Supreme Allied Commander of the Allied Expeditionary Force for the D-day landings in Normandy stimulated everyone who was taking part in the planning and training for it. The rather dismal feeling of lack of constituted authority, from which inevitably Morgan had suffered, was quickly dispelled. A military leader trusted by all had been chosen and charged with 'operations aimed at the heart of Germany and the destruction of her armed forces'.

The event gave a new impetus during the 21 weeks before the anticipated D-day to the great task of converting the numerous volumes of cross-Channel assault plans and projects into precise operational orders. And the momentum began to increase when General Montgomery, former Commander Eighth Army and now Commander (designate) of 21st Army Group, the first expeditionary group of armies, was instructed in Algiers by Eisenhower to begin a thorough study of the OVERLORD outline plan, while the latter, who already had doubts about its feasibility, journeyed to Washington. Montgomery had his first sight of the plan while visiting Churchill at Marrakesh the next day, 2 January 1944. After studying it, his first laconic words were: 'This will not do. I must have more in the initial punch.'

Earlier, in August, the Combined Chiefs of Staff had instructed Morgan to continue preparations for implementing the plan, while at the same time proposing that it should be enlarged. But Morgan had not the power to enlarge it, so the plan had stayed as he and his staff had conceived it in July. Montgomery and General Walter Bedell Smith, Eisenhower's Chief of Staff, began a thorough examination of it on 3 January 1944 at COSSAC Headquarters, Norfolk House, in London's St James's Square, by then temporarily transformed into Supreme Headquarters Allied Expeditionary Force.

A COSSAC chief army planner, Brigadier Kenneth Mclean, gave

them a first detailed briefing on it.[6] 'My immediate reaction', a critical Montgomery wrote later, 'was that to deliver a seaborne assault by one corps of only three divisions against the German Atlantic Wall as then constituted could hardly be considered a sound operation of war.'[7]

At meetings during the next two or three days he developed his criticisms of the limitation of the plan and spoke of the need to extend it substantially. Then at a meeting with army commanders and their chiefs of staff on 7 January at the St. Paul's School headquarters of 21 Army Group in London, he outlined his ideas for a revised plan for this great, but daunting enterprise. This and subsequent talks in January, about which Eisenhower, in Washington, was kept informed, were concerned with the development of the final outline plan for the assault.

Montgomery first explained that to prevent confusion Armies and Corps must 'go in' initially on their own fighting fronts, and not be passed in subsequently through a bridgehead run by another formation. Therefore, the areas originally selected by COSSAC must be extended. This meant that two armies would be committed in the assault, each in charge of their own sectors.[8]

The extended area for the assault, Montgomery went on, would now be from Varreville (east of the Cotentin peninsula) to Cabourg (west of the River Orne). The US First Army (General Bradley) would be on the right and the British Second Army (General Dempsey) on the left, on a front extended from about 25 to 40 miles. The task of the US First Army would be the clearing of the Cherbourg peninsula and the capture of the port of Cherbourg. They would subsequently develop their operations to the south and west.

The task of the British Second Army would be to operate to the south to prevent any interference with the US First Army, from the east. 'It is hoped eventually to get a firm lodgement from Caen to Nantes with the British Army being built up through the Cherbourg peninsula and the American Army through Brittany.' he declared and stressed that it was preferable to land everywhere at once rather than spread the assault over two days. The British effort must be strong in the initial phase if it was to succeed in preventing interference with the United States First Army.

He then showed on the map the area protected by the Havre coast defence guns, which set the limit of the assault to the east. He considered that the marshy areas, in conjunction with the River Orne would help to protect the left flank of the British Second Army.

'The town of Caen', he explained, 'is an important road centre and must be secured. The object of 2nd Army is therefore to seize Caen and the airfield area to the south-east, subsequently exploiting to the south to cover more effectively the flank of the United States 1st

Army.' In view of the urgency of securing the airfields and of ensuring protection to the 1st United States Army, Montgomery considered that five British brigade groups would be required, thus giving United States 1st Army only three brigade landing groups in the assault.

General Omar Bradley, Commander of the United States 1st Army, protested that it would be very difficult to explain to the American public the seemingly small initial American effort. Montgomery was impressed by this argument and a decision on the number of landing groups of each country was therefore deferred until another meeting.[9]

Montgomery had next to convince the naval Commander-in-Chief, Admiral Sir Bertram Ramsay and the Air Commander-in-Chief, Air Marshal Sir Trafford Leigh-Mallory, that his was a better plan than General Morgan's. Outlining it to them at a meeting at St. Paul's School at 3 pm on 10 January 1944, he said that his ideal would be five divisions landed on the first tide and the essentials of two divisions on the second tide, including the 7th Armoured Division on the British front. He would also like the First Airborne Division to land on D-day with first priority, ahead of the American landing on the Cotentin peninsula, followed by the Second Airborne Division 24 hours later, with a detailed plan to be made later.[10].

Admiral Ramsay explained the naval difficulties of the plan. These were the exposure of landing craft and ships to a greater number of enemy coast defence batteries, particularly from the flanks; the extra naval escorts required; the additional sea room that was necessary, and the fact that the new beaches had not been fully examined. He added that he was not prepared to commit himself at this stage, but considered that if the extra resources necessary could be provided, the new conception might be possible.

Montgomery next outlined what he needed from the air forces. These were: between then and D-day the *Luftwaffe* to be so reduced that the assault was possible. Next, to try to conceal our intentions by bombing other beaches; to ensure that the bombing programme, from D-day to D+14, would make rail movement from the east very difficult for the enemy, and for the last 150 miles would compel all movements to be carried out by road. Finally, there should be no bombing of the area itself until the night of D-1-day, with daylight bombing continuing next morning, aimed at the destruction of communications, and later on of the railways.

Air Marshal Mallory responded that by bombing 17 specific places they could ring off the selected beaches. He hoped to paralyse the railways in six weeks. On D-day he proposed concentrated bombing on coast defence guns at night, followed by the destruction of communications. In an extension of the front the whole length of the defences could not be 'drenched' by bombing, but the army would define certain areas, and concentrations would be dropped on these points. 'In general,' he said, 'the extension to the front might mean that the *Luftwaffe* might be able to inflict more damage on us, but certain success could be assured in the end.' He would examine the problem.

Admiral Ramsay then told Montgomery that from the naval point of view the target date of 1 May 1944 was not possible with this revised plan and that the next suitable period with moonlight would be a month later, early in June. Ramsay's reasons were that the proposed increase of the first wave of the assault — nearly double that of the initial plan — added enormously to the need both for naval escort vessels, landing craft for the assault, and for merchant ships carrying the ammunition and supplies to maintain this and the build-up. One of Ramsay's problems was therefore to find these additional resources, while Leigh-Mallory's problem was to acquire 200 more transport aircraft and another eight long range fighter squadrons.[10]

In Montgomery's mind the main obstacle to acquiring the additional 270 landing ships and craft of various kinds that the staff planners estimated would be needed, was ANVIL, the southern France landing scheduled to go in at the same time as OVERLORD. Montgomery had put it strongly to COSSAC (now the American General Bedell Smith, with Morgan as deputy) that ANVIL should be abandoned except as a one-division threat, a proposal with which Bedell Smith entirely agreed.

Eisenhower was not due in London from Washington until 20 January, but Montgomery insisted that meantime planning must go forward. At this meeting on 10 January therefore, COSSAC authorised him to 'plan on the assumption that half the ANVIL lift (of landing craft) would be available for OVERLORD'. It was also decided to send an urgent telegram to Eisenhower supporting this decision. Bedell Smith did so, pointing out in it however that he had refused to recommend the abandonment of ANVIL without 'Eisenhower's personal approval'.[11]

While Eisenhower avoided committing himself until he had studied the issue closely in London, Field-Marshal Dill reported from Washington that the American Chiefs of Staff were considerably irked by Montgomery's proposals drastically to change OVERLORD. And another of those periodic British-American planning wrangles now flared about the issue of staging the southern France landing. It raged in daily messages back and forth across the Atlantic right up to the end of March, when the American Chiefs of Staff finally insisted that OVERLORD should be launched by 31 May, closely followed by a two or three division ANVIL, as promised to Stalin, about whose feelings they were then very respectful. They also had begun to believe that, according to their scales, there were enough landing ships and landing craft in the United Kingdom for as much as a seven-division assault of men and an eight-division lift of vehicles without interfering with ANVIL.

The British view during this wrangle was that 'if the weaker OVERLORD and a two or three division ANVIL are carried out there would be a serious risk of our falling between two stools and of both operations failing'. Priority must therefore be given to OVERLORD — 'the most vital operation upon which we have yet embarked'. They held that this would not conflict with the Teheran agreement, which was that ANVIL should be on the largest scale permitted by the landing craft available at the time.[12]

Churchill intervened, before Eisenhower's arrival in London, with the statement that he was 'strongly in favour of broadening the front for the OVERLORD assault', and for the reduction of ANVIL. 'This strategy', he declared, 'is absolutely sound.' His influence on the argument was one of the reasons for the American Chiefs of Staff's private request to Eisenhower to make a recommendation to the Combined Chiefs of Staff on the issue, without consultation with what they called 'outside agencies', namely Churchill, as British Minister of Defence.

General Eisenhower began his historic task as Supreme Allied Commander, at Norfolk House for the time being, on 20 January 1944, and next day attended his first meeting with General Montgomery, his C-in-C of the D-day assault forces. Montgomery knew that while favouring a strengthened OVERLORD, Eisenhower believed that ANVIL should not be abandoned. It was a momentous meeting that day between the great American staff officer, now Supreme Allied Commander, and the brilliant though austere British field commander, for the scales that influenced the course of history would be moved decisively by Eisenhower's rejection or approval of Montgomery's new plan. For Montgomery this meant convincing Eisenhower — already in favour of a bigger assault — that the former weak OVERLORD plan could mean disaster and that it must be replaced by the stronger one.

He began by outlining the defects of the old plan, and his argument is worth listening to in detail:[13] 'Owing to the narrow frontage of the assault, the enemy reserve formations might succeed in containing the OVERLORD forces within a shallow covering position, with their beaches under continuous artillery fire. The waterlogged areas in the British-Canadian sector canalise the exits for vehicles through a small number of coastal villages which might take some time to capture and clear.

'Owing to the inundations at the foot of the Cotentin peninsula, the capture of Cherbourg from the south is likely to take much longer than estimated. Until Cherbourg is captured, the force will be entirely dependent upon beach maintenance (with hazards of the weather) and upon the untried expedient of the artificial port. Owing to the limitations of landing craft, and to the roads leading inland from the beaches, our rate of build up is unable to compete with the enemy's theoretical rate of reinforcement.'

Describing the main advantages of the new plan Montgomery said: '(a) Owing to the wider frontage of the assault the enemy is likely to be confused in deploying his reserves, and, provided we use our armour to seize quickly ground of tactical importance some miles inland, it will be difficult for him to contain us within a narrow covering position. (b) The wider frontage will to some extent offset the canalisation of beach exits through the coastal villages. (c) There is a good chance of capturing Cherbourg more quickly.'

In considering the new plan, Montgomery stressed, 'It should be borne in mind that the theoretical rate of enemy reinforcement still compares unfavourably with our own build up and there is nothing to prevent him concentrating all his force against the central assault sector, on which we are primarily dependent for maintenance. If the enemy succeeded in defeating us in this sector, it is unlikely that our other landings could survive.'

Moreover, even with additional landing craft, Montgomery admitted cautiously, 'the increased number of divisions in the assault and the faster rate of build up envisaged can only be achieved as a result of reduction in the fighting strength and efficiency of divisions and by taking serious administrative risks'. He also warned that Mulberry, the artificial port, was still an untried expedient and that some of the beaches consisted of peat and clay rather than hard sand.

Montgomery then said that the initial lift of landing ships and landing craft, assuming the addition of half from ANVIL allocations and the later target date, would amount to some 20,000 vehicles, which must provide for both the assault and the follow up. 'Even on the reduced scales, which are comparable to those used in the Mediterranean, it seems unlikely at the present stage of planning that this lift will take more than a total of five and two-thirds divisions, five tank brigades and "overheads".

'The proportion of the initial lift that can be landed on D-day will depend on beach exits and craft beaching limitations which are now under detailed examination. At the present stage of planning it would be optimistic to count on landing on D-day more than the equivalent of five divisions and five tank brigades plus a portion of "overheads", the balance of the initial lift being landed on D+1.' Anything further landed on D+1 would be carried in MT ships or MT coasters and, not being tactically loaded, should be regarded as non-effective before D+2. 'H-hour, the time at which the leading wave of assault craft beached, should be as early as possible on a rising tide.'

Eisenhower approved Montgomery's revision of the COSSAC plan and to avoid loss of time he ordered that planning should proceed on the basis of it while he secured the Combined Chiefs of Staff's agreement.

'Full weight must be given to the fact that this operation marks the crisis of the European war. We cannot afford to fail,' he stressed in an important cable to them on 23 January.[14] Pointing out that the OVERLORD plan was 'on a narrow margin', he contended that to ensure success it was essential to increase the assault force to five divisions. 'Nothing less will give us an adequate margin to ensure success,' he emphasised, and continued:

> Our reasons ... are that an operation of this type must be designed to obtain an adequate bridgehead quickly and to retain the initiative. Three divisions are insufficient for this. The present frontage of assault consequently is too narrow. It will be essential to extend the front to give us a greater opportunity of finding a weak spot through which to exploit success. However, the chances of this success and of the operation, will be greatly increased and the capture of a port speeded up if we could extend our front to the eastern beaches of the Cotentin peninsula west of the barrier formed by the river Vire and its marshy estuary.
>
> Further, the securing of the eastern flank and the early capture of the important focal point of Caen with the vital airfields in its vicinity will be facilitated by the extension of the assault to the beaches just west of Ouistreham.[15]

To assist the assault on the Cotentin, Eisenhower contended in this message, one airborne division should be landed on D-day to seize the exits from the beaches, followed probably by a second airborne division in approximately 24 hours. For this an extra 200 transport aircraft would be needed. By cutting down the scales of vehicles carried in the assault and follow-up he could find enough landing craft from those already assigned to him to lift one more assault brigade and have one brigade in reserve, but the balance of landing craft would have to come from elsewhere.

He estimated that he would need altogether an additional 55 landing ships and 216 landing craft of various kinds. He would need a considerable number of additional naval forces, including destroyers,

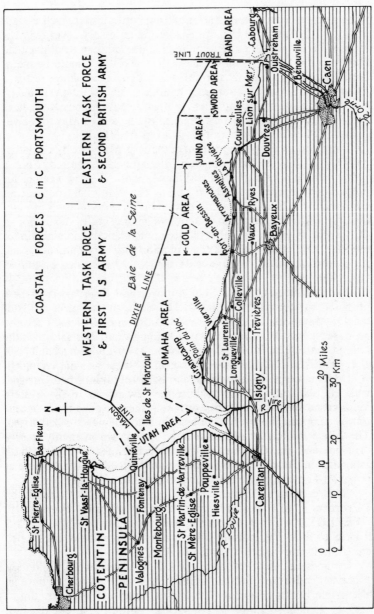

Map shows the final revised area for the D-day landings from Varreville to Cabourg, with the zones assigned to the First United States Army and the Second British Army.

minesweepers, cruisers and one or two old battleships, as well as eight additional fighter squadrons to ensure the necessary cover over the extended areas and the wider shipping lanes. He then recommended that with the five-division OVERLORD, ANVIL should be maintained merely as a one-division threat until enemy weakness justified its active employment. Cautiously he added: 'This solution should be adopted as a last resort and after all other means of alternatives have failed to provide the necessary strength by the end of May for a five-division OVERLORD and a two-division ANVIL.'

He would accept postponement of the early May date by a month if he were assured of then obtaining the strength required. Such a postponement would give an additional month of good weather for preparing air operations and for training the additional troop-carrier aircraft crews. 'It would also make available an extra month's production in the United Kingdom of about 96 landing craft.' Asking for an early decision, he declared that the recommendations contained in his message 'have been made after consultation with my commanders and my own staff, but with no outside agencies',[15] meaning, of course, Churchill.

The Combined Chiefs of Staff approved on 1 February 1944 these proposals for a revised OVERLORD assault, to take place not later than 31 May, with five divisions and two airborne divisions. They also promised a small number of extra landing craft, but said that the United States Chiefs of Staff insisted on a two-division assault soon after OVERLORD in southern France. A threat was not enough.

Oddly enough, the American and British positions had changed, with United States Chiefs pushing for new moves in the western Mediterranean and the British opposing them in favour of concentrating upon the cross-Channel assault. But a new factor had arisen. The Allied landing at Anzio, in Italy, had drawn in enemy reserve divisions and the Germans now clearly intended to fight a hard campaign in Italy so as to keep as many Allied divisions there as possible. The strategic conditions had therefore changed.

'This campaign', General Ismay said in a note to Churchill on 4 February, 'will provide in full measure the diversion to OVERLORD which it had been intended to create by ANVIL. Thus it looks as though Alexander will require a proportion of the French and American divisions allocated to ANVIL.'[16]

In a message on 4 February, the British Chiefs of Staff told their American colleagues that, the situation having changed, 'we have no alternative but to prosecute the Italian campaign with the utmost vigour'. Echoing Churchill's views, they argued that the distance between the ANVIL and OVERLORD areas was so large — nearly 500 miles — the country so rugged and the defensive power of modern weapons so strong, that a pincer argument for it did not apply. 'Thus except for its diversionary effect, which will be equally exerted from Italy or other parts, ANVIL is not strategically interwoven with OVERLORD.'[17]

Eisenhower disagreed with this argument, believing that in the mountainous regions south of Rome — the Cassino Line — only six to eight German divisions could delay the Allied advance, leaving 10 to 15 elsewhere in Italy as well as those in southern France available to stem the Allied assault in northern France. Thus, while supporting ANVIL, at the same time he pressed the American Chiefs of Staff for the additional landing craft he needed for the bigger OVERLORD. 'In my opinion, it is essential to ensure the success of OVERLORD, that requirements for the additional lift which I have put forward be met,' he said in a message on 11 February. 'Any reduction will materially impair the prospects of success of an operation which is to be launched under conditions never yet faced in this war.'[18]

While the argument continued, bringing fresh uncertainty over the vital issue of available landing craft, Admiral Ramsay, General Montgomery and Air Marshal Leigh-Mallory worked with optimism and determination on the draft of a new outline plan, assuming hopefully that the needful vessels would somehow be found.

11 OVERLORD
THE MAGNIFICENT

The revised outline plan for operation OVERLORD, drafted by Montgomery, Ramsay and Leigh-Mallory, was named the Neptune Initial Joint Plan. It was distributed on 1 February 1944, long before the ANVIL controversy was settled, but on the assumption that this enterprise would either be drastically cut, or cancelled, so that the needful extra landing craft and ships would become available.

The object of operation OVERLORD was, of course, the seizure of a lodgement area on the Normandy coast, including Cherbourg port and of airfield sites, from which future offensive operations could be aimed at the heart of Germany with the destruction of her military power. For this purpose, the United States 1st Army and British 21 Army Group were to assault the Normandy beaches simultaneously from the region of Varreville, on the east side of the Cherbourg peninsula, north of the Carentin estuary, and thence 45 miles east along the coast to the river Orne. The 21 Army Group comprised the 2nd British Army (Lt-Gen Dempsey), the 1st Canadian Army (Lt-Gen Crerar) and the British Airborne Troops (Lt-Gen Browning). The American 82nd and 101st Airborne Divisions were attached to General Omar Bradley's 1st United States Army.

Field-Marshal Gerd von Rundstedt commanded the enemy forces in France and the Low Countries, with the title of Commander-in-Chief West. Under him, Field-Marshal Rommel commanded Army Group B, made up of 7th Army in Normandy and Brittany, 15th Army in Pas-de-Calais and Flanders and 88 Corps in Holland. General Johannes Blaskowitz commanded the smaller Army Group G holding the Biscay and southern France coasts.

Early in 1944 the Normandy coastal sector was held by static German troops — 716 Infantry division, a two-regiment division, and a battalion of 709 Infantry Division, both containing, according to an Intelligence report, 'elderly types and a percentage of foreigners'. Two battalions were held in reserve at Bayeaux and Caen respectively. There was also a German tank training school at Carentin and about 70 French tanks.[1]

Infantry in concrete shelters and pillboxes with anti-tank and support weapons in the more important defences defended the coastal sectors. Gaps between these localities were sewn with mines in belts and festooned with barbed-wire defences, but there were no mines in ground believed to be unsuitable for an assault.

Long range artillery in the eastern sectors, to be assaulted by the British, included three batteries of a total of eighteen 155-mm guns and eighteen emplacements for 17-cm guns with a range of about 30,000 yards. In the American sector there were four batteries of a total of 24 150-mm guns; four 17-cm guns near Cherbourg and another four 17-cm mobile railway guns with ranges of 32,000 yards. Two very heavy batteries of two 240-mm guns, one of them at Le Havre, threatened vital sea lanes in the Channel. These were supported inland by 12 to 15 troops of four 105-mm gun howitzers or four 155-mm gun howitzers of divisional and medium artillery.[2]

This was an estimate of enemy coastal defences in late January 1944, but after the appointment of Rommel in February 1944, these defences underwent decisive improvements, including especially, the planting of long double rows of mined obstacles submerged at high water.

The enemy's rate of build up after D-day of fully mobile first class divisions capable of challenging the newly landed Allied forces within a few miles of the beaches was a matter of some concern. Morgan had made a condition for the success of a smaller three-division assault, a maximum arrival of three first class enemy divisions on D-day; five by D+2, and nine by D+8. He also made a pre-condition that the enemy should not be able to move more than 15 divisions from the Soviet Front; and this, in view of the German losses in the East, did not seem possible.

But in May 1944 Allied Intelligence estimated the German first class division build-up as unchanged at three divisions on D-day, then an increase of from six to seven by D+2 and of 11 to 14 by D+8, considerably more than Morgan's cautious pre-condition. However, in view of the Allied assault increase of from three to five divisions, with the additional two and two-thirds airborne divisions by then decided on, as well as the quicker rate of build-up, this German increase was not considered prohibitive.[3]

'The rate of reinforcement of German divisions in the first two months after OVERLORD D-day is now estimated to amount to a maximum of only 13 divisions, as against 15 which COSSAC, estimating when our rate of build-up was slower than now planned, considered acceptable,' a War Cabinet memorandum stated in May 1944.[4]

It was believed that the increased weight and breadth of the initial assault, ensuring the earlier capture of a deep water port and improving weight of the build-up, compensated for the increase in German opposition during the critical phases of the operation, especially in view of the estimated reduction in the likely rate of the German reinforcements in the first two months of the operation.

In the last few anxious weeks before D-day the probable rate of enemy reinforcement was constantly reviewed on the basis of the flow of air reconnaissance reports. Montgomery wrote later that it was then estimated that the Germans would be able to concentrate up to 20 divisions, eight of them Panzers, in Normandy by D+6. 'By D+20', he noted, 'under the worst conditions for ourselves we might expect opposition from some 20 to 30 divisions, of which 9 or 10 would be armoured formations. We had to anticipate the possibility of the enemy having up to 50 in action by D+60.'[5]

This was a very cautious, if not pessimistic view, which seems not to have taken great account of the planned bombing programme to destroy rail and road communications in the approaches to Normandy.

Admiral Ramsay defined the Navy's objects in the Neptune Initial Joint Plan[6] clearly and briefly: 'The object of the naval Commander-in-Chief is the safe and timely arrival of the assault forces at their beaches, the cover of their landings and subsequently the support and maintenance of the build-up of our forces ashore.' The seaborne assault had been increased from three to five divisions and five tank brigades with a follow-up of two divisions on the next tide, the front extended from 25 to about 45 miles, as in the Montgomery plan. In addition, the assault force was to be increased to fifteen and two-thirds divisions by D+8, and as soon as possible to between 26 to 30 divisions, after which it was to be expanded at the rate of from three to five divisions a month, or about one division a week. The daunting assault problems apart, the staggering task of keeping the armies continuously supplied with food, ammunition and equipment, was also that of Ramsay and the Royal Navy.

In terms of warships for escort and for coastal bombardment, it involved an increase of from two to six modern battleships, 18 to 22 cruisers, 78 to 119 destroyers, 75 to 113 frigates, sloops and corvettes, 50 to 80 anti-submarine trawlers and gunboats, 305 to 365 motor torpedo boats, motor gunboats, American P.T. boats and motor launches. Monitors (15-inch gun bombardment ships) stayed at a total of two. The final total amounted to 467 warships, added to which the ten flotillas of minesweepers Admiral Ramsay first requested he now needed to increase to 25 flotillas to sweep clear the wider Channel lanes leading to the beaches of the extended front.

The task of planning and supervising Operation Neptune, as the naval part of the assault was called, and commanding this great armada at sea on D-day was clearly beyond the power of one man. So it was agreed that Admiral Ramsay should have overall command of the two task forces, British and American, the flag officer, Rear-Admiral Sir Philip Vian, should command the Eastern (British) Task Force, while Rear-Admiral Alan G. Kirk commanded the Western (US) Task Force.

The harbour of Port-en-Bessin was the dividing point between the five beaches and assault areas, three British, two American, comprising the lodgement area. These were code-named Omaha, between Colleville and Vierville, west of Port-en-Bessin, and Utah, between Varreville and the Carentin estuary, on the eastern side of the peninsula. Eastwards of it were the beaches, Gold, Juno and Sword, between Asnelles and Ouistreham, to be stormed by the British and Canadian armies. Each of the five divisions was to be ferried across the Channel and landed on its allocated beach by its own naval assault force, distinguished by the first letter of the intended beach. 'Force S' would land its assault forces on Sword beach; 'Force O' on Omaha beach. As well as these five assault forces the two divisions for the immediate follow up were to be landed by 'Force L' (British) and 'Force B' (American).

The initial assault forces would consist of the fighting units of 1st United States Army, comprising three infantry divisions, five tank battalions, two Ranger (commando) battalions, Corps and Army troops, naval and air force detachments, and one, or two, airborne divisions. Second British Army would consist of four infantry divisions less two brigade groups, three assault tank brigades, one armoured brigade, two Special Service brigades (commandos), Corps and Army troops, naval and air force detachments and probably one airborne division. One of the three infantry divisions was Canadian.

These assault formations amounted to approximately 130,000 officers and men with some 20,000 vehicles. They included amphibious assault tanks and engineer assault tanks, flail tanks for clearing a path through minefields and tanks loaded with bridges tailored for crossing anti-tank ditches. There were also self-propelled guns, armoured fighting vehicles, personnel carriers and motor transport. To handle the anticipated scale of the enemy counter-attack, all of these formations were to have landed and be effective by D+3.

The Neptune Initial Joint Plan, repetitive in some respects and bearing other signs of hasty work, passed to the Commanders of the 1st United States and 2nd British Army the task of preparing tactical plans in their sectors. Stating simply the frontages of General Bradley's assault area, it said that the 'main task of the 1st United

States Army will be to capture Cherbourg as quickly as possible'. General Dempsey's 2nd British Army was to 'develop the bridgehead south of the line Caen-St. Lo and south-east of Caen in order to secure airfield sites and to protect the flank of the 1st United States Army while the latter is capturing Cherbourg'. The object of the assault was to 'capture the towns of St. Mere Eglise, Carentin, Isigny, Bayeux and Caen by the evening of D-day'.[7]

Army commanders themselves, after consultation with subordinate commanders if required, were to submit an Outline Assault Plan to the Joint Commanders-in-Chief by 15 February, two weeks later. It was to show: brigade or regimental combat team frontages and objectives; Ranger, Commando and airborne tasks; provisional list of beach defence targets for pre-ranged naval and airfire support and approximate numbers of men and vehicles to be landed on each brigade or regimental combat team beach on each of the four tides; the numbers and types of landing ships and craft involved in each case; tentative list by types of units showing the number of men and vehicles allocated to the initial lift of landing ships and craft.

The Joint Commanders-in-Chief allocated the 1st United States Army Initial Assault forces all the marshalling and embarkation facilities available west of the Dorset harbour of Poole, inclusive; and 2nd British Army all facilities east of Poole. For the build up, British and Canadian formations and the RAF were to move through Southampton, Portsmouth, Newhaven and the Thames. American formations and the 9th USAF were to move through Southampton and the Portland sector and the south-west. Assault and build-up forces were to concentrate in their marshalling areas at least 21 days before sailing.

During daylight on D-1, the plan said, assault forces and naval bombardment forces were to sail in groups from their assembly points on the south coast towards 'a general area south east of the Isle of Wight'. Groups were to be so routed that the chance of a correct enemy forecast as to the exact location of the assault would be so far as possible reduced. Naval escorts and minesweepers were to accompany them, giving special protection to first flight LCT (landing craft, tank), LSI (landing ship, infantry) and transports.

Minesweepers were to sweep 10 channels for the leading groups on reaching the enemy mine barrier and following groups were to pass through these channels, which were to be marked. About seven miles off the Normandy coast the LSIs and transports were to stop and lower their assault landing craft, which carried 30 to 40 men, and together with the tank landing craft and support craft deploy for the assault, approaching the beaches abreast so that the first wave of craft would land simultaneously at H-hour. Meanwhile, bombardment of coast defences from air and sea would have begun, based on lists of targets supplied by HQ 21 Army Group by mid-March. These targets were to have been attacked regularly from the air since then.

Ten fighter squadrons were to be provided as cover for the assaulting forces over the beaches during daylight. Fighters were also during daylight to escort bomber and airborne forces and give cover over the shipping lanes. Air forces were to be directed towards assisting the land forces in their initial attack on enemy coastal positions and, secondly, towards delaying the arrival of the enemy's immediate counter-attack divisions.

'The former will call for night bombing attacks on the coast defence batteries, and for attacks after dawn against coast defences and field artillery still in action; attack on defences covering the beaches and on beach exits may also be required at this stage,' the plan said. Aircraft should be held in readiness on the ground to deliver opportunity attacks against the enemy's concentrations, formations in the field and units approaching the assault area by road or rail.

H-hour, the time at which the first wave of landing craft were to hit the beach, was to be between one-and-a-half and two-and-a-half hours after nautical twilight, and about three hours before high-water, 'so as to allow a minimum period of 30 minutes' daylight for observed bombardment before H-hour and to enable the maximum number of vehicles to be landed on the first tide'.

After the first assault wave, formations were to be landed on the second, third and possibly fourth tides from landing ships and landing craft of the naval follow up forces. On D+1 the landing and build up of personnel, vehicles and stores would also begin from various other vessels. After D+3 the aim was to produce 'a regular daily lift for personnel, vehicles and stores and thus to avoid a succession of loading and discharging peaks'.

Two prefabricated artificial harbours, the famous Mulberries, each about the size of Dover harbour, were to be constructed, one at Arromanches in the British sector, and the other at St. Laurent, in the American sector. They were needed to enable the unloading of stores to go on regardless of weather conditions until sufficient ports had been captured and made usable again.

The Mulberries consisted of an outer floating breakwater called 'bombardons' and an inner one of great sunken concrete caissons, which were hollow steel and concrete cubes about six storeys high displacing 6,000 tons to 1,600 tons of water, according to size. Placed in the correct positions, they were to be flooded by opening seacocks and sunk in some 22 minutes. Altogether 146 caissons of different sizes according to the depth where they were to be sunk were to be towed

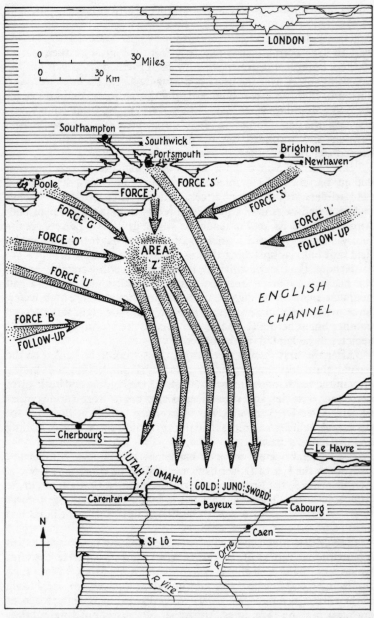

Diagram shows outline plan for the cross-Channel passage of the British and American assault forces bound respectively for Gold, Juno, Sword, and Utah and Omaha beaches.

slowly across the Channel, beginning in the afternoon of D—1. Floating piers anchored to steel posts driven into the sea bed so that they could rise and fall with the tide provided a roadway for loaded vehicles. Seven miles in all of these piers were to be towed to France, in 480-foot lengths.

Within these artificial ports while being unloaded ships would be anchored to what were termed 'spud pierheads', steel pontoons able to rise and fall with the tide placed at the ends of the piers. In all about one-and-a-half million tons of steel and concrete were to be towed to France by a fleet of tugs for this great engineering feat, finally to be carried out under fire from German coast defences.[8]

In addition a fleet of 70 Liberty (cargo) ships with an old British and an old French battleship and two old cruisers were to be sunk at two fathoms at low water elsewhere on the coast to provide shelter harbours for small vessels in rough weather. They were to be code-named, enticingly, 'gooseberries'.

The Overall Air Plan, produced by Air Marshal Leigh-Mallory, set forth the role of the Allied air forces with admirable clarity and logical order. 'The aim of the Air Forces', it declared, 'is to attain and maintain an air situation which will assure freedom of action to our forces without effective interference by enemy air forces, and to render air support to our land and naval forces in the achievement of this object.'[9] Total enemy strength in western France it estimated at 1950, but 850 aircraft represented the maximum that the *Luftwaffe* would be likely to commit directly against OVERLORD. 'The bulk of the remaining fighter force would be reserved for the day and night defence of Germany and of bases and communications in the West.' In other words Allied fighters could expect a four to one superiority over the enemy.

The plan clarified the vexed issue of the air forces' overall command. The Air Commander-in-Chief, Air Marshal Leigh-Mallory, would act for the Supreme Allied Commander, General Eisenhower, in regard to the operation of the Strategic Air Forces, in tactical support of OVERLORD and also in the co-ordination of these operations with those of the Tactical Air Force. The deputy Supreme Allied Commander, Air Marshal Tedder, would act for the Supreme Commander in regard to the operations of the Strategic Air Forces in strategic support of OVERLORD. It meant that General Eisenhower would have no direct command over Bomber Command or the United States Strategic Air Force.

For the preparatory period of D—90 to D-day, the plan charged the Strategic Bombing Forces with bombardment of enemy air frame, engine factories and assembly plants; ballbearing and aircraft accessory plants, and aircraft on the ground. An extensive programme of bombing attacks was called for against railways, missile sites, enemy coast defence batteries, naval installations and airfields, in particular those within 130 miles of the Neptune area.

Shortly before D-day attacks were to be intensified and focused on key points more directly related to the assault area, but still arranged so as not to indicate this area. Attacks on certain coastal batteries were included in this plan in an attempt to stop or delay work on the provision of protective steel armour for them, and thus to assist our effort on D-day by the reduction of enemy fire power opposing the assault.

Not later than D—21 there were to be bombing attacks to neutralise a considerable number of airfields within a radius of 130 miles of Caen. Aircraft repair, maintenance and servicing facilities were to be destroyed and runways rendered unserviceable, in addition to the destruction of aircraft on the ground. From D—30 to D-day there were to be attacks on enemy radar stations from the Pas-de-Calais area to the Cotentin peninsula. Owing to the need for deception, for every one coastal defence battery bombed inside the Neptune area, two outside it were to be bombed.

The air forces were also to intensify strategic and tactical reconnaissance during the preparatory phase. This was to include 'continuous visual and photographic reconnaissance of enemy dispositions and movements, in particular those which might affect the situation in the assault area, as well as detailed reconnaissance of enemy coast defences to detect new construction and/or the strengthening of old installations.'

Hand in hand with continuous aerial observation of ports would go a comprehensive photographic survey of prospective airfield sites to help estimate requirements for constructional needs and for planning the future build-up of Allied air forces on the Continent. The plan again stressed the need for a spread of operations to avoid indicating the Neptune area to the enemy.

From the early hours on D-day to H-hour, RAF Bomber Command was to attack 'with maximum operable strength' 10 selected heavy coastal batteries in the assault area while medium bomber forces attacked as soon as practicable after first light another six coastal batteries and the shore defences. Eighth US Air Force was to 'attack selected points in the beach defence system at H—30 minutes, so timed as to terminate at H-hour.'

From H-hour onwards, fighter bombers were to attack 12 artillery positions in the rear of the beaches, while others were held in reserve to answer urgent calls for air support, and to attack 'opportunity targets'. In general, air tasks were defined as protecting the cross-Channel movement against attack by enemy air and naval forces, neutralising coast and beach defences, protection of landing beaches from air attack, support of the land forces in their advance from the beaches and the reduction of the enemy's ability to counter-attack.

Night fighters were to protect all airborne operations, including cover of the dropping zones during the night preceding D-day, while five fighter squadrons were to undertake beach cover in the British sector, and five in the United States sector, but either sector could be reinforced by aircraft from the other, and six squadrons were to be held in reserve. Another five squadrons would give cover over the main naval approach channels, two at 60 and three at 80 miles from the south coast of England. Escort of bombers and troop carrier aircraft formations was to be made as required from the fighter aircraft pool.

A total force of fighters would be available on D-day of 54 squadrons for beach cover, 15 for shipping cover, 36 for direct air support, 33 for offensive fighter operations and bomber escort, and 33 squadrons as a striking force, including airborne escort.

Each army would be supported initially by one reconnaissance squadron up to noon on D-day and thereafter by two squadrons. Night reconnaissance with the aid of flare illumination and night photography would be undertaken when conditions permitted, to the extent of the equipment available.

Forty Fleet Air Arm aircraft, one RAF fighter squadron and three reconnaissance squadrons, the latter to be returned by noon on D-day to normal duties, were detailed for spotting and direction of naval gunfire against enemy artillery batteries inland in the assault areas. A team of 180 fighter pilots was specially trained for this purpose in the principles of gunnery, recognition of camouflaged targets, shellfire and accurate map reading, all from a height of 4,000 to 6,000 feet.

Spotter pilots, busy with large-scale maps, aerial photographs and powerful field glasses were protected while circling the targets by a fighter aircraft called a 'weaver'.[10] His duty was to weave from side to side above and behind the preoccupied spotter pilot to guard him from attacks by enemy aircraft. Meanwhile, the spotter pilot was to search for and radio back to the naval command at sea, six-figure map references of gunnery targets, then observe the fall of shells and send back corrections of range and angle of fire. The Americans preferred to land a team of gunners with airborne forces, who would then carry out the same observation tasks on land for the naval gunners at sea.

The purpose of these D-day attacks on coastal batteries was to neutralise rather than destroy them by forcing enemy gun crews to take shelter in dugouts and thus to lessen the fire aimed at the assaulting forces. And one of the objects of the first terrific aerial bombardment was so to daze the coastal batteries' gun crews that the warships could come within close range and aim at the steel and concrete gun shelters by visual observation. For of course at Le Havre and near Cherbourg alone there were batteries of big 155-mm guns with ranges of more than 30,000 yards that between them would be able to play havoc with the naval assault forces unless they were put out of action, at least temporarily.

Coastal batteries would also be attacked by some of the airborne forces. At 0200 hours on D-day a 'coup de main' party of 6th Airborne Division would be dropped near Benouville to seize the bridges over the Canal de Caen and the river Orne. Shortly afterwards the British 3rd and 5th Paratroop Brigades were to be dropped by some 264 transport aircraft and 93 tug-glider combinations between the rivers Orne and Dives, to reinforce the earlier party, to destroy the coastal battery at Merville and to destroy bridges over the Dives river and its tributaries. On the evening of D-day some 250 tug and glider combinations were to put down an air landing brigade on zones made ready by the earlier paratroops east and west of the river Orne.

Paratroops of the United States 82nd and 101st Divisions were to be dropped by 432 transport aircraft of 9th Troop Carrier Command in the general area of St. Mère Eglise from about 0020 hours on the night of D—1/D-day, while a glider force would land some 50 gliders of airborne forces at about 0200 hours that night to assist the seaborne assault on the Utah sector, to prevent the movement of enemy reserves into the Cotentin peninsula and to seize the causeways across flooded areas behind the Utah beaches. To confuse the enemy during the airborne landings, and as part of an overall cover operation, dummy paratroops were to be dropped in both the Neptune and Pas-de-Calais areas.

Planning on the basis of the constantly revised Neptune Initial Joint Plan went ahead in the early months of 1944 with great energy at all levels from SCAEF (Supreme Commander Allied Expeditionary Force) to army, corps, division and brigade level. Day by day the air forces intensified their attacks on enemy coastal batteries, railways and communications from Dunkirk to Cherbourg. Combined operations training at special centres from Inverary to Dartmouth was designed so that every officer and man of every battalion, American and British, would experience landing from assault craft with bullets whining over his shoulder and live shells bursting nearby, conditions as near to the real thing as were safe to stage.

Admiral Ramsay, C-in-C the Naval Expeditionary Force, had problems of nightmarish size to overcome. First was the shortage of warships for escort and bombardment. During the Cairo conference in December the British had accepted the American argument that the

Royal Navy alone should supply the entire fleet for this purpose for the cross-Channel assault, but with the increase in its size and extent this was impossible.

Ramsay was able to allocate only one battleship, one 15-in gun monitor, seven cruisers and 16 destroyers to the United States Western Naval Task Force under Admiral Alan G. Kirk. Since these were obviously not enough, in March Ramsay asked for a substantial allocation for this purpose from the United States Navy, and within a few weeks Admiral King had reinforced the Western Task Force with three American battleships, two cruisers and 34 destroyers, thus enabling Ramsay to withdraw from it some of the British vessels needed for the much longer coast of the Eastern Task Force.[11]

Much harder to solve however, was the grave and continuing problem of the shortage of landing craft, caught up as it was with the proposed ANVIL landing in Southern France, over the need for which the British and Americans were still deeply divided. In February, Eisenhower still supported the American view that a compromise should be worked out to save ANVIL without, if possible, harming OVERLORD. 'There is no point in cutting ourselves down and accepting a compromise solution for OVERLORD if ANVIL can never come off,' he argued. 'It would be better to have a really good OVERLORD with a good choice of craft, a good reserve of craft, a good margin all round . . . .'[12]

On 19 February the British Chiefs of Staff urged strongly the complete cancellation of ANVIL. They argued that the stiffer German policy of hard fighting in Italy and the proposed diversion thence of 10 Allied divisions for the southern France landings would face the remaining 20 Allied divisions in Italy with the burden of the entire campaign, and any other development that could arise in the Mediterranean.[13]

Eisenhower, deeply concerned about the landing craft nightmare, began to believe that after all it would be impossible to mount the ANVIL operation concurrent with OVERLORD. On 21 February, in face of his arguments, the American Chiefs of Staff at last agreed that ANVIL might have to be postponed, and Eisenhower supported this view. 'I think it is the gravest possible mistake to allow demands for ANVIL to militate against the main effort in the matter of time and certainty of planning,' he declared at last in a message to Marshall on 9 March.[14] The issue was debated next day during a meeting of Eisenhower with his service commanders. 'Protracted negotiations for provision of the necessary landing craft for OVERLORD had still not been concluded,' the official report of the meeting noted. 'The Supreme Allied Commander had sent a strong telegram to General Marshall urging the need for a final settlement . . . There was little doubt that in the end OVERLORD would be given the necessary craft, but we could not help being anxious whether they would arrive in sufficient time.'[15]

Finally, Eisenhower took the much overdue decision and in a message to Marshall on 21 March urged that ANVIL should be cancelled outright. Three days later on 24 March, the American Chiefs of Staff, evidently anxious not to offend Stalin, stubbornly yielded a little. 'We agree that a date for ANVIL concurrent with OVERLORD cannot be met and that ANVIL must therefore be delayed until 10 July,' they declared. 'We agree that re-allocations of resources from the Mediterranean to the United Kingdom to meet Eisenhower's requirements for OVERLORD should now be directed.'[16] Accordingly, 26 LSTs (landing ship, tank), 40 LCIs (landing craft, infantry) and one LSH (landing ship, headquarters) enough for one division were ordered to be made available for OVERLORD by 30 April. The British Chiefs of Staff accepted this proposal with reservations about the date for ANVIL, which they opposed entirely. (In the end it was launched on 15 August, code-named DRAGOON.)

Even with these extra landing ships and craft coming from the Mediterranean a shortage for OVERLORD still existed, but by postponing it until the 1 June moon period a month's British production of these perpetually scarce vessels to carry the second of the two extra divisions for OVERLORD would become available in time. And this was done.

By late April the build-up of the great force to be landed in Normandy was functioning like a vast, seemingly cumbersome but in fact highly efficient machine, with links across the Atlantic to training camps and arsenals in the United States. American fighting troops and service units were pouring into southern England, occupying vast areas of the south west, spreading huge dumps of food, vehicles, guns, ammunition and equipment across the green fields, as were British forces in central and south-eastern regions.

On 26 April 1944, the relative numbers of Allied troops that SCAEF expected to have landed in Normandy by D+1 were 117,005 British, including Canadian, 93,915 American and 1,100 French; by D+23 it was 711,305 British, 739,585 American and again 1,100 French; by D+42 some 995,900 British, 1,576,000 American, 15,370 French and by D+90 about 1,014,000 British, 1,777,505 American and 15,370 French.

26 April too was the day that the assault forces assembled at their embarkation points, and the day when Admiral Ramsay, Commander-in-Chief of the Allied Naval Expeditionary Force, moved from

London to his battle headquarters at Southwick Park, near Portsmouth.

The stage was now set for Operation OVERLORD, all, that is, except the date of D-day, the time of H-hour and whether this would be in darkness or daylight.

Darkness would of course prevent the enemy shooting accurately at observed targets, and therefore the military commanders at first favoured it. Admiral Ramsay preferred a daylight assault — safer for manoeuvring the huge Neptune armada. Towards the end of April however, aerial photo reconnaissance revealed a dramatic increase in the numbers and extent of submerged beach obstacles visible only near low water. These included thick wooden stakes tipped with mines, concrete pyramids loaded with high explosive shells fused to explode on contact, and cleverly designed timber traps loaded with mines to destroy assault landing craft.

This formidable array of destructive beach obstacles was a major factor in the final decision for a daylight assault. Engineer assault units could make these obstacles safe and mark lanes through them only at low water and in daylight, while the assault craft coxswains similarly needed visibility to avoid wrecking their vessels on the obstacles, and endangering the success of the entire operation.

But unfortunately, at low tide the landing craft would have to hit the sea bed in some parts more than 300 yards from the beaches, so that assault forces would be exposed to a murderous fire from carefully sited enemy automatic arms while crossing this flat sand. There were other factors too that made this a very complex decision, as Eisenhower explained in a letter on 17 May to the United States Adjutant General.[17] An adequate period of morning twilight must be available for aerial bombing and naval bombardment of the coast defences, the field batteries and strongpoints. The engineer assault units must land well before the incoming tide stopped their work, to prepare lanes through the beach obstacles visible above water only near low tide. For certain beaches the depth of water had to be enough to permit clearance of rocks by landing craft carrying the first assault units.

Finally, Eisenhower and Ramsay decided that H-hour was to be 40 minutes after nautical twilight on a day when the tide would at that time be three hours before high water. But this decision too brought its limits, because only on two or three days would low water occur shortly after daylight. And owing to the speed of the incoming tide there would even be variations in these conditions along the 45 mile stretch of coast. H-hour would therefore vary from 0630 hours for the Western Task Force to 0745 hours on the Eastern Sword sector. 1 June had been code-named Y-day, with Y+4, or 5 June, as the target date. Y+5, Y+6 and Y+7 were also possible. Thus there was some flexibility in case of postponement for bad weather, but it was a complex equation.

Eisenhower signalled on 8 May 1944 to his naval, military and air commanders that D-day was to be Y+4, or 5 June; and on 28 May the time for H-hour was finally decided and made known to them as well.

By now the last of the dress rehearsals, operation FABIUS, staged to test loading, unloading and assault, was complete, and in coastal areas closed entirely to visitors the troops were sealed off from all non-military social contacts.

Deception of the enemy was perfect, helped fortuitously during the last week or two before D-day by the necessary re-routeing of all non-military shipping from southern ports to northern ones. This caused an exceptional mass of vessels there, which, observed by the enemy, added to the anxieties Hitler had felt for some time that the Allies were possibly going to invade Norway to try to regain it as easily as he had seized it.

By 3 June all troops were on board their assault vessels, waiting and ready to go on 5 June. Then the high winds forced Eisenhower to order a nerve-racking postponement until 6 June 1944, and on this day operation OVERLORD, that great and dramatic achievement, unique in military history, successfully launched another triumphant fighting front in Europe.

APPENDIX 1

Fuehrer Headquarters
23 March 1942

TOP SECRET

The Fuehrer
and Supreme Commander of the Armed Forces

25 Copies
Copy No. . . .

OKW/WFSt/Op.Nr:001031/42g.Kdos.

DIRECTIVE NO. 40
Subj: Command Organization on the Coasts

(I) General Situation:
In the days to come the coasts of Europe will be seriously exposed to the danger of enemy landings.

The enemy's choice of *time and place for landing operations* will not be based solely on strategic considerations. Reverses in other theatres of operations, obligations toward his allies, and political motives may prompt the enemy to arrive at decisions that would be unlikely to result from purely military deliberations.

Even enemy *landing operations with limited objectives* will — insofar as the enemy does establish himself on the coast at all — seriously affect our own plans in any case. They will disrupt our coastwise shipping and tie down strong Army and *Luftwaffe* forces which thereby would become unavailable for commitment at critical points. Particularly grave dangers will arise if the enemy succeeds in taking our airfields, or in establishing airbases in the territory that he has captured.

Moreover, our military installations and war industries that are in many instances located along or close to the coast, and which in part have valuable equipment, invite *local raids* by the enemy.

Special attention must be paid to British *preparations for landings* on the open coast, for which numerous armoured landing craft suitable for the transportation of combat vehicles and heavy weapons are available. Large-scale *parachute and glider operations* are likewise to be expected.

(II)   General Tactical Instructions for Coastal Defense:

(1) *Coastal defence* is a task for the *Armed Forces*, and requires particularly close and complete co-operation of all the services.

(2) Timely recognition of the *preparations, assembly, and approach* of the enemy for a landing operation must be the goal of the intelligence service as well as that of continual reconnaissance by *Navy* and *Luftwaffe*.

Embarkation operations or transport fleets at sea must subsequently be the target for the concentration of all suitable air and naval forces, with the object of destroying the enemy as far off our coast as possible.

However, because the enemy may employ skilful deception and take advantage of poor visibility, thereby catching us completely by surprise, all troops that might be exposed to such surprise operations must *always be fully prepared for defensive action*.

Counteracting the well-known tendency of the troops to relax their alertness as time goes on will be one of the most important command functions.

(3) Recent battle experiences have taught us that *in fighting for the beaches* — which include coastal waters within the range of medium coastal artillery — *responsibility for the preparation and execution of defensive operations* must unequivocally and unreservedly be concentrated in the hands of *one man*.

All available forces and equipment of the several services, the organizations and formations outside of the armed forces, as well as the German civil agencies in the zone of operations will be committed by the responsible commander for the destruction of enemy transport facilities and invasion forces. That commitment must lead to the *collapse of the enemy attack before, if possible, but at the latest upon the actual landing*.

An immediate counterattack must annihilate landed enemy forces, or throw them back into the sea. All instruments of warfare — regardless of the service, or the formation outside of the armed forces to which they might belong — are to be jointly committed toward that end. Nevertheless, shore-based Navy supply establishments must not be hampered in their essential functions, nor *Luftwaffe* ground organizations and Flak protection of airfields impaired in their efficiency, unless they have become directly affected by ground combat operations.

No headquarters and no unit may initiate a retrograde movement in such a situation. Wherever Germans are committed on or near the coast, they must be armed and trained for active combat.

The enemy must be kept from establishing himself on any island which in enemy hands would constitute a threat to the mainland or coastwise shipping.

(4) *Disposition of forces and improvement of fortifications* are to be so made that the main defensive effort lies in those coastal sectors that are the most probable sites for enemy landings (fortified areas).

Those remaining coastal sectors that are vulnerable to coups de main of even small units must be protected by means of a strongpoint type of defence, utilizing, if possible, the support of shore batteries. *All* installations of military and military-economic importance will be included in that strongpoint defence system.

The same rules apply to offshore islands. Coastal sectors that are less endangered will be patrolled.

(5) The several services will establish a uniform *definition of coastal sectors*, if necessary on the basis of a final decision on the part of the responsible commander named in (III) (1) below.

(6) By means of proportionate allocation of forces, improvement of positions (perimeter defence), and stockpiling of supplies, the *fortified areas and strongpoints* must be enabled to hold out even against superior enemy forces for extended periods of time.

Fortified areas and strongpoints are to be held to the last. They must never be forced to surrender because of a shortage of ammunition, rations, or water.

(7) The commander responsible according to (III) (1) below, issues orders for coastal security, and assures a speedy evaluation, collation, and dissemination to authorized headquarters and civil agencies of intelligence procured by all the services.

Upon the first indication of an imminent enemy operation, that commander is authorized to issue the necessary orders for unified and complementary reconnaissance by sea and air.

(8) All elements stationed in the vicinity of the coast, whether headquarters or units of the Armed Forces, or organizations or formations outside of the Armed Forces, will forego the niceties of peacetime protocol. Their quarters, security measures, equipments, state of alert, and utilization of local resources will be governed solely by the necessity of countering every enemy raid with the utmost speed and force. Wherever the military situation demands, the civilian population will be evacuated at once.

178

(III)   Command

(1) The following authorities *are responsible* for the preparation and conduct of defence on coasts under *German control*:

- (a) in the Eastern Theatre of Operations (excluding Finland), the army commanders designated by OKH;
- (b) in the coastal sector under the control of Army Lapland, the Commanding General of Army Lapland;
- (c) in Norway, the Armed Forces Commander, Norway;
- (d) in Denmark, the Commander of German Troops in Denmark;
- (e) in the occupied West (including the Netherlands), the Commander in Chief West;

In matters pertaining to coastal defence, the commanders mentioned in categories (d) and (e) above are under the direct control of OKW.

- (f) in the Balkans (including the occupied islands), the Armed Forces Commander Southeast;
- (g) in the Baltic and the Ukraine, the Armed Forces Commanders Baltic and Ukraine;
- (h) in the Zone of Interior, the commanding admirals.

(2) Within the framework of coastal defence missions, the commanders designated in (III) (1) above, will have *command authority* over tactical headquarters of the services, the German civil authorities as well as units and organizations outside of the armed forces that are located within their respective areas. In exercising that authority, the commanders will issue tactical, organizational, and supply orders necessary for coastal defence, and ensure their execution. They will influence training to whatever extent is necessary for preparing their forces for ground operations. The required data will be put at their disposal.

(3) Orders and measures implementing this directive will *give priority* to the following:

- (a) inclusion within fortified areas or strongpoints of all installations important militarily or to the war economy, particularly those of the Navy (submarine bases) and the *Luftwaffe*;
- (b) unified direction of coastal surveillance;
- (c) infantry defences of fortified areas and strongpoints;
- (d) infantry defences of isolated installations outside of fortified areas and strongpoints, such as coastal patrol and aircraft warning stations;
- (e) artillery defences against ground targets (in installing new shore batteries and displacing those in position, the requirements of naval warfare will receive priority);

(f) defence preparedness of fortified establishments, their structural improvement, and the stockpiling of reserve supplies, as well as defensive preparedness and stockpiling of supplies in isolated installations outside of those establishments (including supply with all weapons necessary for defence: mines, hand grenades, flame throwers, obstacle material, and similar items);

(g) signal communications;

(h) tests of the state of alert as well as infantry and artillery training within the framework of the defensive missions.

(4) *Similar authority will be vested in the commanders of local headquarters* down to sector commands, insofar as they have been made responsible for the defence of coastal sectors.

The commanders enumerated in (III) (1) above, will generally confer such responsibilities on commanding generals of *army divisions* that are committed for coastal defence, and in Crete, on the Fortress Commander Crete.

In individual sectors and subsectors, and particularly in establishments that have definitely been designated as air or naval bases, the local *Luftwaffe* or Navy commanders are to be put in charge of the entire defence, insofar as their other missions permit them to assume those responsibilities.

(5) *Naval and strategic air forces* are subject to the control of the Navy or *Luftwaffe*, respectively. However, in case of enemy attacks on the coast they are — within the framework of their tactical capabilities — bound to comply with requests from the commanders responsible for defensive operations. For that reason they must be included in the exchange of military intelligence, in preparation for their future employment. Close contact must be maintained with their respective higher headquarters.

(IV) *Special missions of the several services within the framework of coastal defence:*

(1) *Navy:*

(a) organization and protection of coastwise shipping;

(b) training and commitment of the entire coastal artillery against sea targets;

(c) commitment of naval forces.

(2) *Luftwaffe:*

(a) air defence in the coastal areas.

This mission does not affect the right of local defence commanders to direct the assembly of Flak artillery suited and available for commitment against enemy invasion forces.

(b) improvement of the *Luftwaffe* ground organization and its

protection against air and surprise ground attacks on
airfields that have not been sufficiently protected by
their inclusion in the coastal defence system.

(c) commitment of strategic air forces.

Instances of overlapping control resulting from those special
missions must be accepted as unavoidable.

**(V) As of 1 April 1942, all instructions and orders not in
agreement with the present directive are rescinded.**

New combat directives issued by the responsible commander
pursuant to my directive will be submitted to me through OKW.

signed: *Adolf Hitler*

APPENDIX 2

Fuehrer Headquarters
3 November 1943

TOP SECRET

The Fuehrer
OKW/WFSt/Op.Nr.662656/43g.K.Chefs

27 Copies
Copy No. . . .

DIRECTIVE NO. 51

For the last two and one-half years the bitter and costly struggle against Bolshevism has made the utmost demands upon the bulk of our military resources and energies. This commitment was in keeping with the seriousness of the danger, and the over-all situation. The situation has since changed. The threat from the East remains, but an even greater danger looms in the West: the Anglo-American landing! In the East, the vastness of the space will, as a last resort, permit a loss of territory even on a major scale, without suffering a mortal blow to Germany's chance for survival.

Not so in the West! If the enemy here succeeds in penetrating our defences on a wide front, consequences of staggering proportions will follow within a short time. All signs point to an offensive against the Western Front of Europe no later than spring, and perhaps earlier.

For that reason, I can no longer justify the further weakening of the West in favour of other theatres of war. I have therefore decided to strengthen the defences in the West, particularly at places from which we shall launch our long-range war against England. For those are the very points at which the enemy must and will attack; there — unless all indications are misleading — will be fought the decisive invasion battle.

Holding attacks and diversions on other fronts are to be expected. Not even the possibility of a large-scale offensive against Denmark may be excluded. It would pose greater nautical problems and could be less effectively supported from the air, but would nevertheless produce the greatest political and strategic impact if it were to succeed.

During the opening phase of the battle, the entire striking power of the enemy will of necessity be directed against our forces manning the coast. Only an all-out effort in the construction of fortifications, an unsurpassed effort that will enlist all available manpower and physical resources of Germany and the occupied areas, will be able to strengthen our defences along the coasts within the short time that still appears to be left to us.

Stationary weapons (heavy AT guns, immobile tanks to be dug-in, coast artillery, shore-defence guns, mines, etc.) arriving in Denmark and the occupied West within the near future will be heavily concentrated in points of main defensive effort at the most vulnerable coastal sectors. At the same time, we must take the calculated risk that for the present we may be unable to improve our defences in less threatened sectors.

Should the enemy nevertheless force a landing by concentrating his armed might, he must be hit by the full fury of our counterattack. For this mission ample and speedy reinforcements of men and material, as well as intensive training must transform available larger units into first-rate, fully mobile general reserves suitable for offensive operations. The counterattack of these units will prevent the enlargement of the beachhead, and throw the enemy back into the sea.

In addition, well-planned emergency measures, prepared down to the last detail, must enable us instantly to throw against the invader every fit man and machine from coastal sectors not under attack and from the home front.

The anticipated strong attacks by air and sea must be relentlessly countered by Air Force and Navy with all their available resources. I therefore order the following:

(A)   Army:

(1) *The Chief of the Army General Staff* and *the Inspector General of Panzer Troops* will submit to me as soon as possible a schedule covering arms, tanks, assault guns, motor vehicles, and ammunition to be allocated to the Western Front and Denmark within the next three months. That schedule will conform to the new situation. The following considerations will be basic:

(a) Sufficient mobility for all panzer and panzer grenadier divisions in the West, and equipment of each of those units by December 1943 with 93 Mark IV tanks or assault guns, as well as large numbers of antitank weapons.

Accelerated reorganization of the 20 *Luftwaffe* Field

Divisions into an effective mobile reserve force by the end of 1943. This reorganization is to include the issue of assault guns.

Accelerated issue of all authorized weapons to the SS Panzer Grenadier Division Hitler Jugend, the 21st Panzer Division, and the infantry and reserve divisions stationed in Jutland.

(b) Additional shipments of Mark IV tanks, assault guns, and heavy AT guns to the reserve panzer divisions stationed in the West and in Denmark, as well as to the Assault Gun Training Battalion in Denmark.

(c) In November and December, monthly allotments of 100 heavy AT guns models 40 and 43 (half of these to be mobile) in addition to those required for newly activated units in the West and in Denmark.

(d) Allotment of large numbers of weapons (including about 1,000 machine guns) for augmenting the armament of those static divisions that are committed for coastal defence in the West and in Denmark, and for standardizing the equipment of elements that are to be withdrawn from sectors not under attack.

(e) Ample supply of close-combat AT weapons to units in vulnerable sectors.

(f) Improvement of artillery and AT defences in units stationed in Denmark, as well as those committed for coastal protection in the occupied West. Strengthening of GHQ artillery.

(2) The units and elements stationed in the West or in Denmark, as well as panzer, assault gun, and AT units to be activated in the West, must not be transferred to other fronts without my permission. The Chief of the Army General Staff, or the Inspector General of Panzer Troops will submit to me a report through the Armed Forces Operations Staff as soon as the issue of equipment to the panzer and assault gun battalions, as well as to the AT battalions and companies, has been completed.

(3) Beyond similar measures taken in the past, the Commander in Chief West will establish timetables for, and conduct manoeuvres and command post exercises on, the procedure for bringing up units from sectors not under attack. These units will be made capable of performing offensive missions, however limited. In that connection I demand that sectors not threatened by the enemy be ruthlessly stripped of all forces except small guard detachments. For sectors from which reserves are withdrawn, security and guard detachments must be set aside from security and alarm units. Labour forces drawn

largely from the native population must likewise be organized in those sectors, in order to keep open whatever roads might be destroyed by the enemy air force.

(4) The Commander of German Troops in Denmark will take measures in the area under his control in compliance with paragraph 3 above.

(5) Pursuant to separate orders, the Chief of Army Equipment and Commander of the Replacement Army will form *Kampfgruppen* in regimental strength, security battalions, and engineer construction battalions from training cadres, trainees, schools, and instruction and convalescent units in the Zone of the Interior. These troops must be ready for shipment on 48 hours' notice.

Furthermore, other available personnel are to be organized into battalions of replacements and equipped with the available weapons, so that the anticipated heavy losses can quickly be replaced.

(B) Luftwaffe:

The offensive and defensive effectiveness of *Luftwaffe* units in the West and in Denmark will be increased to meet the changed situation. To that end, preparations will be made for the release of units suited for commitment in the anti-invasion effort, that is, all flying units and mobile Flak artillery that can be spared from the air defences of the home front, and from schools and training units in the Zone of the Interior. All those units are to be earmarked for the West and possibly Denmark.

The *Luftwaffe* ground organization in southern Norway, Denmark, north-western Germany, and the West will be expanded and supplied in a way that will — by the most far-reaching decentralization of own forces — deny targets to the enemy bombers, and split the enemy's offensive effort in case of large-scale operations. Particularly important in that connection will be our fighter forces. Possibilities for their commitment must be increased by the establishment of numerous advance landing fields. Special emphasis is to be placed on good camouflage. I expect also that the *Luftwaffe* will unstintingly furnish all available forces, by stripping them from less threatened areas.

(C) Navy:

The Navy will prepare the strongest possible forces suitable for attacking the enemy landing fleets. Coastal defence installations in the process of construction will be completed with the utmost speed. The emplacing of additional coastal batteries and the possibility of laying further flanking mine fields should be investigated.

All school, training, and other shore-based personnel fit for ground combat must be prepared for commitment so that, without undue delay, they can at least be employed as security forces within the zone of the enemy landing operations.

While preparing the reinforcement of the defences in the West, the Navy must keep in mind that it might be called upon to repulse simultaneous enemy landings in Norway and Denmark. In that connection, I attach particular importance to the assembly of numerous U-boats in the northern area. A temporary weakening of U-boat forces in the Atlantic must be risked.

(D) SS:

The Reichsfuehrer-SS will determine what Waffen-SS and police forces he can release for combat, security, and guard duty. He is to prepare to organize effective combat and security forces from training, replacement, and convalescent units, as well as schools and other home-front establishments.

(E)

The commanders in chief of the services, the Reichsfuehrer-SS, the Chief of the Army General Staff, the Commander in Chief West, the Chief of Army Equipment and Commander of the Replacement Army, the Inspector General of Panzer Troops, as well as the Commander of German Troops in Denmark will report to me by *15 November* all measures taken or planned.

I expect that all agencies will make a supreme effort toward utilizing every moment of the remaining time in preparing for the decisive battle in the West.

All authorities will guard against wasting time and energy in useless jurisdictional squabbles, and will direct all their efforts toward strengthening our defensive and offensive power.

signed: *Adolf Hitler*

NOTES

Chapter 1
1. Churchill, *The Grand Alliance*, p. 340
2. op. cit., p. 341
3. op. cit., p. 343
4. ibid.
5. Cab. 68–23
6. Churchill, op. cit., p. 407
7. Cab. 65–23/64
8. Eden, *The Reckoning*, p. 276
9. Cab. 65/23–66
10. ibid.
11. Churchill, op. cit., p. 408
12. Eden, op. cit., p. 276
13. Churchill, op. cit., p. 411

Chapter 2
1. Cab. 69–2/DO.41(64)
2. Cab. 69–3
3. Cab. 69–8/DO.41
4. Churchill, op. cit., p. 413
5. Cab. 69–2/DO.41(69)
6. Churchill, op. cit., p. 420
7. op. cit., p. 485
8. Cab. 69–2/DO.41(71)
9. Gwyer, *Grand Strategy*, III, part 1, p. 335 (Official History)
10. Churchill, op. cit., p. 581
11. op. cit., p. 347
12. Matloff & Snell, *Strategic Planning for Coalition Warfare*, p. 106
13. op. cit., p. 117
14. Cab. 80–33
15. Churchill, op. cit., p. 627

Chapter 3
1. Bryant, *The Turn Of The Tide*, p. 293
2. Cab. 79–56(9)
3. Cab. 79–56(12)
4. Cab. 79–56(15)
5. Matloff & Snell, op. cit., p. 156
6. op. cit., p. 157
7. op. cit., p. 159
8. Eden, op. cit., p. 318
9. Matloff & Snell, op. cit., p. 178
10. Cab. 88–1 (CCS 13th mtg.)
11. Matloff & Snell, p. 182
12. Churchill, *The Hinge Of Fate*, p. 175
13. Stimson & Bundy, *On Active Service In Peace & War*, p. 215
14. Churchill, op. cit., p. 281

Chapter 4
1. Butler, *Grand Strategy*, 111, part 2, p. 675
2. Sherwood, *The White House Papers*, vol. 1, p. ???.
3. Cab. 79–56(23)
4. ibid.
5. Churchill, *The Hinge Of Fate*, p. 283
6. Matloff & Snell, p. 189
7. Cab. 79–56(25)
8. Cab. 79–56(24)
9. Churchill, op. cit., p. 283–5: Cab. 69–4/DO(42)10
10. ibid.
11. Bryant, op. cit., p. 355
12. Churchill, op. cit., p. 287
13. op. cit., p. 289
14. Cab. 65–30(28)
15. ibid.
16. Matloff & Snell, p. 190
17. Cab. 79–56(38): Butler, op. cit.

Chapter 5
1. Churchill, *The Hinge Of Fate*, p. 299
2. Cab. 79–56(46)
3. Churchill, op. cit., p. 303–4
4. Sherwood, *The White House Papers*,
5. Butler, op. cit., p. 596
6. Churchill, op. cit., p. 310
7. Bryant, op. cit., p. 391
8. Cab. 79–56(65)
9. Sherwood, op. cit., Butler, op. cit., p. 622
10. Churchill, op. cit., p. 342
11. Matloff & Snell, p. 240
12. op. cit., p. 242
13. Churchill, op. cit., p. 344
14. Harrison, G., *Cross-Channel Attack*, p. 27

15. Churchill, op. cit., p. 390
16. Cab. 65-31(7)
17. Cab. 65-31(11)
18. Cab. 65-31(16)
19. Churchill, op cit., p. 394
20. Matloff, op. cit., p. 394
21. op. cit., p. 268
22. ibid, p. 268
23. Stimson & Bundy, op. cit., p. 220
24. Matloff & Snell, p. 270
25. Churchill, op. cit., p. 395
26. Harrison, op. cit., p. 28

Chapter 6
1. Churchill, *The Hinge of Fate*, p. 395-6
2. Matloff & Snell, op. cit., appendix B.
3. Churchill, op. cit., p. 399
4. Cab. 79-56(65)
5. Cab. 79-56(22): Butler, *Grand Strategy*, III, part 2, p. 633
6. Matloff & Snell, p. 278
7. Cab. 88-1(32)
8. ibid.
9. Matloff & Snell, p. 282
10. Churchill, op. cit., p. 404
11. Cab. 88-1 (CCS 34th Mtg.)
12. Matloff & Snell, p. 284
13. Cab. 65-31(26)
14. *Stalin's Correspondence*
15. Churchill, op. cit., p. 440
16. op. cit., p. 475
17. op. cit., p. 584
18. op. cit., 585
19. op. cit., p. 583
20. Matloff & Snell, p. 365
21. Churchill, op. cit., p. 590
22. Churchill, op cit., p. 602
23. Matloff & Snell, p. 379

Chapter 7
1. Cab. 88-2(55)
2. Cab. 88-2(57)
3. ibid.
4. Cab. 88-2(58)
5. Bryant, *The Turn Of The Tide*, p. 548
6. Cab. 88-2(59)
7. Cab. 88-2(60)
8. Cab. 88-2 (CCS 155/1)
9. Cab. 88-2(65)
10. Cab. 88-2(67)
11. ibid.
12. Harrison, *Cross-Channel Attack*, p. 44
13. Churchill, op. cit., p. 666
14. op. cit., p. 671, 672

Chapter 8
1. PRM 333/16
2. PRM 333/12
3. PRM 333/13
4. Cab. 76-60(85)
5. Morgan, *Overture To Overlord*, p. 72
6. WO 106-4147 COS(43)101(0)
7. WO 106-4147 COS(43)148(0)
8. WO 106-4147 Cossac(43) 1st Mtg.
9. Morgan, op. cit., p. 70
10. op. cit., p. 66
11. WO 106-4147 COS(43)215(0)
12. WO 106-4222
13. Morgan, op. cit., p. 142
14. op. cit., p. 135
15. Cab. 88-2 CCS 83
16. Bryant, op. cit., p. 620
17. Howard, *Grand Strategy*, vol IV, appendix VIA
18. Harrison, op. cit., p. 65
19. Howard, op. cit., appendix VIB
20. WO 106-4149: Pencil 243
21. Morgan, p. 148
22. op. cit., p. 154
23. WO 106-4149 Cossac(43)28
24. WO 106-4149 Cossac(43)416(0)
25. Morgan, p. 165

Chapter 9
1. WO 106-4149 COS(43)367(0)
2. WO 106-4149 JP(43) 260
3. WO 106-4149 Cossac(43)28
4. WO 106-4149 COS(43)415(0)
5. Stimson & Bundy, op. cit., p. 228
6. Harrison, op. cit., p. 95
7. Cab. 88-3 CCS 303/1
8. Cab. 88-3 CCS 303/3
9. Cab. 88-3 CCS 106th Mtg.
10. Cab. 88-3 CCS 108th Mtg.
11. Bryant, p. 706
12. Harrison, p. 98
13. Cab. 88-3 CCS 303/3 JP(Q)30
14. WO 106-4147 CCS 303/3
15. Morgan, p. 108
16. WO 106-4149 CCS 319/5
17. Harrison, p. 106
18. WO 106-4149 COS(43)206(0)
19. WO 106-4148 COS(43)217(0)
20. WO 106-4148 COS(W)812
21. Morgan, p. 198
22. Harrison, p. 108, quoting CCS 304/3 and 304/4
23. Cab. 88-3 CCS 304/1
24. Cab. 88-3 CCS 124th Mtg.

25. WO 106–4148 CCS 304/1
26. WO 106–4149 COS(W)901
27. WO 106–4149 JSM1303
28. WO 106–4149 COS(W)901
29. WO 106–4148 COS(43)710(0)
30. Harrison, p. 116, quoting Cossac(43)76

Chapter 10
1. Ehrman, *Grand Strategy*, vol V, p. 167
2. Churchill, *Closing The Ring*, p. 312
3. Cab. 88–3 CCS 132nd Mtg.
4. Cab. 88–3 CCS 133rd Mtg.
5. Cab. 88–3 CCS 134th Mtg.
6. Harrison, op. cit., p. 165
7. Montgomery, *Normandy To The Baltic*, p. 7
8. WO 205–16: Notes of a meeting of Army Commanders and their Chiefs of Staff on 7 Jan 1944
9. op. cit.
10. WO 205–15: Notes of C-in-C's meeting with Navy and Air Cs-in-C at St. Paul's School on 10 Jan 1944
11. Harrison, p. 167
12. WO 106 OZ243
13. WO 205–16: Notes of C-in-C's meeting with Supreme Allied Commander on 21 Jan 1944

14. WO 106–4150 (SH-2)
15. ibid.
16. COS(44) 35th Mtg. WO 106–4150
17. WO 106–4150 COS(W)1126
18. WO 106–4150 OZ786

Chapter 11
1. 21 AG 00/253/Ops WO 106–4148
2. ibid.
3. WO 106–4148 JIC(44)210(0)
4. ibid.
5. Montgomery, op. cit., p. 19
6. WO 205–15: The Neptune Initial Joint Plan
7. ibid.
8. Edwards, Operation Neptune, pp. 59–60
9. WO 205–645: The Overall Air Plan, 15 April 1944
10. Edwards, op. cit., p. 91
11. Harrison, p. 194
12. WO 205–5G
13. WO 106–4150 COS(W)1156
14. Harrison, p. 173
15. WO 205–12 SCAEF 7th Mtg. 10 March 1944
16. WO 106–4150 JSM 1593 24 March 1944
17. WO 205 SHAEF 187

ACKNOWLEDGEMENTS

For kind permission to reproduce extracts from these books, grateful acknowledgements are due to the following publishers: The Hutchinson Publishing Group Ltd., *Normandy to the Baltic* by Field-Marshal Montgomery; Wm. Collins Sons & Co. Ltd., *Turn of the Tide* by Arthur Bryant; Cassell Ltd., *The Second World War* by Sir Winston Churchill.

The extracts from *Overture to Overlord* by Sir Frederick Morgan, published by Hodder & Stoughton Ltd., are reprinted by permission of A.D. Peters & Co. Ltd.

BIBLIOGRAPHY

Official Documents
The War Cabinet Minutes, Chiefs of Staffs' Papers, the Prime Minister's File, COSSAC Records and SHAEF Records — all of which are to be found in the Public Record Office.

Official Histories
British Foreign Policy in The Second World War. Vols I & II. WOODWARD, Sir LLEWELLYN: HMSO: Vol I 1970, Vol II 1971.
Grand Strategy. Vol II, BUTLER, J.R.M.: HMSO, 1957; Vol III, Parts 1 and 2, GWYER, J. & BUTLER, J.R.M.: HMSO, 1964; Vol IV, HOWARD, MICHAEL: HMSO, 1972; Vol V, EHRMAN, J.: HMSO, 1956.
HARRISON, G.A.: *Cross-Channel Attack*. US Army.
MATLOFF, M. and SNELL, E.: *Strategic Planning for Coalition Warfare*. US Army.

Published Works
AVON, The Earl of: *The Reckoning*. London: Cassell, 1965; Boston: Houghton Mifflin, 1965.
BAYNES, NORMAN: *The Speeches of Adolf Hitler*. London: Royal Institute of International Affairs, 1942; New York: Oxford University Press, 1943.
BRYANT, ARTHUR: *The Turn of The Tide*. London: Collins, 1957; New York; Doubleday, 1957; Toronto: Collins, 1957.
BUNDY, MCGEORGE and STIMSON, H.L.: *On Active Service In Peace and War*. New York: Harper & Row, 1948; Toronto: Musson, 1948; London: Hutchinson, 1949.
BUTCHER, HARRY: *My Three Years With Eisenhower*. London: Heinemann, 1946; New York; Simon & Schuster, 1946; Toronto: Musson, 1946.
CHURCHILL, SIR WINSTON: *The Second World War*. (Vols I to V) London: Cassell, 1948–53; Boston: Houghton Mifflin, 1948–53; Toronto: K. Allen, 1948–53.
DRIBERG, TOM: *Beaverbrook*. London: Weidenfeld and Nicolson, 1956; Toronto: Ambassador Books, 1956.
EDWARDS, KENNETH: *Operation Neptune*. London: Collins, 1946; Toronto: Collins, 1946.
EISENHOWER, DWIGHT: *Crusade In Europe*. New York: Doubleday, 1948; London: Heinemann, 1949.
FEIS, HERBERT: *Churchill, Roosevelt & Stalin*. London: Oxford University Press, 1957; Princeton: Princeton University Press, 1957; Toronto: S.J.R. Saunders, 1957.

FULLER, J.F.C. (Major-General): *The Second World War*. London: Eyre and Spottiswoode, 1948; Toronto: Collins, 1948; New York: Duell, Sloan and Pearce, 1949.

HIGGINS, TRUMBULL: *Winston Churchill and The Second Front*. London and Toronto: Oxford University Press, 1957.

HULL, CORDELL: *Memoirs*. (Vol II) London: Hodder & Stoughton, 1948: New York: Macmillan, 1948.

ISMAY, General Lord: *Memoirs*. London: Heinemann, 1960; New York: Viking Press, 1960.

MAISKY, IVAN: *Memoirs of A Soviet Ambassador*. London: Hutchinson, 1967; New York: Scribner, 1968.

MONTGOMERY, Field-Marshal Viscount: *Normandy to the Baltic*. London: Hutchinson, 1947; Boston: Houghton Mifflin, 1948.
Memoirs. London and Toronto: Collins, 1958; Cleveland and New York: World Publishing Company, 1958.

MORAN, Lord: *Winston Churchill: The Struggle For Survival 1940–1965*. London: Constable, 1966; Boston: Houghton Mifflin, 1966, as *Churchill: The Struggle For Survival 1940–1965*.

MORGAN, Lieutenant-General SIR FREDERICK: *Overture to Overlord*. London: Hodder and Stoughton, 1950; New York: Doubleday, 1950; Toronto: Musson, 1950.

PARKINSON, ROGER: *Blood, Toil, Tears and Sweat*. London: Hart-Davis MacGibbon, 1973; New York: McKay, 1973.

ROOSEVELT, ELLIOT: *As He Saw It*. New York: Duell, Sloan and Pearce, 1946.

SALISBURY, HARRISON: *The Siege Of Leningrad*. London: Secker and Warburg, 1969; New York: Harper & Row, 1969, as *The 900 Days: The Siege Of Leningrad*.

SHERWOOD, ROBERT: *Roosevelt and Hopkins; An Intimate History*. New York: Harper & Row, 1948; Toronto: Musson, 1948; London: Eyre and Spottiswoode, 1948–49, as *White House Papers of Harry L. Hopkins; An Intimate History*.

SHIRER, WILLIAM: *Rise and Fall Of The Third Reich*. London: Secker and Warburg, 1960; New York: Simon & Schuster, 1960.

STALIN *Correspondence*. New York: Capricorn Books, 1965.

TREVOR-ROPER, H. (ed.): *Hitler's War Directives 1939–45*. London: Sidgwick & Jackson, 1964; New York: Holt, Rinehart and Winston, 1965, as *Blitzkreig to Defeat: Hitler's War Directives, 1939–1945*.

WARLIMONT, HANS: *Inside Hitler's Headquarters*. London: Weidenfeld and Nicolson, 1964; New York: Frederick A. Praeger, 1964; Ontario: Burns and MacEachern, 1964.

WERTH, ALEXANDER: *Russia At War*. London: Barrie & Rockliff, 1964; New York: Dutton, 1964; Toronto: Smithers & Bonellie, 1964.

WHEELER-BENNETT, Sir JOHN (ed.): *Action This Day; Working With Churchill*. London: Macmillan, 1968; New York: St. Martin's Press, 1969.

Other Sources

The Times, The Daily Telegraph, The Daily Express, The Guardian, Keesings Contemporary Archives.

INDEX